INSIGHTS

FROM A PROPHET'S LIFE

RUSSELL M. NELSON

INSIGHTS
FROM A PROPHET'S LIFE

RUSSELL M. NELSON

SHERI DEW

DESERET
BOOK

Salt Lake City, Utah

Library of Congress Cataloging-in-Publication Data

Names: Dew, Sheri L., author.
Title: Insights from a prophet's life : Russell M. Nelson / Sheri Dew.
Description: Salt Lake City, Utah : Deseret Book, [2019] | Includes bibliographical references and index.
Identifiers: LCCN 2018058581 | ISBN 9781629725918 (hardbound : alk. paper)
Subjects: LCSH: Nelson, Russell Marion. | The Church of Jesus Christ of Latter-day Saints—Presidents—Biography. | LCGFT: Biographies.
Classification: LCC BX8695.N42 D49 2019 | DDC 289.3092 [B] —dc23
LC record available at https://lccn.loc.gov/2018058581

Printed in the United States of America
Publishers Printing, Salt Lake City, UT

10   9   8   7   6   5   4   3   2

CONTENTS

Introduction
vii

PART ONE
LAYING A FOUNDATION FOR SERVICE
1924 to 1955
1

PART TWO
HEALING HEARTS AND BUILDING A HOME
1955 to 1984
51

PART THREE
THE QUORUM OF THE TWELVE APOSTLES
1984 to 2015
155

PART FOUR
PRESIDENT OF THE TWELVE,
PRESIDENT OF THE CHURCH
2015 to Present
273

Epilogue
429

Sources Cited
433

Index
437

Image Credits
451

President Russell M. Nelson's official portrait.

INTRODUCTION

Prophets are always teaching. They teach by what they say—and they say a lot. But they also teach by what they do. Their lives teach volumes, even sermons.

We learn from prophets by the choices they make, particularly under duress; by how they deal with grief and recover from their mistakes; by how they treat others; by how they respond to visibility and acclaim; by how and why they repeatedly choose obedience and faith over the alternatives; and by how they endure.

If this learning were not important, Nephi and Alma and Mormon and Moroni and a host of others through the ages would not have expended extraordinary effort recording the *life experiences* of prophets—Lehi and his family leaving Jerusalem, Nephi building a boat and being harassed by his older brothers, Alma and Amulek in prison, Abinadi before the court of King Noah, Moroni's description of the collapse of the Nephite civilization, and on and on.

Very simply, there are lessons to be learned, insights to be gained, by studying the lives of prophets. In 2003, Elder Spencer J. Condie of the Seventy authored an important biography of then-Elder Russell M. Nelson. There is no need to duplicate that significant documentation of Elder Nelson's remarkable life.

But much has happened since then. That book was published before Elder Nelson lost his beloved Dantzel to a heart attack. Before he created the first stakes in Rome, Yerevan, Moscow, and elsewhere.

Before he married Wendy Watson. Before he and Wendy were attacked by robbers with pistols and AK-47s in the mission home in Mozambique. Before he dedicated six countries on the Balkan peninsula in four days. Before he chaired the Missionary Executive Committee that put forward the recommendation to lower the ages of missionaries. Before he dedicated the restored Priesthood Restoration site, which at that point he considered the most important priesthood assignment of his life. Before he became President of the Quorum of the Twelve. And before he was ordained President of the Church.

The attempt of this book is not only to highlight signal events in President Nelson's life since Elder Condie's biography was published, but, in particular, to examine major episodes from the life of the living prophet and extract the insights embedded in them.

Some of these episodes in President Nelson's life took place in a matter of minutes or hours; others spanned several years. I selected each episode either because he learned something or because we can learn something from him, or both. I initially attempted to articulate the insights from each episode but ultimately abandoned that approach because impressions, thoughts, learnings, and insights will vary with each person. Personal revelation is just that—personal.

That you will learn from President Russell M. Nelson's life, though, is a given. It is certain.

———

President Gordon B. Hinckley once told me, referring to himself as well as his Brethren of the General Authorities, "We are ordinary men called to do an extraordinary work."

I partly agree with him. Taking the gospel to every nation, kindred, tongue, and people *is* an extraordinary work—and really, when you think about it, beyond the capacity of anyone or even any group of people. But this is not the work of man. It is the Lord's. And He has chosen and prepared prophets to lead us, guide us, warn us, counsel us, and convey His love to us.

The part of President Hinckley's statement that doesn't resonate with me is the "ordinary man" part. He likely meant to convey what King Benjamin told his people—that they shouldn't regard him as anything more than a mortal man. "I am like as yourselves," he said, "subject to all manner of infirmities in body and mind" (Mosiah 2:10–11).

But prophets are not ordinary. There is nothing ordinary about their foreordination. There is nothing ordinary about the burden and privilege they assume when they are called to lead the Lord's Church. And there is nothing ordinary about the tutorial and course work the Divine Schoolmaster puts them through.

Each prophet's mortal schooling is singular. In studying a prophet's life, we see how the Lord molds, prepares, and tutors a man so that at the appointed hour, he is able, worthy, and ready to be His mouthpiece and to lead His people.

Like those who have preceded him, President Russell M. Nelson is no ordinary man. His professional accomplishments as one of the earliest pioneers of open-heart surgery are well documented. His contributions to the Church as a General Authority and General Officer now span four decades. His personal attributes are exemplary. He is exceptional in so many ways.

And yet he, like King Benjamin and every other prophet who has ever lived, has felt pain, made mistakes, fallen short at times, and been called upon to do things that at the time looked impossible. These experiences have led to one of President Nelson's favorite phrases—that the Lord uses the unlikely to accomplish the impossible, and he has often used himself as a perfect example of that truth.

———

Some may accuse me of bias in the writing of this work, and I can understand why. I first met Wendy Watson in 1997, four days after I had been called to serve as a counselor in the Relief Society General Presidency. She was then a professor of marriage and family therapy at BYU and, as it happens, the keynote speaker for the BYU Women's Conference that year. To the surprise of both of us, we became the dearest of friends.

Since her marriage to Elder Nelson in 2006, he too has become a treasured friend. So have I selected and interpreted the material in this book from a biased perspective? Perhaps. May I suggest, however, that my association with the Nelsons has given me access to information, conversations, and personal experiences that likely would not have been available to another writer. I hope my point of view is more informed than it is biased.

In that regard, if quotations from President and Sister Nelson were published elsewhere, I have included the appropriate references. If they came from interviews I conducted, I have not referenced the dates of those interviews—and simply acknowledge hours of recorded conversation with them both over about a year's period of time.

My acquaintance with the Nelsons notwithstanding, I acknowledge a much greater bias, a definite frame of reference, that has had the greatest influence on this selection of episodes from President Nelson's life.

I believe that one of the hallmarks of The Church of Jesus Christ of Latter-day Saints is that we are led by a living prophet. And I have believed—in fact, I have *known* this—for a long time.

The first time I ever saw a prophet in person was 1966. I was twelve, and our family had driven from Ulysses, Kansas, to Salt Lake City, Utah, to attend general conference for the first time. We stood in long lines outside the Tabernacle to get in. Once we found seats in the balcony, the benches were hard and the meetings long for an antsy preteen. I will admit to being more fascinated with the KSL camera-man, who in that era sat on a seat that was raised and lowered by a small hydraulic lift, than with the speakers. But after the last session, something unforgettable happened. President David O. McKay, wearing that patented white suit of his and with his signature white, flowing hair that made him look every inch a prophet, walked out of the Tabernacle onto Temple Square and stopped and talked to a group of youth waiting for him. I was one of those youth, and I've never forgotten how I felt as he talked to us. I did not get to shake his hand, but at one point he looked right at me, and as he did I felt a sensation run the length of my body. I don't know that I understood what I was feeling at that moment, but I can track the beginning of my testimony of the living prophet to that experience. It is a moment frozen in time for me.

Since then, I've had the unique privilege of associating closely with four prophets—Presidents Ezra Taft Benson, Gordon B. Hinckley, Thomas S. Monson, and Russell M. Nelson—and have been in their presence hundreds of times. This familiarity has not bred contempt or anything remotely related to it. To the contrary, the more closely I've worked with them, and the more I have observed them in a wide array of settings, the more remarkable they have become in my eyes. And the Spirit has borne witness again and again that I am in the presence of a prophet.

I know that the Prophet Joseph Smith saw what he said he saw in a grove of trees in upstate New York. He is the presiding high priest of this dispensation. I believe it. I know it. I have received countless witnesses that this is true.

In the same way I know Joseph Smith to be a prophet, I know that President Russell M. Nelson is the Lord's mouthpiece today, the sixteenth successor to Joseph Smith and a living prophet in every sense of the word.

The heavens are open. God is our Father, and His Son Jesus

Christ is our Savior. They speak to Their prophet. Our spiritual safety hinges upon our willingness to hear his counsel and heed his words.

There is a telling moment in Nephi's life when, after finally arriving in the promised land, Laman and Lemuel become increasingly angry with him, and the Lord warns Nephi to flee into the wilderness. His account of what transpires is interesting and, at first glance, basically a passenger list: "I, Nephi, did take my family, and also Zoram and his family, and Sam, mine elder brother and his family, and Jacob and Joseph, my younger brethren, and also my sisters." But then he adds a line laden with meaning: "and all those who would go with me. And all those who would go with me were those who believed in the warnings and the revelations of God" (2 Nephi 5:6). In short, they were all who believed in the words of a prophet.

The question is the same in our day, for each of us: *Will we go with the prophet?* When President Russell M. Nelson testifies of Christ and points us to the covenant path by asking us to minister, read the Book of Mormon, spend more time in the temple, and be more careful about the media we consume, will we heed and follow? *Will we go with him?*

With my witness about the importance of following the prophet as my frame of reference—my bias, if you will—I offer these insights from a prophet's life.

PART ONE

LAYING A FOUNDATION FOR SERVICE

———

1924 TO 1955

"I expected Daddy to be upset, but he never said a word."

—Russell M. Nelson

All eight of Russell Nelson's great-grandparents joined the Church in Europe and immigrated to the United States during the early part of the nineteenth century, when gathering to Zion was the aim of most European converts. They all ended up in the small central Utah town of Ephraim. "Each of these stalwart souls sacrificed everything to come to Zion," he later said. During subsequent generations, however, not all of his ancestors remained faithful, and as a result, Russell and his siblings—Marjory, Enid, and Robert—were not raised in a gospel-centered home.

Nonetheless, Russell adored his parents, Marion Clavar Nelson and Floss Edna Anderson Nelson. "My mother and father were just so wonderful," he said. "Every night was family home evening. Daddy may have been smoking a cigar, but it was family home evening nonetheless."

The second of four children, and the eldest son, Russell flourished in the happy home life his parents provided for him and his two sisters and brother. They spent lots of time together, enjoyed summer vacations as a family, went on frequent outings, and were fully engaged in each other's lives. When Russell ran for student-body

Russell as a young child.

3

Russell (front row, center) with his family.

office in junior high, he asked his father to help him with his campaign speech. Marion was happy to take a look at his son's draft. "Daddy wouldn't lift a pencil until I'd made the effort," Russell said.

The family didn't attend church together, but his mother taught him how to pray and, for some reason, saw that he attended meetings—though his siblings usually didn't. Russell wasn't above skipping out from time to time to play football with friends in a nearby lot, but he went to church enough to begin to understand that, as much as he loved his family, he was missing something.

One day he jumped on the streetcar and went downtown to the Deseret Book store. When a kind sales clerk greeted him, he asked if she could help him find a book he could read about The Church of Jesus Christ of Latter-day Saints. "I wanted to know about the Church, because my family didn't give me that," he explained. "One of the salesladies took me by the hand and began to teach me. I don't remember what book she gave me, but she helped me. I loved learning about the gospel."

One of the things he learned about was the Word of Wisdom, and he wished his parents would live that law. One evening, after his parents had indulged in some social drinking, they raised their voices against each other—something young Russell hadn't seen much of in their home. And he didn't like it.

That night he went to the basement, where he knew his parents stored some of their alcohol, broke every bottle, and poured the contents down a drain in the concrete basement floor. "I expected Daddy to be upset, but he never said a word," Russell remembered. "He knew that I was right."

As it would turn out, Russell Nelson was a standout in

Russell (front row, right) is made an honorary lieutenant in the U.S. Army at Camp Williams, Utah.

Russell's parents, Edna and Marion Nelson.

anything he touched, and he seems to have done almost everything early. He graduated from high school early, went to the university early, graduated from medical school early, and so on. The one thing he did late was get baptized.

He was sixteen years old and a senior in high school when he was baptized and confirmed a member of The Church of Jesus Christ of Latter-day Saints and received the gift of the Holy Ghost. Curiously, though, throughout his growing-up years, Russell had continued to attend church—usually alone. His closest friends were not in his ward, he wasn't wowed by the lessons, and he thought the music conductor was intimidating. "He had a baton," Russell remembered, "and he loved to shake it at my nose and at the other boys as well. 'Master, the Tempest Is Raging' was a favorite, and he was quite energetic with that baton of his during that song."

Something inside, however, kept him going. At the time of his baptism, Sterling W. Sill, who would later serve as a General Authority, was his bishop, and Bishop Sill took a special interest in

The Provo Utah Temple, where Russell and his parents and siblings were sealed in 1977.

the teenaged Russell. "By that point, I had a testimony. I knew the gospel was for real," Russell said.

It would be decades before his parents would become active in the Church. "As I matured and began to understand the magnificence of Heavenly Father's plan, I often said to myself, 'I don't want one more Christmas present! I just want to be sealed to my parents'" (Nelson, "Revelation").

That gift finally became a reality, but not until 1977. On February 6 of that year, Russell, then General President of the Sunday School, ordained his father an elder in the Melchizedek Priesthood, and the following month, on March 26, Marion and Edna were sealed in the Provo Utah Temple, and their four children were sealed to them. That was the day Russell M. Nelson finally received from his parents the gift he had dreamed about for decades.

> "'Father, can you see us at all times,
> and do you know what we are doing?'
>
> "'No, my son, I cannot. . . .
> There is . . . much more order here in
> the Spirit world than in the other world.'"
>
> —Andrew Clarence (A. C.) Nelson, Russell M. Nelson's
>   paternal grandfather

Despite the lack of gospel training in Russell Nelson's childhood home, many of his forebears were fully engaged in the gospel of Jesus Christ. Over time, as the young Russell grew and matured, he would learn more about his spiritual heritage, which he cherished.

A. C. Nelson, Russell's paternal grandfather.

One treasured experience involved his paternal grandfather, Andrew Clarence Nelson, who went by "A. C." Russell's Grandfather Nelson died of cancer on December 26, 1913, just four weeks shy of his fiftieth birthday—and more than a decade before his grandson Russell would be born. A. C. enjoyed some prominence in Salt Lake City and served as Utah's State Superintendent of Public Schools from 1900 until his death in 1913.

On the night of April 6, 1891, when A. C. was just twenty-seven, he had a dream, perhaps even a

8

night vision, in which he saw and talked with his father, Mads Peter Nielsen, who had died on January 27th of that year. A. C. recorded the experience in his journal, which later became a prized family memory for his grandson Russell.

In A. C.'s journal entry, he said he realized there were those who wouldn't believe his account and would even "scorn and laugh at the idea of such a visitation," but he knew it was real.

It began after A. C. had gone to bed. His "father came in or entered the room; he came and sat on the side of the bed" and began to talk. "Well, my son, as I had a few spare minutes, I received permission to come and see you a few minutes. I am feeling well, my son, and have had very much to do since I died."

When A. C. asked what his father, Mads, had been doing in the spirit world, he answered, "I have been travelling together with Apostle Erastus Snow ever since I died. That is, since three days after I died. I received my commission to preach the gospel. You cannot imagine, my son, how many spirits there are in the spirit world that have not yet received the gospel. But many are receiving it, and a great work is being accomplished."

Mads told his son that one of the reasons he had come to visit A. C. was because he and his sisters weren't yet sealed to Mads and his wife, Margrethe Christensen. "That, my son, is partly what I came to see you about. We will yet make a family and live throughout Eternity."

A. C. asked, "Father, can you see us at all times, and do you

Russell's paternal grandmother, Amanda Jensen, wife of A. C. Nelson.

know what we are doing?" "No, my son, I cannot. . . ." his father replied. "There is just as much, and much more, order here in the Spirit world than in the other world. I have been assigned work and that must be performed."

A. C. told his father that he was very grateful he'd died in full fellowship in the Church. "Well, my son, your father always did know since he joined the Church that the Gospel was true. . . . I got a little stubborn, but who is there of us that has not been a little cross and naughty at times. The short time that I was cross does not amount to 15 minutes in comparison to Eternity."

A. C. then asked if it felt natural to die, and, being reassured that it felt very natural, he asked if the Resurrection was a reality. "Yes, my son, as true as can be. You cannot avoid being Resurrected. It is just as natural for all to be Resurrected as it is to be born and die again. No one can avoid being Resurrected. There are many spirits in the Spirit world who would to God, that there would be no Resurrection."

Finally, A. C. asked his father if the gospel, as taught by The Church of Jesus Christ of Latter-day Saints, was true. "My son, do you see that picture," pointing to a picture of the First Presidency on the wall. When A. C. said yes, he saw it, his father said, "Well, just as sure as you see that picture, just so sure is the Gospel true. The Gospel of Jesus Christ has within it the power of saving every man and woman that will obey it. . . . My son, always cling to the Gospel. Be humble, be prayerful, be submissive to the Priesthood, be true, be faithful to the covenants you have made with God."

Russell's grandfather's visit with his departed father occurred twenty-seven years before President Joseph F. Smith's 1918 vision of the redemption of the dead, which became section 138 of the Doctrine and Covenants. "From President Smith's experience, he taught that the faithful elders continue doing missionary work after they depart from this mortal life," Russell Nelson would say years later. "And I'm sure that's not just the elders. It would be the sisters, too. So many of our sisters are exceptional missionaries" (Nelson and Nelson, RootsTech).

While young Russell Nelson was not aware of his grandfather's experience during his youth, in time his gospel heritage would become increasingly sweet to him—and would intensify his natural interest in the gathering of Israel and in the turning of the hearts of fathers to their children and vice versa. "It is so precious to me that my grandfather would leave that record for us," he later said. "We learned that his children were subsequently sealed to him. So the reason for that visit was accomplished."

A. C. Nelson's family in 1907. Left to right: A. C., holding Clyde; Marion (Russell's father); Claron; Aunt Chloe; Amanda, holding Lucile; Lamar; Irv; Cliff; Clarence, holding Lloyd.

"I was curious."

—Russell M. Nelson

How did you go from being told in medical school that you could not touch the human heart, or you would be discredited as a physician, to helping build the first heart-lung machine?" Russell Nelson would be asked many times in his life. "Oh, I was curious," he would answer.

Russell's unbridled curiosity manifested itself early. Well before his teenage years, he obtained his own library card to the old Salt Lake Public Library, located then at 15 South State Street. On Saturdays and summer days, he would hop on the streetcar, go downtown to the library, and spend hours pulling book after book from the stacks and reading, reading, reading. He read books on the nervous system, baseball, mammals, American history—you name it. Even the Dewey decimal system used to catalog books intrigued him. "I was fascinated by just the methodology about how they maintained a library. So, basically, I would go downtown on weekends and educate myself and then get on the streetcar and go home."

The old Salt Lake Public Library building.

Russell's curiosity and appetite for learning also motivated him inside the classroom, and his native intellect typically landed him at the head of the class. He skipped the fifth grade and, despite being the youngest member of his class at East High School, graduated in 1941 as the valedictorian when he was all of sixteen.

When he entered the University of Utah, World War II was raging, and the air force, navy, and army all needed more doctors. During high school, Russell had decided he wanted to go into medicine. That decision had temporarily disappointed his advertising executive father, who imagined his son following in his footsteps. But ultimately both his mother and father were supportive, so by the time he enrolled in the university, Russell was clear on his intent to become a doctor. The pressure of war affected the school's calendar, and he attended year-round, working ultimately on his bachelor's and MD degrees simultaneously.

The young Russell Ballard was several years behind Russell Nelson at both East High School and the University of Utah. "He was a legend at East High School," President M. Russell Ballard later

The University of Utah, where Russell received bachelor's and MD degrees.

Russell (second row, third from left) with his fellow interns in Minneapolis.

reflected. "He was outstanding as a leader at East High School, out-standing as a leader at the University of Utah. He became a leader of just about everything he ever touched. Ever since then I have counted him as one of my role models" (*Church News*/KSL Interview, January 9, 2018).

"He was a young genius," Elder Gregory A. Schwitzer, also a medical doctor, would later confirm. "I've talked with people who were medical school classmates of his, and they always knew he would be number one in the class. When you go to medical school, there are just certain physicians who are not just confident or bright, they are brilliant, they shine. He would fit that category" (*Church News*/KSL Interview, January 8, 2018).

Prior to 1942, when the University of Utah board of regents approved a four-year medical school, those studying medicine there could take only two years of course work and then needed to go

The young college graduate.

elsewhere to graduate. Russell was in one of the first classes of the new, four-year school, and "we had a bright, aggressive faculty anxious to make a good name for the school," he remembered. Only twenty-six of the fifty-two who began in his class graduated in 1947. (Some had to repeat a year or two.)

The training was outstanding. Several of his professors became father figures to him. "I adored them. I respected them. I learned as much as I could from them," he said simply (Greenberg, Interview).

They in turn took special interest in the bright young medical student. Dr. Leo T. Samuels invited Russell to join in his research on Von Gierke's disease. Dr. Max Wintrobe taught him in internal medicine, and Dr. Louis Goodman in pharmacology. Dr. Philip B. Price, the son of a Presbyterian minister born in China, considered him a protégé in surgery. Price's background as a professor of surgery at Qilu University, Shandong Province, in Jinan, and then at Johns Hopkins—all before coming to Utah—fascinated Russell. And when Russell was about to graduate from the U and Dr. Emil Holmstrom learned he was interested in surgery, Dr. Holmstrom picked up the phone and made arrangements for Russell to do his internship and postgraduate work at the University of Minnesota, then regarded as one of the most prestigious universities in the world for surgical training. Dr. Owen H. Wangensteen taught there, and, in Russell's assessment, he was "arguably one of the most outstanding trainers of surgeons that we've had in this country" (Greenberg, Interview). In every class and from every professor, Russell was the proverbial sponge, absorbing and soaking up as much knowledge and information as he could.

It worked in his favor that, from its earliest days, the University of Utah medical school worked to provide cutting-edge medical training. Over the years, notable alumni would include William DeVries, a renowned cardiothoracic surgeon who performed the first successful permanent artificial heart implant; Robert Jarvik, the inventor of the artificial heart; J. Charles Rich Jr., a neurosurgeon named as president of the American Association of Neurological Surgeons; Dale G. Renlund, noted cardiologist and later a member of the Quorum of the Twelve; and Robert Metcalf, a pioneer in arthroscopic surgery and sports medicine.

When Russell graduated first in his class with both his bachelor's and MD degrees from the University of Utah in August 1947, he was twenty-two years old.

Ready to move on.

"Dantzel made it clear that nobody was going to marry her unless they could do so in the temple."

—Russell M. Nelson

Russell Nelson's interests were multifaceted, and his heavy load at the university didn't keep him from exploring extracurricular activities. Among other things, he was talented musically. Though he learned to read music, he had perfect pitch and an almost uncanny ability to play the piano (and later the organ) by ear—and could do so as well as he could with music in front of him. Plus, he had a beautiful baritone voice. In fact, had it not been for his singing voice, he might never have met Dantzel White.

One day in 1942, Gail Plummer recruited Russell to accept a role in the play *Hayfoot, Strawfoot* he was directing at Kingsbury Hall on the University of Utah campus. Russell at first declined. His premed course work was all-consuming. But Plummer persisted, and finally Russell relented. When he walked into the theater for the first rehearsal on April 16, 1942, Russell was instantly fixated on a beautiful brunette onstage who had the most hypnotic soprano voice he'd ever heard. She caught his eye and his ear.

"Who is that beautiful girl singing up there?" he asked Plummer. Her name was Dantzel White, and Russell could not believe his good fortune when he learned that the role he had agreed to play was opposite her. As he left this first meeting, he had a vivid, and perhaps hopeful, feeling come over him: "She was the most beautiful girl I had ever seen," he said, and he sensed and hoped that she was the girl he would marry. For him, it was love at first sight.

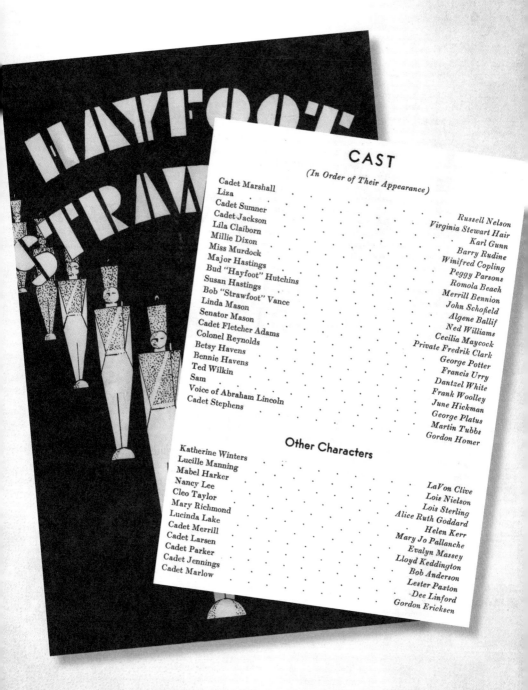

CAST

(In Order of Their Appearance)

Cadet Marshall	
Liza	
Cadet Sumner	
Cadet Jackson	Russell Nelson
Lila Claiborn	Virginia Stewart Hair
Millie Dixon	Karl Gunn
Miss Murdock	Barry Rudine
Major Hastings	Winifred Copling
Bud "Hayfoot" Hutchins	Peggy Parsons
Susan Hastings	Romola Beach
Bob "Strawfoot" Vance	Merrill Bennion
Linda Mason	John Schofield
Senator Mason	Algene Ballif
Cadet Fletcher Adams	Ned Williams
Colonel Reynolds	Cecilia Maycock
Betsy Havens	Private Fredrik Clark
Bennie Havens	George Potter
Ted Wilkin	Francis Urry
Sam	Dantzel White
Voice of Abraham Lincoln	Frank Woolley
Cadet Stephens	June Hickman
	George Platus
	Martin Tubbs
	Gordon Homer

Other Characters

Katherine Winters	
Lucille Manning	
Mabel Harker	
Nancy Lee	LaVon Clive
Cleo Taylor	Lois Nielson
Mary Richmond	Lois Sterling
Lucinda Lake	Alice Ruth Goddard
Cadet Merrill	Helen Kerr
Cadet Larsen	Mary Jo Pallanche
Cadet Parker	Evalyn Massey
Cadet Jennings	Lloyd Keddington
Cadet Marlow	Bob Anderson
	Lester Paxton
	Dee Linford
	Gordon Ericksen

Playbill from the production where Russell and Dantzel met.

A young Russell and Dantzel enjoying time together.

The young premed student began to date the darling girl studying elementary education, and, fortunately, Dantzel felt the same attraction to him. In fact, shortly after their first meeting, she made a trip home to Perry, Utah, to visit her parents, Maude Clark White and LeRoy Davis White. Though she'd known Russell for just a short time, she told them that she had met the man she wanted to marry.

"I fell madly in love with Dantzel," Russell said, "and she made it clear that nobody was going to marry her unless they could do so in the temple. That was a given for her."

For a young man whose gospel education thus far in life had been modest, though increasing in his later teenage years, marrying Dantzel in the temple became great motivation for Russell to learn more about the gospel and to prepare to go to the temple.

Three years after their first meeting—on August 31, 1945—they were married in the Salt Lake Temple. In doing so, Dantzel, whose

Russell M. Nelson married Dantzel White on August 31, 1945.

gorgeous operatic soprano voice had won her a full scholarship to the famed Juilliard School in New York City, put her own career aside to marry the love of her life.

They were young—Dantzel was nineteen and Russell just twenty, though he was already a sophomore in medical school. Russell's parents and siblings could not attend the sealing in the temple, and "they were not cheerful about that," he admitted. "But they *loved* Dantzel and were in favor of our marrying, so that helped them deal with the fact that their inactivity in the Church prevented their presence in the temple."

Dantzel and Russell had dated as World War II raged, with all the uncertainty and unique challenges that era posed. And now that they were married, she supported him, financially and otherwise, as he completed medical school in 1947. Then off they went to Minnesota for what would be the beginning of a long road of graduate school and advanced medical training.

They were young and naive about what lay ahead of them. And they were young in the gospel as well. While Dantzel came from a devout Latter-day Saint home, Russell did not, and their combined understanding of the gospel was modest. "When we married in the temple, we didn't know many scriptures," Russell would later explain. "But we did know Matthew 6:33: 'Seek ye first the kingdom of God, and his righteousness; and all these things shall be added unto you.' . . . That became the lodestar for every decision we made together" (Nelson, "Faith and Families").

"Leaving the nest is the best marriage glue
I can imagine."

—Russell M. Nelson

Making the break with Salt Lake City, where Dantzel and Russell were surrounded by family and lifelong friends, was a great adventure and a bit unnerving all at the same time. Many years later, however, Russell would say, "Leaving the nest is the best marriage glue I can imagine, because a husband and wife have to deal with their challenges together. They can't go running home to Momma or to Daddy. You tough it out and figure it out."

The Nelsons put that theory to the test. They loved each other

Russell and Dantzel on their honeymoon at Bryce Canyon, Utah.

Russell and Dantzel, embarking on their new life together.

dearly: that was a given. But in 1947, in the aftermath of a world war, nothing else came easy. Just finding transportation to Minneapolis was a feat. With the country in the thick of rebuilding and retooling, no one was yet manufacturing new cars, so vehicles were in short supply. Russell's father, ever supportive of his son, somehow managed to get them a car, and Russell and Dantzel headed to Minneapolis. There, once again, he set out to do two things at once—report for duty as an intern at the University of Minnesota hospitals and also get his PhD with a major in surgery and a minor in physiology.

The Nelsons didn't know a soul in Minnesota, so they were on their own. There weren't enough apartments to accommodate all the students now flocking to the university, so Russell and Dantzel had to "audition" for an apartment space. When a landlord finally decided to take a chance on them, their rent was a staggering $72.50 a month— half of what Dantzel earned as a schoolteacher. She was basically their sole means of support, so spending half of what she made on their small apartment seemed extreme. But this was just the beginning of dealing with thin income. The greatest financial challenges for the young couple lay ahead, because Dr. Nelson was embarking on years of post-doctoral training, which would be interrupted even further when he enlisted in the army at the outbreak of the Korean War.

"There were twelve and a half years from the time I received my doctoral degree until I sent my first bill for surgical services," Russell recalled. "We borrowed money. Dantzel earned some. I made a little here and there. Somehow we survived."

The move to Minnesota was an adjustment for both of them. Russell's internship was both compelling and consuming, and he was often required to stay at the hospital for days at a time. This left Dantzel often traversing the icy Minneapolis streets alone, only to come home to an apartment that felt vacant. One night when Russell called from the hospital to check on her, she said with some emotion, "I've got to have something *live* around the house!" Russell "recognized that this was a reasonable request—so I bought her a goldfish!" (Condie, *Russell M. Nelson*, 65). Soon thereafter, she found she was expecting their first child and her days of being alone at home were soon to end.

During subsequent years and decades, when Russell would hear young couples question whether they could afford to have children, he would say, "If we had waited until we could afford a child, we would have missed Marsha, Wendy, Gloria, Brenda, and Sylvia—half of our children. Who would we have done without? And over time, we would have missed their husbands and their children and their children's children. Everything in our family would have been cut in half."

Despite their poverty and the educational mountain ahead of

them, Russell and Dantzel had their first little girl, Marsha, on July 29, 1948, just as Dr. Nelson completed his internship.

Through those early days, they learned to rely on each other—to work through problems together; share the load of family, school, and work; and make a place for themselves in the world. They knew stress and pressure, but their lives were full and, if asked, they would have insisted they felt rich because they had each other.

Dantzel with Marsha (left) and Wendy.

"Don't forget to pay tithing on my blood money!"

—Dantzel White Nelson

Russell and Dantzel were stretched financially from the day they got married. Two days after their wedding, the Japanese signed documents of surrender aboard the *USS Missouri,* marking the official end of World War II. The impact of war on the United States, however, would linger much longer. Rationing, shortages of housing and food, and a wounded economy disrupted everyone's lives—and certainly that of a young couple with schooling and specialized training ahead of them. To say their early years of marriage were lean financially would be soft-pedaling the reality of their meager monetary resources.

While still attending the University of Utah, Dantzel and Russell eagerly accepted any invitations to dinner from their parents and friends. At one point, Dantzel worked two jobs—as a teacher by day and clerk in a music store by night—to keep her husband in medical school. On one occasion while in medical school at the U of U, when they found themselves short by thirty-seven dollars at the end of the month, Russell picked Dantzel up after school and took her to LDS Hospital, where they

Russell's desk from his medical school days.

27

The young Nelson family: Dantzel, holding Gloria; Russell, holding Wendy; and Marsha.

each sold a pint of blood for twenty-five dollars. As the needle was withdrawn from Dantzel's arm, she said to Russell, "Don't forget to pay tithing on my blood money!"

Russell's mother-in-law was none too happy when she realized her daughter was working two jobs and giving blood on top of that. "I got the general feeling that she didn't think Dantzel had married much of a husband," Russell said many years later. "We laughed about it later, but at the time it was no laughing matter. Giving blood had to be our low point financially. But even then, Dantzel's first concern was that we pay our tithing."

Later, in Boston, on a rare evening together while Russell was still receiving advanced medical training, they strolled down Boylston Street, window shopping as they went—which was about all they could afford to do. As they passed a furniture store, Dantzel pressed her nose against the windowpane, looked for a few moments, and then asked her husband, "Do you think we'll ever be able to afford a lamp?"

During their years in Minnesota, Dantzel was the breadwinner, teaching school for all of $135 a month. Russell contributed another $15 monthly, his pay as an intern. One evening, Dantzel asked her husband if he was paying tithing on his monthly wage. "Frankly," he said, "I had regarded that as just a token payment designed to keep my teeth clean, hair cut, and shoes polished. But when she confronted me with that question, I realized that she was right and I was wrong, and so our tithing was increased to include a tenth of that $15 every month. I have been a full tithe payer ever since" (Nelson, *From Heart to Heart,* 68).

The lean years stretched into a couple of decades. Two doctor's degrees and surgical specialization in a new field took years. Then, though the pioneering days in open-heart surgery were exciting, dramatic, adventurous, filled with pressure, and rewarding, they were not particularly lucrative. As their young family continued to grow, the children didn't seem to know that it wasn't normal to sleep in sleeping bags on army cots. But somehow they managed, and over time, their financial situation modulated. And, said Russell, "I'm happy to report that the day came when I could afford to buy Dantzel both a table and a lamp."

"We have worked so hard all of these years to support you, now to find out that you are only a dog doctor."

—Marion C. Nelson, Russell's father

Russell's fortunate pattern of working with, and being mentored by, excellent professors and clinicians at the University of Utah continued at the University of Minnesota Medical School.

Dr. Maurice Visscher, a critically acclaimed physiologist, mentored the young Dr. Nelson in his PhD, though Visscher made it abundantly clear that he didn't think much of Latter-day Saints. "I've still got scars on my adrenal glands from him," Dr. Nelson admitted years later, "but I learned a great deal from him, and he greatly influenced my PhD dissertation."

Others were also key in Dr. Nelson's training. Dr. Owen H. Wangensteen, the chief of surgery at the University of Minnesota hospitals, went on to enjoy a fabled career as an innovator and trainer of future leaders in the field of surgery. Other important members of the faculty included Drs. Clarence Dennis, Richard L. Varco, and K. Alvin Merendino. Russell also studied with a group of bright, talented residents, including Dr. Christiaan Barnard, a South African surgeon who would later perform the first human-to-human heart transplant in 1967. Russell's curious, innovative mind was in great company, and both his professors and fellow students challenged him and enhanced his learning.

Russell relished being in Minnesota and counted his blessings frequently for the privilege. But it wasn't all roses. Dr. Wangensteen didn't much care for his bright young intern's lifestyle, which was too squeaky-clean for him. And Wangensteen's chief resident, Ivan Baronofsky, liked him even less. When Russell turned down cocktails at a Christmas party, Baronofsky threatened, "Nelson, you take this drink or I will make life mighty rough for you around here."

"Well, Doctor, you do what you have to do, and I will do what I have to do," Russell replied.

Baronofsky made good on his promise and gave young Dr. Nelson all the tough cases to scrub on and denied him nights or weekends off. "He was as mean as he could be," Russell remembered, "but meanwhile I was learning how to do surgery because I was on all of the long, tough cases. So what he thought was punishment actually turned to my benefit."

Then something happened that changed the direction of young Russell Nelson's career and life. Dr. Clarence Dennis received what was then considered to be an enormous research grant—$25,000, disbursed over five years—to develop an artificial heart-lung machine. The minute Dr. Nelson heard about the project, he wanted to be part of it and approached Dr. Dennis about joining his team. Dr. Dennis was happy to have an extra pair of free hands, not to mention a fertile young mind, as they launched into this new territory. At that point, they weren't even completely sure what a heart-lung machine would be used for. But they set out to build a machine that would essentially take over a patient's circulation and allow surgery on a heart that wasn't beating.

This was a leap into the unknown. Ironically, Russell had never contemplated heart surgery—because there was no such thing as heart surgery. He and his fellow med students had been taught that they must never touch the human heart or it would stop beating. One of his textbooks, by T. Billroth, published in 1913, famously declared that "a surgeon who would attempt such an operation [on the heart] should lose the respect of his colleagues."

At that time, said Russell, the "only intersection between disease of the heart and surgery was, 'Do not operate!' It was not even contemplated, because everybody knew that you could not touch the heart. God made the body in such a way that the brain is protected with a skull and the heart with a sternum. So, hands off!" During World War II, there were cases reported in which wounds to the heart were treated with stitches, but rarely—and almost never successfully.

It didn't take long for Dr. Dennis's heart-lung machine team to do a review of the scientific literature, because there basically wasn't any. A French surgeon, Dr. Alexis Carrel, had tried to help famed aviator Charles Lindbergh, who had a family member dying of mitral valve disease. Lindbergh asked the French physician why a valve couldn't be repaired. "At that time," Dr. Nelson explained, "there was no way to fix the valve any more than you could fix a valve in an airplane motor while it was running." But Dr. Carrel, along with a handful of other surgeons around the globe who were coming alive to the notion of heart surgery, first contemplated the idea of somehow taking care of a person's circulation for a short period of time in an alternative way while repairs could be made on the heart.

One of Dr. Nelson's first experiments in Dr. Dennis's lab was to see if he could open the chest of a dog, touch its heart, and have it survive. The team built a respirator, injected novocaine into the sac surrounding the heart, and numbed the nerves. Lo and behold, it worked! Russell held the beating heart in his hand. "This shows just how primitive our knowledge was at that point," he recalled. "We were finding our way, taking small steps into the dark and hoping that greater light and knowledge would come as we did. But the first thing we showed was that you could touch the heart and it would continue to beat."

From this point on, they used dogs as patients to test the primitive heart-lung machine they were building and gradually improving. "I didn't realize that the task which lay before us was impossible," Dr. Nelson admitted, "and so I started out with the very naive assumption that it wouldn't be very hard to build a heart-lung machine."

Dr. Dennis and Russell, along with doctors Karl E. Karlson, W. Phil Eder, Frank Eddy, and others, made every piece of that first heart-lung machine themselves. Russell and his colleagues basically learned to run a machine shop. He learned to blow glass, work a lathe, and operate a drill press. In order to merge tubing, they had to have glass connectors; and to make a Y connector so that two lines could merge into one, they had to blow glass.

There were medical challenges as well, and plenty of them. "We had no idea about oxygen consumption rates or minimum flow rates or the influence of temperature on the rate of metabolism," Russell explained. It took them about a year to learn how to have blood flow outside the body without clotting. "So a year was spent just learning how to render the blood incoagulable and then coagulable again so healing could take place in the surgical incision," he added. They learned to make blood fluid with heparin and then reverse the effects with protamine sulfate (Greenberg, Interview).

Little by little, they improved their processes and their machine, but they kept encountering one major hitch: the dogs they operated on did fine while on the heart-lung machine, but then later died of a mysterious illness characterized by bloody diarrhea.

It was then that Dr. Dennis left for Europe to fulfill professional obligations there, leaving Dr. Nelson in charge of the lab. While Dennis was gone, Russell discovered the cause of the problem. Though they had sterilized the machine after each use, they hadn't thought to replace the tubing attaching the machine to the animals. The toxins the bacteria manufactured during the operations were still attached to the tubing.

"I was able to show that one could die of bacterial toxemia even without the bacteria around," Dr. Nelson explained. "When Dennis came back, I said, 'I've solved our problem.'" When they started

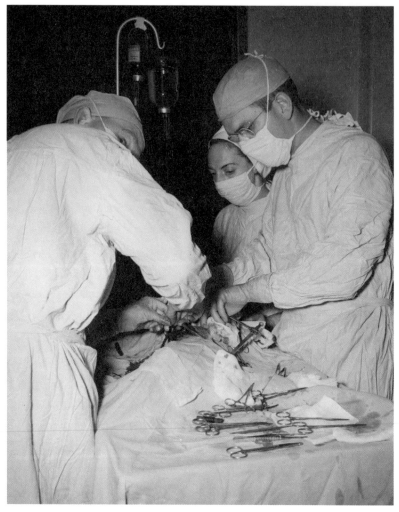

Dr. Nelson and colleagues operating on a dog.

replacing the tubing with each new operation, the dogs stopped dying. Dr. Nelson wrote his PhD dissertation about the research that came from this discovery, on the metabolic effects of paracolon bacterial toxemia. "The dog is the great hero of the development of heart surgery," Russell declared, "because everything we learned, we learned on dogs" (Greenberg, Interview).

About this time, Russell's parents came to visit him and Dantzel in Minnesota. He was eager to show them his research lab, and the first thing he did after they arrived was to take his father to the lab for a grand tour. Among other things, Russell introduced his father to the first dog ever to survive thirty minutes of total circulatory support with a heart-lung machine. "When I showed this mangy-looking critter to my father, which I considered to be a medical triumph, he turned his back to me, pulled out his handkerchief, and began to wipe his eyes. I thought he was overcome with the significance of what we had accomplished, but instead he said, 'Your mother and I have worked so hard all these years to support you, now to find out that you are only a dog doctor.'"

There were early failures and early triumphs. Despite the latter, Dr. Dennis's team had overlooked a seemingly simple but severely limiting problem. The machine they built worked perfectly for a dog, who could be rolled into the small lab. But the machine itself was so big they couldn't get it out the door of their lab and into an operating room where it could be used with a human. "Our machine," Russell described, "was like a ship built in a bottle" (Greenberg, Interview).

The reality of this limitation became instantly clear when, in 1951, Dr. Richard L. Varco, a faculty member at the University of Minnesota hospitals, approached the heart-lung team about using the pump-oxygenator to allow him to operate on a patient. When they couldn't figure out how to get the six-by-four-foot monstrosity out of the lab, they started all over to build a more compact model.

While in the midst of this grueling but fascinating process of discovery, Russell had a pivotal experience that put a human face on the need for cardiac surgery—and helped him solidify his interest in that specialty. In Minnesota, the Nelsons had become close friends with Dr. Don and Netta Davis, another young couple in the medical program. When Netta developed rheumatic mitral stenosis, which then progressed to full-fledged heart failure, Russell and Dantzel watched helplessly as their friend wasted away physically and succumbed to the effects of a diseased valve that at the time could not be repaired. Russell resolved to devote his professional career to helping patients with heart disease.

In March 1951, Dr. Dennis and others performed the first open-heart operation on a human being using the machine his team, including Dr. Nelson, had built. The pump worked well and supported the patient's circulation, but she did not survive. What doctors had believed to be a simple hole in the heart turned out to be a more complicated congenital abnormality.

Despite the death of the patient, details of this pioneering operation were subsequently presented at the American Surgical Association meetings in April 1951. "The significance of that first operation can't be overstated," Dr. Nelson summarized. "With that operation, the story changed. The question had been, 'Can we gain surgical access to the interior of the human heart?' Now the new question was, 'Can the anatomic abnormality in the human heart be corrected surgically?' A whole new world of surgical repair of the heart had become possible."

Russell was not in the operating room the day that first heart-lung machine, the one he had helped build, was used. The onset of the Korean War had made him highly susceptible to the draft. Rather than wait for the inevitable, he took control of the process and enlisted in the army. Dr. Nelson had gone to war.

"I sensed that my rifle was more of a hazard to me than a protection."

—Lieutenant Russell M. Nelson

The euphoria and sense of contribution Dr. Nelson was experiencing in Minnesota because of his studies and work on the heart-lung machine were interrupted by war—the Korean War—for which doctors were desperately needed. Because Russell had served in the naval reserves, and the navy had helped put him through medical school, he knew he was a prime candidate for the draft. So, one year

Dr. Nelson holding his daughter Marsha in Washington, DC, in April 1951.

shy of finishing his residency and getting his PhD degree, he enlisted in the army.

When the surgeon general learned about his training, Dr. Nelson was selected to form a surgical research unit at the Walter Reed National Military Medical Center in Washington, DC, and he and Dantzel headed for the nation's capital.

Soon thereafter, however, the army changed its mind and issued orders for his immediate transfer to active duty in Korea. This news was unsettling for Russell and for Dantzel, who had just given birth to their second daughter, Wendy. He would never have brought his wife to a new city to fend for herself with two small children had he known he was leaving for Asia.

Thankfully, history intervened. President Harry S Truman unexpectedly fired General Douglas MacArthur as commander in chief of military operations in the Far East, and Lieutenant Nelson's travel orders were canceled for a few weeks. That merciful intervention gave him time to arrange for his small family to travel to Utah, where they could live with Dantzel's family while he was overseas. After he'd had just enough time to make all those arrangements, new orders

Dr. Nelson with his rifle.

Dr. Nelson with some Korean villagers.

arrived, and he was off to Tokyo and then Korea as a member of a four-man surgical research team headed by Dr. Fiorindo A. Simeone. During the next several months, they visited every M.A.S.H. unit on the Korean peninsula. "I went into the army in March," Lieutenant Nelson said, "and in June I went over to Korea and started out right at the front lines, at the battlefront where cannons were firing" (Greenberg, Interview).

As it turns out, at least some of what would later be depicted in the popular television sitcom M*A*S*H wasn't all that far from the truth. Television doctors Hawkeye Pierce and B. J. Hunnicutt didn't know one end of a rifle from the other, and neither did Dr. Nelson. On the flight from Tokyo to Taegu, Korea, a superior officer handed him a rifle and told him to carry it. When Lieutenant Nelson protested, saying he'd never used a rifle and had no idea how to fire one, he was instructed, "Carry it anyway." One day, while he was walking through a Korean village, guerillas in surrounding hills started

Lieutenant Nelson poses with a Korean man and his oxcart.

Dr. Nelson in front of a M.A.S.H. unit in Korea.

Captain Russell M. Nelson.

shooting at him. He couldn't see where the shots were coming from, and he didn't know how to use the gun anyway. "I sensed that my rifle was more of a hazard to me than a protection," he said (Nelson, *From Heart to Heart,* 77).

His research team was charged with determining why soldiers died once they entered the military's medical care system. Some soldiers, of course, died immediately from wounds incurred in battle. But the team's task was to determine the major causes of death for those who entered M.A.S.H. units and were later treated in military hospitals.

The research team learned several things: that those who experienced frostbite during Korean winters had a harder time getting blood flow to their extremities if they smoked, or even if they experienced secondhand smoke; that many burn patients did better with more open treatment of their wounds than with massive dressings; that renal failure was exacerbated during the oppressive summer months when already dehydrated men were subjected to bleeding, blood transfusions, and further dehydration; and that many of the major blood-vessel injuries could be helped by the vascular surgical techniques the team introduced.

Lieutenant Nelson also learned something else: that foxholes invite serious introspection. One evening the M.A.S.H. unit where he was working came under attack. He and Dr. Simeone shared a foxhole for most of the night. "Dr. Simeone, a devout Catholic, and I, a devout Latter-day Saint, prayed unitedly in our foxhole that our lives might be preserved," he recalled. Lieutenant Nelson reflected later how much it meant to face life-threatening danger with a man of faith whose beliefs may have differed from his but who looked to the same Source for comfort and strength. Their combined faith was a boon to both that stressful night.

At another M.A.S.H., Russell met a young Latter-day Saint soldier who had been paralyzed by a gunshot wound. He wondered how to comfort the young man and ended up being the one comforted when the soldier said, "Don't worry about me, Brother Nelson, for I know why I was sent to the earth—to gain experiences and work out my salvation. I can work out my salvation with my mind and not with my legs. I'll be all right!" Russell recorded afterward that "the faith of that young man has motivated me ever since" (Nelson, *From Heart to Heart*, 79).

Dr. Nelson with a tank on Wake Island.

> "That was like giving a boy a red wagon! . . .
> I loved Boston. I loved Harvard.
> I loved Mass General Hospital."
>
> —Dr. Russell M. Nelson

After twenty months of military service, Russell was promoted—or, as he explained it, "Because I'd managed to inhale and exhale for twenty months, I was promoted to captain." The work Captain Nelson did in the Korean theater as well as research he conducted on bacterial toxemia in shock patients caught the attention of Dr. Edward D. Churchill, professor of surgery at Harvard Medical School and chief of surgical services at Massachusetts General Hospital in Boston. Russell was eager to return to Minnesota to complete his residency and PhD degree, but Dr. Churchill convinced him to come to Boston for a year and "contribute to the educational ferment at Harvard." So he and Dantzel were off for a year-long Ivy League experience on the Harvard Service at Mass General.

"Well," Russell recalled, "that was like giving a boy a red wagon! Wow! I just loved it there! I loved Boston. I loved Harvard. I loved Mass General Hospital. It was just a wonderful privilege."

There he was an assistant resident in surgery, charged with "helping wonderful, famous, world-class surgeons in the operating room. It was a dream. I had learned a lot in Minnesota, but the surgeons in Boston were so good, so experienced, so very polished. They did surgery like an artist paints a painting. It was beautiful. I learned how to operate without incurring the kinds of complications that surgeons had become accustomed to. It was a step up for me, a chance to increase my knowledge and improve my skills exponentially."

With his experience in Korea and now Boston, in a span of less than two years Dr. Nelson was exposed to the most rudimentary kind of surgery designed to keep soldiers alive on the front lines—"meat-ball" surgery, as the characters on *M*A*S*H* sometimes described it—and some of the most skilled, refined surgery in the world at Massachusetts General. In terms of training for what would lie ahead, the contrast and range of experience were ideal.

The year in Boston was invigorating and stressful all at once. Dr. Nelson's schedule put him on call every other night and every other weekend. That meant he kissed Dantzel and their daughters good-bye one morning at 6:00 a.m. and didn't see them again until late the next day. He averaged seven of every forty-eight hours at home, and most of those either he or the children were asleep.

The Nelson family in Boston: Dantzel, holding Brenda; Marsha; Gloria; Russell, holding Wendy.

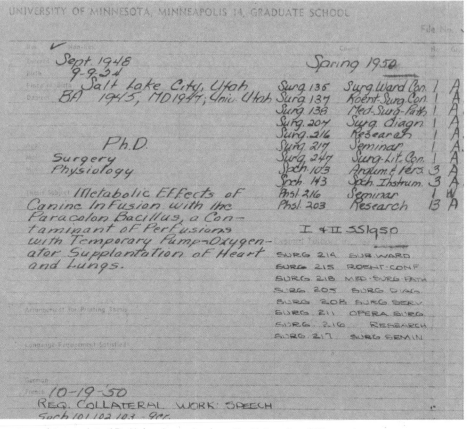

A transcript of Dr. Nelson's grades from the University of Minnesota.

Both Dantzel and Russell felt the sacrifices were worth it and somehow managed to keep the stress between them at a minimum—no doubt a tribute to Dantzel's patience and commitment to her husband's training. In Boston, Russell experienced firsthand that few things are more valuable than knowledge, there is no way to put a value on skill and talent, and there is no substitute for truth.

After a year at Harvard and Mass General, the Nelsons returned to Minnesota, where Russell finished his residency and was awarded his PhD. It was now 1954. Seven years had passed since he finished medical school and began his advanced training. Finally, Dr. Nelson was ready to practice medicine.

361409

Name Russell Marion Nelson

Addre 848 - 20th Ave. S.E. Mpls.14

Sheet 2

Course	Hr.	Gr.	Course	Hr.	Gr.	Memoranda
Fall 1950						Granted permission to make foll. changes on program for the Ph.D. (Coll. field)
Surg. 101 Outpt. Clinic	1	A				
Surg. 135 Surg. Ward Con.	1	A				
Surg. 134 Roent. Surg. Con.	1	A				Remove FROM COLL. Field
Surg. 138 Med. Surg. Path.	1	A				Speech 101 3cr.
Surg. 205 Surg. Diagn.	1	A				Add to coll. field
Surg. 208 Surg. Service	1	A				Speech 143 3cr.
Surg. 211 Oper. Surg.	1	XA				2-26-52
Surg. 216 Research	1	A				PD $10.00 GRAD. FEE
Surg. 245 Surg. Lit. Con.	1	A				PH D
PhSl. 116 Seminar	2	A				PD $5.00 LARGE DIPLOMA FEES
						11-19-54
FALL 1954						
	STAFF					
SURG. 200	OPD IN SURG.	1	A			
SURG. 205	SURG. DIAGN.	1	A			
SURG. 208	SURGIC. SERV.	1	A			
SURG. 211	OPER. SURG.	1	A			
SURG. 214	SURG. WARD CONF.	1	A			
SURG. 215	ROENTG. S. CONF.	1	A			
SURG. 216	RESEARCH	1	A			
SURG. 217	SEMINAR	1	A			
SURG. 218	M.S.P. CONF.	1	A			
SURG. 245	S. LIT. CONF.	1	A			

Doctor of Philosophy In Surgery

Granted December 16, 1954

Giving an address in his doctoral robes in later years.

"It always works, because divine law is irrefutable."

—Dr. Russell M. Nelson

During Russell's internship and residency, his appreciation for the predictability and power of natural law increased exponentially. Even with the finest skills a medical school could teach, surgeons have no healing power themselves. They must depend upon law to help the body heal.

In the early stages of pioneering work in open-heart surgery, Russell was drawn to three verses in the Doctrine and Covenants that seemed to have particular application for his work: "All kingdoms have a law given; And there are many kingdoms; for there is no space in the which there is no kingdom; and there is no kingdom in which there is no space, either a greater or a lesser kingdom. And unto every kingdom is given a law; and unto every law there are certain bounds also and conditions" (Doctrine and Covenants 88:36–38). These verses combined with another clear scriptural promise from the Doctrine and Covenants inspired him—that "when we obtain any blessing from God, it is by obedience to that law upon which it is predicated" (Doctrine and Covenants 130:20).

Surely, he reasoned, there were laws that governed the beating heart, laws that, if understood and obeyed, would result in blessings—and in the case of his responsibility for patients, the blessing of being able to cure and heal their damaged hearts.

In his early experiments, he found that the heart didn't mind being held and would keep beating because doing so did not violate a law. Then he and others discovered that if they simply altered the sodium/potassium ratio in the blood that flows into the coronary arteries to nourish the heart, the heart would stop instantly. At that point, it looked like a piece of salmon, flaccid and limp.

By the same token, they learned that when they washed the potassium chloride out with normal blood, the heart would spring back to life again because they had restored the normal ratio. "This process is what surgeons use today to turn the heartbeat off and do their surgical repairs," Russell explained. "You have to have the heart still. You can't splice spaghetti in motion."

Russell Nelson learned about the incontrovertibility of divine law in the operating room, and he learned to respect the power and blessings that result from obeying law.

"In other words," he later explained, "whenever a blessing is received, it's because a law has been obeyed. And that means certain procedures will *always* work—not just most of the time, not just some of the time, but every single time without exception. That takes the pressure off an individual who is willing to study the laws that govern the physical body and be obedient to them. Otherwise we'd be crazy

Dr. Nelson took meticulous notes in this small notebook.

49

to take these patients down to death and back every day" (Johnson, "Russell M. Nelson").

Decades later, Dr. Vivian Lee, then dean of the University of Utah Medical School, invited Elder Nelson to speak to the current class of medical students. After he described the process they'd gone through to learn how to turn the heartbeat on and off based upon the law it operated on, Dean Lee, as moderator, asked: "What if it doesn't work?"

"It always works," Elder Nelson responded, "because divine law is irrefutable." On another occasion, he added that it's similar to the principles that allow an airplane to fly. "You'd never climb into an airplane if you didn't have confidence that there are laws that, when obeyed, give an airplane lift and allow it to take off. An airplane will always work if the pilots obey the law that governs lift correctly, because air is buoyant and will support weight. Likewise, everything a doctor does is predicated upon the fact that if the laws are obeyed, the results are certain." As he told a group of university students, "It was through the understanding of the scriptures and 'likening' them to this area of interest that the great field of heart surgery as we know it today was facilitated for me" (Nelson, "Begin with the End in Mind").

On one occasion a medical colleague chastised Dr. Nelson for failing to separate his professional knowledge from his religious convictions. "That startled me," he admitted, "because I did not feel that truth should be fractionalized. Truth is indivisible" (Hafen, *Disciple's Life*, 165).

Blessings depend on truth and obedience to law. Said Elder Nelson years later, "You can pray all you want, you can hope all you want, but until the law is fulfilled upon which that blessing is predicated, it won't happen."

PART TWO

HEALING HEARTS AND BUILDING A HOME

1955 TO 1984

"Our competition wasn't with each other.
It was with death, disease, and ignorance."

—Dr. Russell M. Nelson

With his residency completed at the University of Minnesota, stints at Walter Reed Army Hospital in Washington, DC, the front lines of Korea, and Massachusetts General in Boston, and a PhD in hand, it was time for the Nelsons to determine what came next. They now had four little girls, and Russell had received tempting offers to stay in Minneapolis or return to Boston. But he and Dantzel felt drawn home to Utah and wondered if his training wouldn't be best put to use there. So, despite having no job offer in hand, they moved their small family back to Salt Lake City.

The job situation resolved itself quickly. As soon as Dr. Philip B. Price, his earlier mentor and professor of surgery at the University of Utah College of Medicine, found that his accomplished protégé had returned to Utah, he offered him a position as assistant professor of surgery at the university. He also provided Russell with a rudimentary lab in a temporary army barracks near the medical school so he could continue his research on the heart-lung machine. It was all he could have hoped for.

Russell split his time between the operating room and the lab, where he began to build another heart-lung machine—"because I could see a better way of doing it," he said.

One evening he found himself telling Dantzel about the latest dilemma he was trying to solve on the new-and-improved heart-lung machine he was building. The challenge was to figure out how tiny air bubbles could be introduced into a column of blood gently enough to oxygenate it without destroying its formed elements. As they talked, they reasoned that "the foamed blood could be defoamed and collected in a settling chamber where it could be pumped back to the arterial system of the patient" (Nelson, *From Heart to Heart*, 97).

With four children and a fifth on the way, the Nelsons were in the baby business. As they looked at the baby bottles, nipples, and screw caps around the house, they had an idea. They put a rubber membrane on the bottom of a baby-bottle nipple, and Dantzel used her sewing machine to perforate the membrane with a hundred little holes to create the needed bubbles. They then screwed the modified nipple onto a glass column "into which the venous blood flowed. By turning the oxygen gas on, tiny bubbles were created which ascended along with the blood up the oxygenating column. Then as this column of foamy blood erupted over the top of the oxygenating column, we provided a zone of contact so that that blood would pass over some copper 'Chore-girls,' which were originally made to scrub pots and pans. The 'Chore-girls' were daubed with a compound known as a silicone antifoam which changed the surface tension of the bubbles so that they burst, allowing the gas to escape into the atmosphere. The liquid blood surrounding the bubbles cascaded down the walls of the outer receiving chamber and settled without bubbles, awaiting passage through a pump back to the heart" (Nelson, *From Heart to Heart*, 97–98).

Scrubbing pad similar to the "Chore-girls" pads Dr. Nelson used in his machine.

Russell tested the oxygenator he and Dantzel built on animals, and it worked well enough that he later used it to perform his first open-heart operation on a human being. A few years later, after Dr. Nelson had performed a number

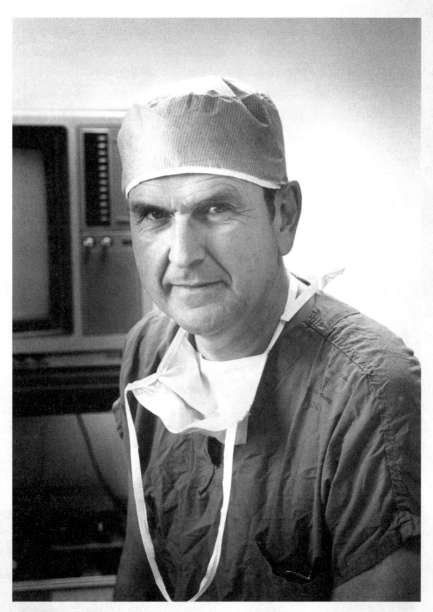

Dr. Russell M. Nelson.

of operations using this device, he took it to an engineer and asked him to make a more refined version. When the appliance came back from the engineer, housed in a beautiful chassis, Dantzel inspected the new-and-improved version and teased, "Why didn't you build it this way in the first place?"

Dantzel's contributions to Russell's research and thinking were significant enough that, decades later, in June 2018, when the University of Utah established a Presidential Endowed Chair of Cardiothoracic Surgery, they did so in the names of both Dr. Russell M. and Dantzel White Nelson.

Because of Dr. Nelson's extensive specialized training, accentuated by his personal involvement in helping build the first heart-lung machine and then a subsequent, improved model, it was just a matter of time until he was approached about performing an open-heart operation in Utah. That day came in November 1955 when Dr. Hans

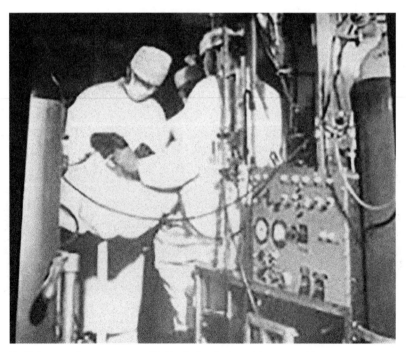

Dr. Nelson performs surgery with the help of a heart-lung machine.

Hecht, the head of cardiology at the U of U, told Dr. Nelson he had a patient for him—Vernell Worthen, who had an atrial septal defect.

Dr. Nelson faced a crossroads: he could refer the patient to his colleagues in Minnesota, where they were doing cutting-edge work in heart surgery and had performed many open-heart procedures, or he could attempt it for the first time. "I had a frank talk with the patient and with my chief of surgery," he said. "I told Vernell that this operation had never been performed previously in Utah, that as the senior resident in Minnesota I had assisted surgeons doing this operation many times, and that I felt ready to perform it. But I also told her that I would happily refer her to my colleagues in Minnesota if she preferred that."

The patient chose Dr. Nelson to perform the operation, and the chief of surgery gave him the green light. So, on November 9, 1955, he scrubbed for his first open-heart operation as surgeon in charge, walked into the operating room, and, with a sense of confidence punctuated by a few butterflies, opened the patient's chest and performed the procedure he had assisted with many times as a senior resident in Minnesota.

Gratefully, the operation was a success. At the age of thirty-one, Dr. Nelson had put himself and the University of Utah on the open-heart surgery map. Utah was only the third state in the nation where this medical feat had been performed—the first west of the Mississippi—and with this, the professional floodgates opened for Dr. Nelson.

Doctors started sending him patients, and surgeons from around the world came to Salt Lake City to learn from an open-heart surgery pioneer. In coming months and years, on any given day, there might be surgeons from Holland, Sweden, China, India, and a host of other countries working side by side with him in his lab and observing or assisting him in the operating room.

Remarkably, Dr. Nelson shared what he knew with as many as

cared to come. When he traveled to professional meetings, he and the relatively few other surgeons operating on the heart conferred about what they were learning—what worked, what didn't, what increased the chance of survival and quality of life after surgery, the best post-operative practices, and so on.

During that pioneering era, there was no such thing as propri-etary information. No one, least of all Dr. Nelson, seemed concerned about getting credit for new procedures, securing patents or copy-rights, getting royalties, or turning their knowledge into financial windfalls. Said Dr. Nelson in retrospect, "In those days we charged an operating fee. But in research and development, there was no money. Our professional ethics were such that there were no such things as trade secrets. Truth was truth, and we would share every-thing we learned."

When, decades later, he was asked why there wasn't a more fierce sense of competition among him and his colleagues, he responded, simply: "Our competition was not with each other. It was with dis-ease, ignorance, and death. That was our competition. But never with each other."

Such collaboration might have been unheard of in other disci-plines or professions, but Dr. Nelson's approach worked for him, driven in part because in those early years of open-heart surgery, mortality rates were high. Each time surgeons entered the operating room, they faced life-and-death situations and decisions. Often they peered into the unknown as they pioneered a long list of procedures on the heart. Nonetheless, as Russell's career accelerated, he expe-rienced firsthand that as he shared the insights and knowledge God gave him, God gave him more.

He was, as it turned out, a natural teacher. From 1968 through 1984, he served as director of the thoracic surgical residency pro-gram at the University of Utah and was directly involved in training at least seventy-five residents in open-heart surgery from around the

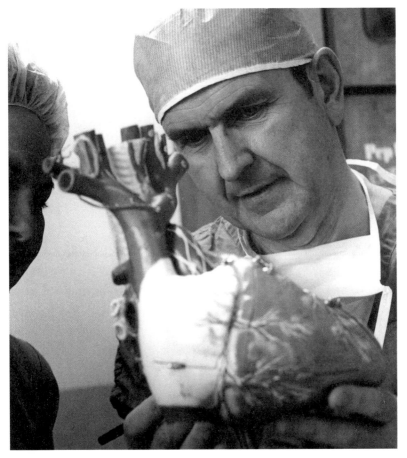

Dr. Nelson examines a model of the human heart.

world. Students came from China, India, Iran, Mexico, Turkey, the Netherlands, Greece, and Italy, to name a few places, and after completing their training they fanned out around the globe and trained others.

Later, as Elder Nelson traveled the world for the Church, he was frequently reunited with former students. Just one example was his meeting Dr. Devendra Saksena in New Delhi, India, in 2015. Dr. Saksena had been Dr. Nelson's resident from 1968 to 1970 and went on to become India's number-one cardiac surgeon. Another resident,

Lyle Joyce, went on to the Mayo Clinic, where many years later he would in turn train Dr. Nelson's grandson Dr. Stephen McKellar in open-heart surgery. Dr. Nelson's influence had cascading, multi-generational, worldwide impact.

Dr. Nelson taught in other ways as well. Elder Gregory A. Schwitzer of the Seventy, himself an MD, first met Dr. Nelson when his ninth-grade class went to LDS Hospital to meet with a surgeon who had agreed to tell them what it was like to be a doctor. That surgeon was Dr. Nelson. "I remember him standing in front of our class," Elder Schwitzer recalled, "holding an artificial heart valve in his hand and explaining how it worked."

The experience was unforgettable, even life-changing for the young Greg Schwitzer: "I didn't really remember or understand everything he said medically. I do remember how he inspired me. I believe, in part, my decision to choose my life profession was because of the influence and the inspiring nature of that first intersection of my life with his. He looked so dedicated, and he was so kind. I'll never forget the feeling I had" (*Church News*/KSL Interview, January 8, 2018).

In terms of teaching, Dr. Nelson would also, over time, write more than seventy peer-reviewed papers for medical publications. He found that he had a knack for languages and studied a number of them to help him as he lectured widely around the world, teaching open-heart procedures. Most important, he focused intently on the nearly seven thousand patients who would submit to his scalpel. "The duty of a doctor, primarily, is to teach," Dr. Nelson explained. "A doctor is really functioning at his highest level when he is teaching his patient what is wrong and what can be done about it" (Condie, *Russell M. Nelson,* 140).

During a career that would span another thirty years, he would be the instrument in saving literally thousands of lives.

"Are you finished crying yet? . . . Go back to the lab."

—Dantzel White Nelson

___

O ver time, Dr. Nelson experienced tremendous success. Those early days of open-heart surgery, however, were tenuous.

Surgeons lose patients. Pioneering surgeons lose even more.

Those initial open-heart operations were "like sailing an uncharted sea," Dr. Nelson admitted. There were days of sheer elation. When he completed successful operations and improved or perfected or invented procedures in the process, the relief, sense of accomplishment, and pure joy were exhilarating. But there were also days of high stress, days and weeks of bone-numbing fatigue, and, sometimes, moments of pure despair.

One of the most defeating experiences involved the Hatfield family. The first three children of Ruth and Jimmy Hatfield were born with congenital heart disease. Jimmy Jr., the eldest son, died before Dr. Nelson met the Hatfields—and before the advent of cardiac surgery. He met Ruth and Jimmy in 1958 when they brought their second child and oldest daughter, Laural Ann, to him for help. She was gravely ill, and Russell was not optimistic about her chances to survive an open-heart operation, but the Hatfields pleaded with him to try to save her, so he did. Despite his best efforts, Laural Ann died.

The following year, in 1959, the Hatfields brought another daughter to Dr. Nelson. Sixteen-month-old Gay Lynn had been born with a malformed heart, and again, they implored him to try to save their daughter. He explained that it was unlikely anything could be done to address her abnormalities, and he did not recommend surgery. But

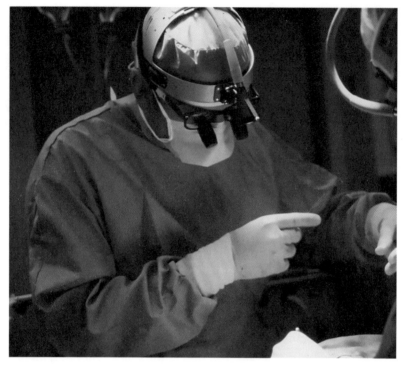

Dr. Nelson performing another delicate surgical procedure.

again, they pleaded with him to try. He performed the operation, and that night Gay Lynn died.

Russell drove home distraught, overcome with grief. "This third heartbreaking loss in one family literally undid me," he explained. "Words cannot describe my feelings of pain. Despair, grief, tragedy— these characterizations only scratch the surface of the torment raging in my soul, which caused me to determine that my failures and inadequacies would never be inflicted on another human family" (Nelson, *From Heart to Heart,* 99).

The minute Russell walked in the door, Dantzel could see that her husband was in deep distress. He threw himself on the living-room floor and sobbed. This went on for hours. He stayed there, kneeling next to a chair in the living room much of the time, all night long. Dantzel stayed with him, listening as his grief came tumbling out and as he repeatedly declared that he would never perform another operation on the heart. He simply could not risk putting another family through what he felt he had put the Hatfields through.

Dantzel saw his grief and understood his pain. But she also saw something he could not see. Around 5:00 the next morning, she uttered words that would shape his future. With love in her voice but also a strong dose of backbone, she asked, "Are you finished crying yet? Then get dressed. Go back to the lab. Go to work! You need to learn

Dantzel was her husband's greatest support.

more. If you quit now, others will have to painfully learn what you already know" (Nelson, "Plea to My Sisters").

Her words stunned him. At a pivotal moment in his career, a moment when he might have abandoned heart surgery, Dantzel spoke with a perfect mixture of confidence, love, and urgency. She was her husband's voice of authority at one of the most important professional moments of his life.

Russell went back to the lab. He went back to the surgical suite. And he learned more—much, much more.

Through it all, he not only increased his skill and knowledge but came to understand the healer's art. Twenty-five years after the devastating loss of the second Hatfield daughter, he would say: "Nowadays doctors have a very high rate of success in these operations, but we can't save everyone—that would be impossible. Sometimes all we can do is offer comfort. We don't ever want to destroy hope. The doctor's job is to cure sometimes, to relieve suffering frequently, but always to comfort" (Johnson, "Russell M. Nelson").

"A person who is out of control is . . . out of control."

—Dr. Russell M. Nelson

Even when he was a young surgeon, Dr. Nelson's operating room was calm and orderly and had an attitude of respect for everyone in the room. "Things can go wrong in a hurry in the operating room," he explained, "particularly if you're working with circuits and connectors and things where an aorta can blow apart in front of your eyes, or the tubing can split open. You've got to be ready to make instant decisions and take instant actions. The only way you can do that is to demand absolute control over your emotions. Absolute control. I learned this the hard way."

As a young intern in Minneapolis, Dr. Nelson found himself assisting a surgeon who was amputating a gangrenous leg. "Not ischemic gangrene but gas gangrene, botulism," he described. "And the surgeon was just jittery." The operation was difficult and not proceeding as desired. At one point, one of the surgical team members failed to perform a function exactly as prescribed, and the surgeon became furious and spewed one insult after another while deriding his colleague. As he did so, and while cutting through tissue loaded with disease, he lost control of his scalpel and jabbed the knife infected with botulism through Dr. Nelson's forearm. The danger to the young intern was immediately apparent to everyone in the room, but even this costly, unprofessional mistake didn't humble or calm the surgeon in charge.

"I didn't like that very well," Dr. Nelson said in understated fashion. "I said right then and there, 'Russell, you will never lose control in the operating room. You will always be able to handle things without getting upset. I resolved that I would discipline my body to be subject to the dominion of my spirit."

There were other learning experiences that reinforced his resolve. While assisting a surgeon during his time in Boston, Russell was tying a knot on a crucial bleeder when the thread broke. "It broke!" he said to the more experienced surgeon. Seizing the teaching moment, the surgeon stopped the operation, laid out a suture on the table, and asked, "Now, Dr. Nelson, will that suture ever break?"

"No," Russell responded.

"You broke it," said the surgeon. "It won't ever break on its own. You have to break it for it to break. So take responsibility."

Such early training in responsibility and self-mastery paid dividends throughout Russell's life. He became a model of discipline. Though blessed with a lean body, he weighed himself every day and held back a little on what he ate if he went up a pound. Many years later, his Brethren would say they had never seen him out of control, never seen him lose his temper during even the most intense discussions about critical issues. As his international travel increased, he learned to adapt to time zones with the attitude, "If I'm flying to this time zone, I'm now in that time zone." In like manner, the environment in his operating room was distinctive among surgeons.

In November 2015, President Russell M. Nelson was honored by the University of Utah Medical School upon the sixtieth anniversary of the first open-heart operation in the state. Heart surgeons came from far and wide to celebrate one of their professional heroes and mentors, a true pioneer in their field.

Elder Gary E. Stevenson of the Quorum of the Twelve was in attendance and found himself seated next to a former student of Dr. Nelson's from when he was the head of the thoracic surgery residency program at the medical school. This man, now an accomplished surgeon in his own right, described Dr. Nelson's unique teaching style, which resulted in a great deal of notoriety.

Heart-surgery residents, he explained, do much of their learning in the operating room, where they perform surgery under faculty supervision. The environment in some operating rooms was, this student said, "chaotic, competitive, pressure filled, and even ego driven." The experience could be demeaning and frightening all at once because young resident surgeons knew their careers were on the line.

But he described Dr. Nelson's operating room as distinct from the others: "It was peaceful, calm, and dignified. Residents were treated with deep respect." Soft music played over an intercom, and despite the life-or-death situations they might encounter, the surgical team worked with deliberate concentration and no sense of drama.

This is not to say the environment was lax, however. Once Dr. Nelson demonstrated a procedure, he expected near perfection from the residents. As a result, said this former student, "The best patient outcomes and the best surgeons came out of Dr. Nelson's operating room."

Elder Stevenson summarized, "This is no surprise to me at all. This is what I have observed firsthand and been truly blessed by in the Quorum of the Twelve. I feel like I have been, in a sense, one of his 'residents in training'" (Stevenson, "Heart of a Prophet").

Elder Gregory A. Schwitzer of the Seventy concurred: "I have never met a surgeon who was trained under Russell M. Nelson who didn't have the highest accolades for the training he received. He taught them what you might call the 'unwritten laws of medicine,' in terms of bedside manner, caring for the individual, and looking into their hearts figuratively as well as literally" (*Church News*/KSL Interview, January 8, 2018).

When residents and other members of the operating team needed to be corrected, Dr. Nelson did so with respect. During one quadruple coronary arterial bypass operation—surgery to bypass obstructions in four arteries—at one point in the delicate operation the patient's blood pressure suddenly dropped, much to the surgical team's surprise. Dr. Nelson quickly identified the problem—a clamp that should have been left on one of many tubes in the procedure had been removed. With the clamp replaced, he said to the operating team member responsible for the mistake, "I still love you." Moments later he added, "Sometimes I love you more than other times." Despite the error, the atmosphere remained positive.

About that incident, Dr. Nelson explained, "It's a matter of extreme self-discipline. Your natural reaction is, 'Take me out, coach! I want to go home!' But of course you can't. A life is totally dependent on the whole surgical team. So you've got to stay just as calm and relaxed and sharp as you ever were" (Johnson, "Russell M. Nelson").

Said Elder Schwitzer, "Russell M. Nelson is renowned for what he did in his career. He was an innovator and a pioneer. But I don't think there is another senior physician on the medical staff who consistently is also described with the word *inspiring*. He certainly inspired me" (*Church News*/KSL Interview, January 8, 2018).

"What are you going to do for his tricuspid regurgitation?"–Dr. Maunsel B. Pearce

"I don't know. I have no idea."–Dr. Russell M. Nelson

In the early days of open-heart surgery, Dr. Nelson often found himself staring into the unknown and confronting problems no one had tackled before. This was exactly the situation when Brother E. Lyman, a stake patriarch living in southern Utah, came seeking his help. Russell's extensive review revealed that his patient had two problems: mitral stenosis and tricuspid valve regurgitation. In layman's terms, this man had two faulty valves—one that could be repaired surgically and one that couldn't, the tricuspid valve. So Dr. Nelson declined to operate.

Brother Lyman left that day but later returned to ask again if Dr. Nelson would operate. Again Dr. Nelson declined. It was neither moral nor responsible, he felt, to put someone through open-heart surgery when it wouldn't solve the problem.

But Brother Lyman returned a third time, and on this visit he was not going to take no for an answer. With some emotion, he said to the heart surgeon: "Dr. Nelson, I have prayed for help and have been directed to you. The Lord will not reveal to me how to repair that second valve, but He can reveal it to you. Your mind is so prepared. If you will operate upon me, the Lord will make it known to you what to do. Please perform the operation that *I* need, and pray for the help that *you* need" (Nelson, "Sweet Power of Prayer").

This was 1960, and cardiac surgery was still less than a decade old. At the time the patriarch pleaded for his help, Dr. Nelson had performed seventy-three operations—not an insignificant number, considering the infancy of the discipline. By today's standards, however, his surgical experience was still limited. Cardiothoracic surgeons today complete three hundred or more cardiac operations by the time they finish their residency and begin their careers. Further, Russell's work on diagnoses most closely connected to Brother Lyman's situation was even more limited. He had performed only eight open-field operations on the mitral valve, the closest surgical comparable to the tricuspid valve, and he had performed just two repairs on mitral valve insufficiency. Even contemplating operating on a defective tricuspid valve was venturing entirely into the unknown.

No one was more aware of this than Dr. Nelson. He recalled, "I was still a young surgeon, and to my knowledge no one had ever attempted to correct such a problem."

But Brother Lyman's repeated requests were compelling. Elder Nelson would later explain that "his great faith had a profound effect upon me. How could I turn him away again?" (Nelson, "Sweet Power of Prayer").

With no small amount of trepidation, Dr. Nelson agreed to operate, and he set the date of May 24, 1960, for the procedure. "Don't think I didn't pray about that procedure," he said. "I prayed and prayed and got absolutely *zero*. As we opened Brother Lyman's chest, my resident, Dr. Maunsel B. Pearce, looked at me and asked, 'What are you going to do for his tricuspid regurgitation?' and I said, 'I don't know. I have no idea.'"

He and his surgical team first relieved the obstruction in the first, reparable valve. So far, so good. They then exposed the second valve and found it to be intact. The only thing wrong with it was that it was badly dilated. "I could put my whole hand in his tricuspid valve orifice instead of three fingers, which is what it should have been," Dr. Nelson explained.

Thankfully, the tissue was good. There seemed to be nothing wrong with the tricuspid valve other than the fact that the hole had

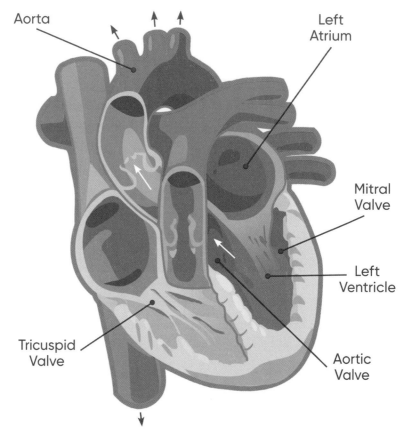

A diagram of the human heart.

been stretched to the point where the tissue could not close properly. It was while Dr. Nelson surveyed this situation that he had a distinct impression: "Reduce the circumference of the ring." His immediate thought was: "I don't know how to do that. If it were a pair of pants, I'd tighten the belt. But you can't put a belt around the heart."

Then a diagram appeared in his mind showing him where to place sutures to essentially do a series of tucks and pleats that would reduce the circumference so that the valve tissue would cover the hole. It was roughly comparable to cinching up the belt on a pair of trousers worn by someone who has lost weight.

"I still remember that mental image—complete with dotted lines where sutures should be placed," he explained years later. He completed the repair on the tricuspid valve as it was diagrammed in his mind. As the surgical team tested the valve and concluded the procedure, Dr. Pearce said, no doubt speaking for everyone in the room, "It's a miracle." Russell responded simply, "It's an answer to prayer." He knew exactly from Whom the help had come.

Later, Dr. Nelson admitted: "I had no idea what I was going to do as I began that operation. Today there are all sorts of ways to reduce the circumference of the ring, but I knew none of those procedures at the time. I had not experienced pure revelation like that, surgically, before. But that was pure revelation. I had that man's heart open, and if that revelation had not come, he would have died."

In his postoperative dictation, Dr. Nelson wasn't even sure what to call the procedure he'd just performed. He named it *tricuspid commissurorrhaphy* at the time, but future surgeons would rename the procedure *tricuspid valve annuloplasty*.

As it turned out, a close personal friend and colleague at the University of Southern California, Dr. Jerome Kay, had completed a first-ever repair technique for tricuspid insufficiency two months earlier, in March of that year. But Russell had not heard about the procedure and didn't have the advantage of Dr. Kay's experience (see "Discovering a Surgical First," 319–37).

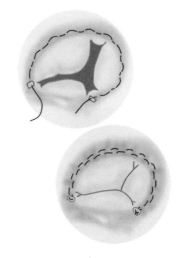

With time, the fundamental technique Dr. Nelson used, which was distinct from Dr. Kay's, was seen as even more remarkable. A team of medical reporters later wrote: "Nelson's annuloplasty technique would

The tricuspid valve.

prove a remarkably effective solution to the problem of tricuspid regurgitation, one that would anticipate problems with contemporary approaches years before they were appreciated by the surgical community at large. In the intervening . . . decades medical science has progressed considerably. . . . However, as a group of modern surgeons recently noted, the message impressed on the mind of a scrubbed-in, nervous surgeon as he peered into a dilated right atrium in 1960 has remained a fundamental principle in surgical correction of tricuspid insufficiency through the present day: reduce the circumference of the ring" ("Discovering a Surgical First," 319–37).

Precisely as Brother Lyman had declared at the outset, it was Dr. Nelson's rare combination of knowledge and ability to receive inspiration that led to this surgical discovery—and success. Brother Lyman lived many more years.

It all began, however, with the faith of the patient that inspired his surgeon to try. "It was a step into the dark," Russell said. "I thought about Joshua coming back into the Promised Land with his people and crossing the waters of the River Jordan at flood time. It wasn't until they put their feet in the water that they saw the hand of the Lord manifest in their lives. And that is what I experienced that day."

"My life is ready for inspection."
—Mickey Oswald

During the early days of open-heart surgery, when mortality rates were still very high, Dr. Nelson felt he must address the potential of death every time he consulted with a patient in heart failure.

In 1956, Dr. Nelson performed ten consecutive open-heart operations without a death. He reported the feat to the American College of Surgeons because, at the time, the accomplishment was noteworthy. In time, he would perform a hundred consecutive operations without a death, but in the early days, that was not the case.

"We had to live with our own conscience," Russell said. "I would tell patients and the referring physicians that if we thought the patient could live more than a year, we should not operate. But if the patient's life expectancy could be measured in a few days or weeks or perhaps months, we might be able to help and should operate. The patients couldn't be at death's door or they wouldn't be able to survive the operation. So they had to be strong enough to tolerate the operation but sick enough that they would die fairly soon without it."

One memorable patient was Mickey Oswald, Russell's high school football coach. Though Russell had made the football team at East High School, he didn't play much. For one thing, though he was athletically inclined and would become a beautiful snow and water skier, his lean frame wasn't built for football. For another, he was already contemplating a career in medicine, and the idea of some beefy lineman stepping on his hands or mangling some other body part wasn't very appealing. So he rode the bench most of the time.

Coach Oswald was grateful Russell's career as a football player was short-lived, because years later he would need his former player's services when he faced heart failure.

After Dr. Nelson evaluated his coach's condition, he told him that his prognosis was not good. If they were to proceed with an operation, it would be at an extremely high risk and he could not guarantee survival. But Russell agreed to do surgery because death was certain otherwise. "I'll never forget his response," Russell related. "'My life is ready for inspection,' Mickey said. 'Let's proceed.'"

"Those words, 'My life is ready for inspection,' have stayed with me ever since," Russell said years later. "He meant it most sincerely, and I have often contemplated the power of being able to face the next world with that kind of spiritual confidence."

Coach Oswald did not survive the operation, making his declaration to Dr. Nelson all the more poignant.

> "Nelson is a labeled Mormon and our appointment of him would be offensive to our donors."
>
> —Max Wintrobe

D r. Philip B. Price's mentorship of Russell Nelson dated to medical school. When Russell and Dantzel wanted to return to Utah in 1955, he hired Dr. Nelson as an assistant professor of surgery at the U. When Dr. Nelson was contemplating performing the first open-heart operation in Utah, Dr. Price was one of his most vocal champions.

When Dr. Price was named dean of the university's medical school in the late 1950s, the vacancy he created as chair of surgery at the U was up for grabs. Dr. Nelson, who had been back at the university for four years and would have been Dr. Price's pick to succeed him, looked to be an ideal candidate.

But Dr. Max Wintrobe, an influential man at the University of Utah and chairman of the search committee, had other ideas. "Nelson is a labeled Mormon and our appointment of him would be offensive to our donors," he declared. Dr. Walter J. Burdette was named to the post, and Burdette's plans going forward didn't include Dr. Nelson.

Further complicating the situation, in 1957, the John and Mary R. Markle Foundation had awarded Dr. Nelson a Markle scholarship, a prestigious grant of $6,000 annually for five years to support his continuing cardiovascular research. To be known as a "Markle scholar" was akin to being crowned a prince in the medical field. But with Burdette's arrival at the U, it became evident that Dr. Nelson's remaining on the faculty was not in Dr. Burdette's plan. It felt unfair, but there was nothing for Dr. Nelson to do but resign his faculty

The Salt Lake Tribune

Salt Lake City, Utah — Saturday Morning — April 7, 1956

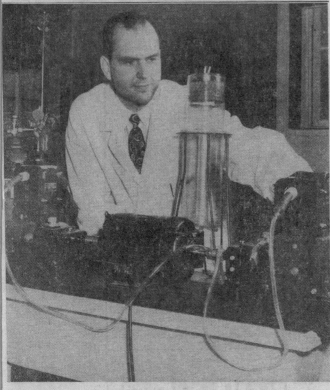

Dr. Russell M. Nelson, University of Utah College of Medicine, demonstrates improved type of heart-lung machine which he developed lately at Salt Lake General Hospital.

Direct-Vision Open Heart Surgery

S.L. Achieves Another Medical Stride

By William C. Patrick
Tribune Medical Editor

Salt Lake City is now one of the few medical centers in the world in which direct-vision open heart surgery is being performed with the aid of a heart-lung machine.

This was disclosed Friday in a talk before the first annual scientific session of the Utah Heart Assn. at the Veterans Administration Hospital, Fort Douglas.

The device being used here is a less complex but efficient version of heart-lung machines employed elsewhere.

children and adults with heart defects. All survived to gain a new release on life, except the last, a 7-year-old girl, who died of kidney failure two days after the operation.

The great advantage of the by-pass technique is that it enables the surgeon to cut into the wall of the heart at the level of the ventricles, the large pumping chambers at the lower end. With blood coursing through the chambers this would be impossible.

Many successful heart operations have been performed by other techniques, but in these the surgeon has to feel his way through small incisions cut into the upper portion.

One Method

One method used to reduce the activity of the heart and the amount of blood being pumped is to take the patient's body temperature down below normal by packing him in ice, and thus lower the demand for oxygen. This is known as hypothermia.

Another advantage of using the heart-lung machine, Dr. Nelson said, is that it gives the surgeon more time to work in the heart. In hypothermia the surgeon is given about 10 minutes for actual work on the heart; with by-pass of the blood the heart can be kept open for as much as an hour.

Described at Meet

It was described to physicians attending the meeting by Dr. Russell M. Nelson, assistant professor of surgery, University of Utah College of Medicine, who developed the machine with the co-operation of his association in the college.

Five operations for the correction of structural heart defects have been performed while blood was by-passed away from the human heart and the lungs. The machine took over the job of pumping, purifying and supplying the blood with oxygen, while the surgeon operated on a relatively quiet, bloodless heart.

Mother First Patient

Dr. Nelson said his first operation with the new heart-lung machine was performed last Nov. 9 at Salt Lake General Hospital on a 39-year-old mother of three children from Price. She had suffered circulatory difficulties all her life because of a defect consisting of two holes between the upper chambers of the heart, which the surgeon was able to close.

She left the hospital a week after the operation, now has a normal heart and is enjoying full activity for the first time in her life.

This is believed to be the first time a heart operation was performed with circulation by-pass west of Minneapolis, where a heart-lung machine was first used on a human patient undergoing heart surgery in March 1951.

Since November four other operations have been performed at Salt Lake General, on both

Promising Field

Dr. Nelson said one of the most promising fields for use of circulation by-pass is correcting the condition known as tetralogy of Fallot, in which there are four heart abnormalities causing serious impairment of circulation. This is what makes the so-called "blue babies."

The usual operation involves surgical changes to rearrange the blood flow to provide a better functioning heart, but which actually adds a fifth abnormality to the four existing ones. With the circulation by-passeed through a heart-lung machine the surgeon can operate inside the heart and correct the original difficulties.

Dr. Nelson said the by-pass technique holds great promise in facilitating surgery to cure ventricular septal defects (holes in the walls of the ventricles).
See Page 28, Col. 4

Dr. Nelson with the heart-lung machine.

position at the University of Utah and release his Markle grant after having held it just two years.

Russell couldn't help but be worried. He had been in practice for four years, and his expertise and reputation were growing. But he was still a young doctor in a new field, he had a growing family to care for, and he was now out of a job.

He and Dantzel were grateful when he was invited to join the ranks of the Salt Lake Clinic. At the same time, he applied for and received staff privileges at LDS Hospital. So, in essence, he simply moved his surgical practice across town.

In time, Dr. Burdette was asked to leave the university. Russell never returned to the University of Utah as a full-time employee, but the day came when he was instrumental in pulling together resources from LDS Hospital, Primary Children's Hospital, Veteran's Hospital, and the University of Utah to create an almost matchless thoracic surgical training program benefiting all entities. "I had a lot of good helpers," Russell Nelson remembered. "I had Conrad Jenson and Kent Jones and, in time, Don Doty. The University had Keith Reemtsma, a very able leader. And at the LDS Hospital there was not only my group, but the Rumel group, the Salt Lake Clinic, and many others."

Utah was proving to be a seedbed for cardio-thoracic expertise.

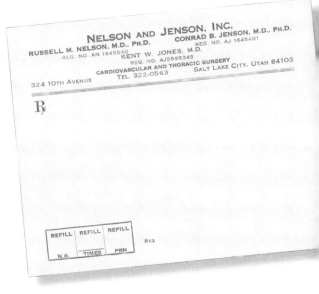

A prescription pad from Dr. Nelson's practice.

"I saw a baby boy."

—Dantzel White Nelson

I t was early fall in 1957 when Dantzel woke Russell in the middle of
the night to tell him about a vivid dream she'd just had. With some
exuberance, she announced that she and Russell were going to have
a baby boy. "During the night, I had a vision," she said. "It was more
than just a dream. I saw a baby boy. He had a round face and lots of
hair and he looked just like you. I had a wonderful visit with him."

Russell was interested, to say the least. Dantzel was pregnant
with their sixth child, and after five daughters, the prospects of
having a son were exciting. They adored their daughters—Marsha,
Wendy, Gloria, Brenda, and Sylvia—but also loved the idea of having
a son. When Emily, their sixth daughter, was born shortly thereafter,
they both wondered about Dantzel's nighttime experience but were
quickly smitten with their newest baby girl.

Sixteen months later, they had another child—a girl, Laurie. And
then three years later, another girl, Rosalie. And then three and a half
years after that, another girl, Marjorie. Following Dantzel's first vision of the chubby-faced, dark-haired little boy, the Nelsons made
four more trips to the hospital to deliver babies and returned home
each time with a precious bundle wrapped in pink.

Curiously, throughout this entire expanse of time—the better part of a decade—Dantzel's nighttime experiences with the boy
continued. "I saw him again," she would tell Russell in the morning.
"He's such a sweet and a special young boy."

They now had a large family by anyone's standards—nine daughters—and Dantzel's age had become an issue. With each successive

pregnancy, she had found it increasingly difficult to both carry and deliver their babies. Stopping was not an option, though. Her experiences with the little boy were so vivid that she felt certain their family was not yet complete.

So, despite the fact that she would be forty-six when she delivered this baby, she became pregnant a tenth time. It had been more than five years since she had delivered Marjorie, their youngest daughter.

While in Sun Valley, Idaho, speaking at a meeting of the Idaho Heart Association, Russell awoke in the middle of the night with the clear impression that this time Dantzel was carrying the son she had been seeing for years. And he also had the impression that the little boy's name should be Russell Marion Nelson Jr. With each previous pregnancy, Russell and Dantzel had selected both a girl's and a boy's name, but they'd always shied away from labeling a son as "Junior." This time, however, it felt different.

When Dantzel went into labor, pitocin was given to strengthen her contractions. But then her blood pressure soared. Russell was at her side and became increasingly nervous as her labor did not progress. When her blood pressure hit 220/120, he insisted that her obstetrician take the baby by cesarean section. On March 21, 1972, Dantzel delivered a beautiful, *twelve-pound, twenty-three-inch* bundle of joy—a dark-haired, chubby-faced baby boy!

As Dantzel awakened from the anesthesia and Russell handed her bundled son to her, she exclaimed, "He's the one! He's the one I've seen and known for all these years." Finally the Nelsons had a son, and, as Russell would quip later, "Our home was like a girls' dormitory until our one and only son came along. Poor boy! He didn't know who his real mother was for his first couple of years" (Nelson, "Faith and Families").

As Russ Jr. grew, he, like his sisters, loved spending time with his father, who seemed to have a knack for making even mundane things seem like fun. Russell would spread his papers out on a table and ask

boy
oh boy!

Birth announcement for Russell M. Nelson Jr.

Russell's family showing off his first son and first grandson, born two months apart. When Russ Jr. was born, he was already an uncle.

Nine beautiful daughters . . .

| Marjorie 6 | Rosalie 10 | Laurie 12 | Emily 14 | Sylvia 16 | Brenda 18 | Gloria 19 | Wendy 20 | Marsha and Christopher |

And now, a SON! Russell Marion Nelson, Jr. Born: March 21, 1972
Weight: 12 lbs. Length: 23 in.

Dantzel and Russell

And a GRANDSON too!
Nathan Christopher McKellar
Born: February 13, 1972
Weight: 7 lbs. 5 oz. Length: 20½ in.

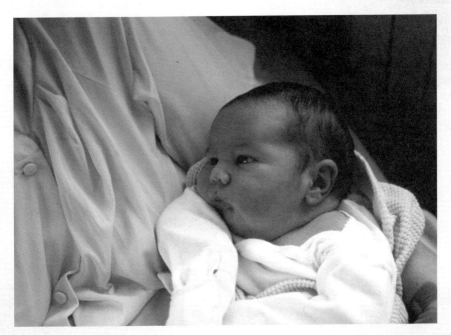

Baby Russ with his mother.

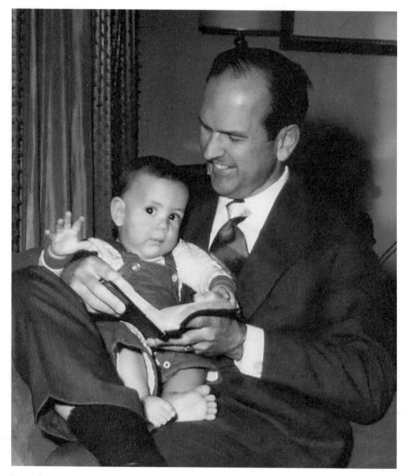

Russell with his son Russ Jr.

who wanted to help him with his taxes, knowing none of the children could, but inviting them to be nearby. "He could make taking out the garbage a fun routine," Russ Jr. said years later. "He's always been the same, and that normalcy made growing up comfortable and more reliable."

While he was still young, Russ Jr. had the distinct thought: "I can ask my dad anything and he always knows the answer. He took me once to the hospital and taught me how to read angiograms. He would always take time to explain things so that I could learn. Even on a fishing trip, he would carve the lens out of the fish's eye and say, 'See how it magnifies'" (Russell M. Nelson Jr., Remarks).

Family was everything to Russell. He loved his work and was immersed in it; he cherished calls to serve in the Church; but family meant everything to him. Through the years when Dantzel or the children would be asked about their relationship with their busy husband or father, each would predictably respond, "When he's home, he's home."

But between the hospital and Church responsibilities, he wasn't home much. Dantzel carried the lion's share of the load at home, and rather than resent her lot, she loved it. Somehow the fact that her intensely busy husband still wasn't bringing home much money, paired with the chaos of a large and ever-growing family, did not wear her down. Surely the challenge of it all must have been a burden at times, and she made countless personal sacrifices, but her children did not see them. She seemed born to be a mother and chose to love almost everything about it. Through the years, she taught her husband volumes about the unique bond between mother and child.

After Laurie was born, Russell and Dantzel were waiting for the nurse to bring their new baby to them. Dantzel had been under anesthetic during delivery and hadn't yet seen her little girl. Suddenly she said, "I hear our baby crying."

"You're kidding," Russell replied. "You haven't even seen her yet."

But Dantzel insisted, "That's our baby. I know her voice."

She asked Russell to check, so he walked into the corridor and down to a large cart that carried babies in their bassinets from the nursery to their mothers' rooms. There was only one baby crying. "They all looked alike to me, so I checked the I.D. tag and found that the one crying was labeled 'Baby Girl Nelson, Room 571.' That was an inspiration to me. Dantzel knew her child's voice even before she had ever heard it. I couldn't help but think about the Savior's statement

Surrounded by his growing, energetic family.

that 'my sheep know my voice.'" In this case, the "shepherd" knew the voice of her sheep.

Dantzel was, as Russell would later declare, "the fountain from whom flows the nourishing love in our home" (Nelson, "Call to the Holy Apostleship"). Despite all the acclaim, recognition, responsibility, and visibility that would come to him throughout his life, he was quick to say that the blessings that meant the most to him came because of her. And the eternal reality lodged with Russell that, when all was said and done, the purpose of God's plan was to seal and exalt families.

President Nelson's love for his family extends through all the generations. Here he holds a new great-grandson in 2009.

"If I have to change professions, I'll do it.
If I am called, I will serve."

—Russell M. Nelson

In December 1964, Elders Spencer W. Kimball and LeGrand Richards of the Quorum of the Twelve Apostles were assigned to preside at the conference of Salt Lake City's Bonneville Stake and to call a new stake president.

As they interviewed members of the high council, bishops in the stake, and other priesthood leaders who might be considered for such a calling, Russell Nelson's name kept coming up. But anyone who suggested him also said that he was too busy and that his lifestyle as a heart surgeon wouldn't allow it.

There was no doubt about it, he was busy. The same year he had the revelatory experience while operating to repair a tricuspid valve problem, he also joined a small group of surgeons at the forefront in their field when he performed coronary arteriography and coronary thromboendarterectomy. He published frequently, had a busy clinical workload, carried a significant administrative and educational load as the director of Utah's only cardiothoracic surgical training program, for a year had been serving on the stake high council, and, if that weren't enough, served as a Temple Square missionary for nearly ten years (between 1955 and 1965), helping visitors from 4:00 to 5:00 each Thursday. His workload and commitments were dizzying.

When the Brethren interviewed Russell and asked him to describe his workload, he admitted that during every post-operative period, he was metaphorically tied to each patient for several days. But he also said he would never turn down a call from the Lord. "Of

President of the Bonneville Stake.

course I have time," he told them. "I'll make time. If I have to change professions, I'll do it. If I am called, I will serve."

Dr. Nelson also explained that the intensity of his schedule was in part because, in those early days of aortic valve surgery, the mortality rate was about 25 percent—meaning, he was losing one in four patients. "I am married to each patient night and day, almost one-on-one, for many hours and sometimes for many days," he admitted. "I stay close to them until we get them through" ("Elder Russell M. Nelson of the Quorum of the Twelve Apostles").

Russell's schedule notwithstanding, Elder Kimball and Elder Richards felt directed to extend the call for him to serve as the new stake president. Elder Kimball's words to him were inauspicious: "We feel that the Lord wants you to preside over this stake. During our many interviews, whenever your name has come up the response has been rather routine: 'Oh, he wouldn't be very good,' or 'He doesn't have time,' or both. Nonetheless, we feel that the Lord wants you. Now if you feel that you are too busy and shouldn't accept the call, then that's your privilege" (Nelson, *From Heart to Heart,* 114).

Russell answered simply that "that decision was made August 31, 1945, when Sister Nelson and I were married in the temple. We made a commitment then to 'seek . . . first the kingdom of God.'" (Nelson, *From Heart to Heart,* 114).

He would later joke that he wondered if he had been called because of a musical performance his eight little girls (his youngest, Marjorie, wasn't born yet) had given the night before at a dinner program held in the stake cultural hall for the visiting General Authorities. "Our girls were just adorable," he said, "and I always wondered if that was what sold them on me."

Elder Kimball was voice in setting him apart, and he made it clear that this call was from the Lord. He also blessed Russell that the quality of his work as a surgeon would increase, that he would continue to acquire more skill quickly, and specifically that the mortality rate would decline particularly in his pioneering efforts with aortic valve surgery.

The following year, the mortality rate on Dr. Nelson's aortic valve surgery fell from 25 to 2 percent. Surgeons throughout the country envied the progress he was making. Asked why the mortality rate improved, he said, "Well, we just got better at it. We did better a little each day. But I may have gotten better faster than others because of that blessing and ordination."

Eight years later, Dr. Nelson would perform a complex operation on Elder Kimball that included replacing his aortic valve—the very procedure Elder Kimball had blessed him with the capacity to improve.

"It doesn't feel good to me."

—President David O. McKay

It was late in 1965 when Dr. Nelson received an unexpected but intriguing invitation. His work had caught the eye of the University of Chicago Medical School, and they knocked on his door with a prestigious, almost too-good-to-be-true offer. Would the accomplished young heart surgeon move to Chicago and accept the position as professor of surgery and chairman of the Division of Cardiovascular and Thoracic Surgery at the acclaimed university?

This offer was guaranteed to propel him forward in his career in a way that his work in Salt Lake City likely would not—and the young Dr. Nelson knew it. Russell and Dantzel traveled to Chicago to explore the attractive, not to mention lucrative, offer and liked what they saw. Professionally, this was an advancement. Personally, it offered a change of scenery and new opportunities for their nine daughters (their one son was yet to be born). And financially it would be a boon.

And there were other perks. A highly respected young law professor by the name of Dallin H. Oaks was firmly entrenched at the university, and the school's administration—understanding full well the importance Dr. Nelson

The University of Chicago.

placed on his faith—invited Dallin and his wife, June, to host the Nelsons on their visit to Chicago.

On November 21, 1965, the two couples had Sunday dinner together at their home, and they hit it off. Russell called meeting the Oaks family one of the highlights of the trip, and Dallin and June found the Nelsons delightful. "Of course we did everything we could to persuade him to accept an offer that we knew was being extended," Dallin Oaks later said. "I was taking the role of an advocate, for which I'd been trained professionally, and I was trying to convince them it was a good thing to come and live in Chicago" (*Church News*/KSL Interview, January 10, 2018). The prospect of having a distinguished colleague of his own faith, along with another strong Latter-day Saint family, nearby was appealing.

The stars seemed to be aligning. The university rolled out the red carpet, including in their offer the kind of research lab and staff support that would thrill any serious academician. And there was one further inducement that reassured the Nelsons: "One of the reasons we want you," the dean said, "is that we know you are a good Mormon. We want you on our faculty. We need you here to bring the influence to this University that a Mormon could bring" (Nelson, *From Heart to Heart*, 149).

Russell and Dantzel decided to accept the offer. They found a neighborhood where they felt they could put down roots and put earnest money down on a home, then returned to Salt Lake City with a move to Chicago in their near future.

Dr. Nelson, who was also President Nelson—president of the Bonneville Stake in Salt Lake City—told his high council that he had received an offer in Chicago and their family would be moving. But when Joseph Anderson, a member of President Nelson's high council and also secretary to the First Presidency, heard the announcement, he suggested that President Nelson might want to talk about his pending move with President David O. McKay. "The President of the

Church can't be concerned about the occupational changes of stake presidents," Russell challenged. "Oh, yes he can," Brother Anderson countered. So, at Brother Anderson's insistence, Dr. Nelson agreed to meet with the President of the Church.

On December 14, 1965, Dr. Nelson went to President McKay's apartment on the tenth floor of the Hotel Utah. An aging but smiling David O. McKay was leaning on a metal walker as he greeted him at the door. "You'll have to pardon my use of this walker," he said, smiling. "Sometimes these days my legs are a bit disobedient."

The young surgeon explained the reason for his visit and asked the President if he had counsel for him. President McKay's body may have been frail, but his mind was razor sharp as he quizzed Russell about the offer from the acclaimed university. Why were they considering making this move? How many children did they have, and what would this mean for them? Where did they live in Salt Lake City? Was this about fame? Was it about money? What impact would it have on his career? The prophet left no stone unturned.

Yes, the University of Chicago was a more prestigious institution, with its medical school highly regarded. Yes, this would mean a substantial increase in Dr. Nelson's compensation—the university had offered an annual salary of $60,000, which for a young doctor then living on $300 a month seemed like financial nirvana—not to mention other perks, such as full tuition for all of his children regardless of where they decided to attend college. And yes, this would likely result in even more professional acclaim.

It would also mean uprooting their large family, but they would have each other and felt confident they would make many new friends in Chicago—in fact, they had already met Dallin and June Oaks and their family and sensed they would become fast friends. And experiences they'd had living previously in Minneapolis, Washington, DC, and Boston had been rich and rewarding. They were not concerned about moving away from Utah again.

President David O. McKay.

After some discussion, President McKay leaned his head back on his chair and closed his eyes for a long, almost uncomfortable period of time. At one point, Russell wondered if something had happened to the President and if, as a doctor, he should check his vital signs. Finally, President McKay opened his eyes, looked at Russell directly, and said, "Brother Nelson, if I were you, I wouldn't be in a hurry to change neighborhoods. It doesn't feel good to me. No, Brother Nelson, your place is here in Salt Lake City. People will come from all over the world to you because you are here. I don't think you should go to Chicago" (Nelson, *From Heart to Heart,* 150). And then he added, with a hint of a smile, "You will find your fame and fortune here. You're already famous. I know about you."

"That was it," Russell said. "A prophet had spoken. If the prophet didn't feel right about it, we were not going to go."

In an instant, the potential for more notoriety, more money, and more acclaim was gone.

When Russell called the university and declined the offer, most of his colleagues felt he was making a tragic professional mistake. "But I had no intention of seeking the counsel of a prophet and then not taking it," he explained.

Elder Jeffrey R. Holland would later describe the extent of the University of Chicago's aggressive recruitment of Dr. Nelson: "He would be made head of the department. He would have a salary through the roof. They would pay for all of his children's education, wherever those children went on the face of the earth." But when the prophet spoke, continued Elder Holland, "Russell Nelson made the decision on the spot. He was not going to go." This episode demonstrates the "childlike humility and simplicity of Russell Nelson's faith" (Weaver, "Get to Know President Russell M. Nelson").

Some years later—in 1982, just two years before being called to the Quorum of the Twelve—Russell Nelson would say, "I never ask myself, 'When does a prophet speak as a prophet and when does he not? My interest has been, 'How can I be more like him?'" He then added, "My [belief is that we should] stop putting question marks behind the prophet's statements and put exclamation points instead" (Johnson, "Russell M. Nelson").

> "Verily my Sabbaths ye shall keep:
> for it is a sign between me and you."
>
> —Exodus 31:13

The dilemma of keeping the Sabbath day holy was a complicated issue for the young surgeon. How does a busy doctor handle the Sabbath? "This was not a theoretical question for a doctor," Dr. Nelson explained. "We were dedicated to healing and saving lives, and I wrestled to know how to handle this."

Russell wanted to be in church with his family. After an intense week of performing operation after operation and scrubbing his hands with soap, water, and a bristle brush so many times that the skin was raw, he needed the personal, physical, and spiritual healing the Sabbath allows as well as a breather from the relentless, life-and-death pressure of his profession.

And yet, there were always operations to be performed, and sometimes there were lives at stake. During at least one season of his career, he dealt with a hospital administrator who wanted to keep the operating suites busy on weekends and who applied pressure for the surgeons to operate on Sundays. The issue was complex and confusing. During his formative years as a surgeon, Dr. Nelson even studied lists compiled by others who suggested dos and don'ts for the Sabbath day. But he found them all wanting.

Then one day Dr. Nelson came across a passage in Exodus that triggered new spiritual understanding: "Verily my Sabbaths ye shall keep: for it is a sign between me and you" (Exodus 31:13).

When he realized what he did on Sunday was a sign to the Lord about how he felt about Him, his dilemma was resolved. He said,

94

'Too Busy, But—'

'Make Time' For Church, Doctor Says

By Maurice A. Jones
Tribune Church Editor

How does a busy surgeon find time to handle an important church assignment?

Dr. Russell M. Nelson answered, "You never find time to do anything. One can always make time to do things he feels are important."

Dr. Nelson, Salt Lake heart surgeon, last Sunday was sustained as president of the Bonneville Stake, Church of Jesus Christ of Latter-day Saints, succeeding Frank B. Bowers, 1166 Harvard Ave. (1105 South).

'Great Counselors'

"I know this assignment will be time-consuming but I have some great men as counselors to help me and the members of the Stake High Council will be of great assistance," he said.

Named and sustained by a vote of the stake membership as a new first counselor was Albert R. Bowen, 1847 Laird Ave. (12th South). Joseph B. Wirthlin, 932 Military Dr. (1745 East) was sustained as second counselor.

Selected as new members of the Stake High Council were Francis Gibbons Benn E. Broadbent and Paul W. Cox.

Alternate Members

New alternate High Council members are Orvil Rex Warner, Frank D. Parry and Alton B. Sorenson.

Dr. Nelson attributes his perspective in cardiac research to his study of the scriputres and his work as a member of the LDS Church

Dr. Nelson, his wife, Danzel, and their eight daughters ranging in age from 16 to 2 years, live at 1347 Normandie Cl. (1325 East).

Dr. Nelson serves as president of the Utah Heart Assn.

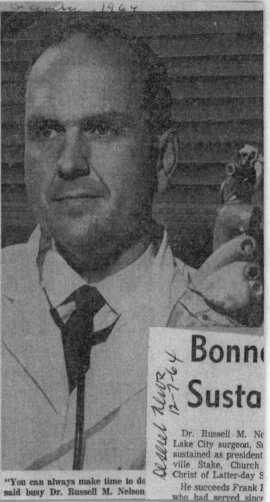

December 1964

"You can always make time to do said busy Dr. Russell M. Nelson

Deseret News 12-7-64

Bonne Susta

Dr. Russell M. Ne Lake City surgeon, Si sustained as president ville Stake, Church Christ of Latter-day S

He succeeds Frank I who had served since

Newspaper article highlights Dr. Nelson's commitment to the Sabbath day.

"I no longer needed lists of dos and don'ts. When I had to make a decision whether or not an activity was appropriate for the Sabbath, I simply asked myself, 'What sign do I want to give to God?' That question made my choices about the Sabbath day crystal clear" (Nelson, "Sabbath Is a Delight").

He determined he would not operate on anyone on Sunday unless he knew the person would not live until Monday. If a patient came in with a bleeding aorta or a crushed chest, yes, he would operate on Sunday. Every cardiac surgeon operated on Sundays to save lives that wouldn't last another day. Sometimes the bleeding had to be stopped immediately. But if the patient could wait until Monday, Dr. Nelson waited.

"Once I had the Sabbath day concept figured out," he explained, "and understood that what I did on Sunday was a sign of my love for God, I realized that just as it wouldn't show my love for Him by operating on Sunday when it could wait until Monday, it also wouldn't show love for God if I let someone die on Sunday who could have been saved. For a cardiovascular surgeon, that scripture was lifesaving for my conscience and for my heart."

"Do you really want me to be the head of a union?"

—Russell M. Nelson

One day in June 1971, Dr. Nelson received an unexpected phone call from President N. Eldon Tanner, then Second Counselor in the First Presidency to President Joseph Fielding Smith. That day, unlike many, he was able to drop everything and go immediately to President Tanner's office, where he also found President Harold B. Lee, First Counselor in the First Presidency, waiting.

The new General Sunday School Presidency with family members and Church leaders. Front row, left to right: President Harold B. Lee, Joseph B. Wirthlin, Russell M. Nelson, Richard L. Warner, President N. Eldon Tanner. Dantzel is directly behind her husband.

A new office and new responsibilities.

Forgoing any small talk, the men quickly explained the reason
for their summons: they wished to call Russell to lead the Sunday
School organization of the Church—if, and only if, it would not take
him away from his work as a surgeon.

Russell, still serving as stake president, was shocked. He hadn't
seen anything like this coming. But he responded as he had with
every request to serve, that he would accept any call from the Lord,
even if it meant leaving his medical practice. The two counselors in
the First Presidency insisted that they would extend the call only if he
could continue his work as a surgeon as well.

Russell and his new counselors, Joseph B. Wirthlin as first

counselor and Richard L. Warner as second, were sustained during the closing session of the MIA June Conference on Sunday, June 27, 1971. And thus began Russell Nelson's term of more than eight years as General Sunday School President.

Shortly thereafter, the *Salt Lake Tribune* published a headline indicating that Church authorities had just named a new "head" of the Deseret Sunday School Union. Russell found the phraseology disturbing and immediately asked for

General Sunday School President Russell M. Nelson with his counselors, Joseph B. Wirthlin (left) and Richard L. Warner (right).

a meeting with President Lee. "Do you really want me to be the head of a union?" he asked President Lee.

Later that year, as part of the Church's priesthood correlation program, the name of the Deseret Sunday School Union was changed to simply the Sunday School, and the Sunday School general "superintendent" became the General Sunday School President. Russell served in this capacity until 1979, when he was called as a regional representative of the Twelve.

"Don't worry. Things will work out."

—President N. Eldon Tanner

Russell's call to serve as General President of the Sunday School was still brand-new when, just two months later, he received a letter from the First Presidency inviting him and Dantzel to attend the first area conference of the Church, to be held in Manchester, England, from August 27 to 29, 1971.

Russell and Dantzel were honored by the invitation but immediately realized they had a major conflict: Dr. Nelson had agreed to attend and present a significant professional paper at meetings of the International Surgical Society and the International Cardiovascular Society in Moscow, Russia. The Manchester area conference was right in the middle of Russell's Russian commitment. Wondering what to do, he sought counsel from President N. Eldon Tanner, who seemed nonplussed by the conflict and said, simply, "You will be able to do both. Don't worry. It will work out."

Russell talking with President N. Eldon Tanner and his wife, Sister Sarah Tanner.

In a leap of faith, Russell and Dantzel left for Russia, where the situation became even more complicated when Russian officials took their Russian visas from them as they entered the country. They could leave the USSR to

Dantzel often traveled with Russell on his assignments.

attend the Manchester conference, but now they had no way of get-ting back in. The situation seemed impossible.

Russell tried everything he could think of, negotiating in Russian, French, and English as the need arose, to try to obtain permission to leave Russia for several days and then return. Finally, a government official told them their only hope was to appeal to the office of the foreign minister, Andrei Gromyko, who would later become the pres-ident of Russia. They went to Gromyko's office and literally waited all day seeking help. Just four hours prior to their flight to England, Gromyko's office finally granted them unusual visas allowing them to leave the country and return.

When President Tanner learned what had transpired, he said, "I told you it would work out."

"It was a faith-promoting experience for us," Russell said, "to see President Tanner's promise fulfilled."

President Joseph Fielding Smith.

All of the visa hassle and worry was worth it. President Joseph Fielding Smith, then President of the Church, had just lost his wife Jessie Evans Smith, and everyone was concerned about his well-being. Yet it was from the aging Church President that the new General President of the Sunday School learned a compelling lesson in leadership.

Shortly after the Nelsons' arrival in Manchester, they joined President Smith and other General Authorities and General Officers there in a special meeting. President Smith called upon many in the room to report on their individual areas of responsibility. After hearing what everyone else had to say, President Smith stood and said: "I want you to know of my great love for you. All my life I've tried to prepare to be able to be of assistance to you in your great ministry. So, if I can be of help to you in any way in the great responsibilities that you carry, that is what I want to do" (Condie, *Russell M. Nelson,* 165).

Russell was struck with the realization that the prophet had not delivered a volley of dos and don'ts but instead had expressed his love and desire to help. It was a lesson he would rely on often in coming years and one that shaped his natural instincts to mentor, teach, and encourage rather than lead through displays of personality and power.

"As a surgeon, I cannot recommend an operation on Elder Spencer W. Kimball."

—Dr. Russell M. Nelson

Three days in the presence of the First Presidency and other senior leaders of the Church at the Manchester area conference was a spiritual feast for Russell and Dantzel. But that trip also opened Dr. Nelson's eyes to something of which he had been unaware.

While in Manchester, Elder Spencer W. Kimball of the Quorum of the Twelve confided in him that he had been having recurring chest pain and that he didn't feel well. Once back in Salt Lake City, Dr. Nelson performed a selective coronary arteriogram and other tests that revealed two serious problems: a major obstruction in the left anterior descending artery and a deteriorating aortic valve.

Elder Kimball was seventy-seven years old and had had health issues for years. The risk of an aortic valve replacement alone in a man of that age was high. The risk of a coronary graft operation at that age was also high. Doing both at the same time was unthinkable, and Dr. Nelson told Elder Kimball so.

With this sober diagnosis from his surgeon, in early March 1972, Elder Kimball called a meeting to discuss his situation with President Harold B. Lee. Sister Camilla Kimball, Dr. Ernest Wilkinson (Elder Kimball's medical doctor), and Dr. Nelson were also in the meeting. Elder Kimball began the meeting by saying, in essence, "I'm doing poorly and am not going to live long, and I want my internist to explain it to you."

Dr. Wilkinson then confirmed that Elder Kimball had an aortic valve malfunction, that the valve was deformed and leaky, and that he also had a severe narrowing of the main coronary artery. At that point, Elder Kimball could barely get out of bed. Dr. Wilkinson confirmed that the best he could offer Elder Kimball through traditional medical care was a life expectancy of a few weeks.

President Lee then asked Dr. Nelson if an operation could correct these problems and what the odds were of survival.

"Surgically you would have to have two operations at the same time, one to replace the defective aortic valve and the other to graft that obstructed coronary artery to make a bypass graft," Dr. Nelson explained. "We have no experience operating on a seventy-seven-year-old man in heart failure doing these two operations at once—a valve and a coronary heart operation. It's never been done before that I know of. It would entail extremely high risk. As a surgeon, I cannot recommend the operation."

President Lee then asked what the risks would be if Dr. Nelson were to proceed with the operation: "They are incalculably great," Russell responded, again repeating, "I would not recommend an operation."

At that point, Elder Kimball said: "There you have it, Brethren. I am an old man and ready to die. It is well for a younger man to come to the quorum and do the work I can no longer do" (Condie, *Russell M. Nelson,* 154).

With this, President Lee rose to his feet, pounded the desk with his fist, and declared with no small amount of energy: "Spencer, you have been called! You are not to die. You are to do everything you need to do in order to care for yourself and continue to live!"

Elder Kimball instantly responded, in an act of faith, "All right, then I will have the operation."

Elder Kimball's declaration made Sister Kimball cry and nearly gave the heart surgeon a heart attack. The weight of the decision, the gravity of the situation, passed instantly to Dr. Nelson. "My heart sank," Russell said. "I knew what he needed, and I also knew I'd never done this before. I didn't know if anyone had done it, but I knew I hadn't.

"I was sitting right by Elder Kimball," Dr. Nelson continued, "and I had just said I didn't advise the operation. I had just explained that this had never been done before in a man in heart failure who was his age. I knew I would have to correct two major problems in one operation or he wouldn't have a chance of surviving. The thought came clearly to mind, 'Oh no! You're in a corner you can't get out of now.' But Elder Kimball didn't make the decision based on medical advice but on inspiration through his priesthood leaders, and he was faithful to his leaders to a fault."

The group agreed to wait until after general conference, just weeks away, and then proceed with the operation on April 12. For the balance of March, Dr. Nelson thought about the unprecedented procedure he was to perform on a prophet, seer, and revelator. He prayed about it and contemplated how he might approach it. The weight of what he considered a mandate from the First Presidency pressed upon him. He wasn't at all confident that it was doable, though all eyes were on him to perform what would be nothing short of a miracle.

Elder Kimball was so weak that he attended only one of the seven sessions of the April 1972 general conference. "His breathlessness and inability to exert

President Spencer W. Kimball and Russell M. Nelson had a special bond.

himself because of his congestive heart failure forced him to listen to the other sessions from his bed," Dr. Nelson explained.

The evening before the surgical procedure, Russell went to President Lee and President Tanner and asked for a priesthood blessing. President Tanner was voice, and in the blessing he instructed Dr. Nelson not to worry about his own inadequacies. He also promised him that "you have been raised up by the Lord to do this operation, and you will do it with great success."

Dr. Nelson left feeling encouraged but with the weight of the world on his shoulders. The next day, however, true to the promises in the blessing, he had a singular experience in the operating room. From the moment he made the incision and his resident assistant exclaimed, "He doesn't bleed!" through to the end, everything went perfectly. "From the beginning," said Dr. Nelson, "we could see that this operation was different. As just one small example, usually you have to use a cauterizer to take care of small bleeders, but that day we didn't."

They put in a new prosthetic aortic valve and then grafted the left internal mammary artery to Elder Kimball's left coronary artery. After they evacuated all of the air and took the clamp off the aorta, one shock got the rhythm of the heart back, and the power of Elder Kimball's pulse surprised even Dr. Nelson. "I took one look at that oscilloscope, saw the power of his pulse, and thought, 'My goodness, his powerful heart has been dealing with a bad valve all these years.' He had a huge heart with great power. It's similar to trying to water your lawn with a kink in the hose. When you unkink it, you have much more flow. That is what it felt like with Elder Kimball. He had more power in his heart than most of the people I'd been operating on.

"Most of all," Russell continued, "heaven magnified the experience. That day, it was as though we pitched a perfect game—no hits, no runs, no errors, no walks. There wasn't a broken stitch or a dropped instrument. Nothing unexpected occurred. There was not

At a dinner with President Spencer W. Kimball and his wife, Camilla.

one technical flaw in a series of thousands of intricate manipulations. Each step was perfect. We were servants of the Lord that day. There is no question about it. My resident could hardly believe what he was seeing."

As though participating in a flawless surgical procedure on an aging patient weren't enough, there was one additional highlight to come. As Dr. Nelson was concluding the operation, while still in the surgical suite in his scrubs and mask, he had an unmistakable spiritual impression—that this man would live to be the President of the Church. "I knew that President Kimball was a prophet," Dr. Nelson said. "I knew that he was an Apostle, but now it was revealed to me that he would preside over the Church!" (Condie, *Russell M. Nelson,* 156).

The impression was so strong, so clear, that Dr. Nelson could hardly contain himself as he performed the routine maneuvers to conclude the operation. "No one ever thought Elder Kimball would outlive President Harold B. Lee," President Nelson said years later in reflection, "but that day, the Spirit of the Lord spoke to me and told me Spencer W. Kimball would become President of the Church. At that moment, I understood why heaven had been so involved in that perfect operation."

It was a moment, and a feeling, the surgeon never forgot. Later that week, as Elder Kimball convalesced, Dr. Nelson shared his impression with Elder Kimball. They both wept, but, said Russell, "I know that he did not take this feeling as seriously as I did because he knew that President Harold B. Lee, who was senior to him in the quorum, was younger and healthier than he was. But I could not deny the impression I had had."

Once Elder Kimball was home from the hospital, Dr. Nelson made frequent house calls, often stopping by to be the Apostle's postoperative walking partner. There were days when Elder Kimball was discouraged, as convalescing patients often are. "The thing that President Kimball feared most was disability," Dr. Nelson remembered. "He did not fear death, but he did not want to be a drain on the Brethren, the Church, or his beloved Camilla. He was concerned that although his life might have been prolonged, he might not be able to return to full service in the Church" (Condie, *Russell M. Nelson*, 156–57).

During this period, Dr. Nelson came to understand how wise Camilla Kimball was. Several weeks after the operation, she said one day to Russell, "Brother Nelson, I think we need to push Spencer a little more now. I think we've been babying him long enough."

"She was right," Russell said. "There comes a time in the convalescence from an illness when all of the attention and caring and feeding with assistance should stop and the patient should work a little harder. She sensed that timing in the most amazing way."

Elder Kimball was still recovering from this operation when, on July 2, 1972, President Joseph Fielding Smith passed away. President Harold B. Lee was next in line to become President of the Church, which meant Spencer W. Kimball was now second in the line of succession and, as the new President of the Quorum of the Twelve Apostles, would have additional responsibilities. Dr. Nelson was there to help Sister Kimball get Elder Kimball dressed so that he could attend the meeting of the Quorum of the Twelve when the First Presidency was reorganized.

These experiences surrounding major open-heart surgery and the postoperative recuperative period were some of many with Spencer W. Kimball that would have lasting impact on Russell Nelson. They created a unique bond that would lead President Nelson, many decades hence, to declare, "Other than my father, President Kimball has had more impact on my life than any other man."

"Each time I tried to find air, I hit the underside of the raft. My family couldn't see me, but I could hear them shouting, 'Daddy! Where's Daddy?'"

—Russell M. Nelson

During that unusual and eventful summer of 1972, Russell and Dantzel decided to take their family on a vacation that would give their teenage daughters some distance from telephones and boyfriends. A rafting trip down the Colorado River through the majestic Grand Canyon seemed to be just the ticket.

The first day was beautiful, but on the second they had an experience Russell would never forget. As they approached Horn Creek rapids and saw the looming precipitous drop, Russell admitted he was "terrified" as he imagined his family plunging over what was essentially a waterfall several stories high. He instinctively put his arms around Dantzel and his youngest daughter, Marjorie, to protect them. But as they reached the drop and the raft began to bend, it acted like a giant slingshot and flung Russell into the air and then smack-dab into the middle of the rapids. He was a strong swimmer but was nearly powerless against the strength of the churning river,

Russ Jr. on a subsequent rafting trip.

and he felt like an egg in an eggbeater as he tried to fight his way to the surface. Each time he tried to find air, he hit the bottom of the raft. His family couldn't see him, but he could hear them shouting, "Daddy! Where's Daddy?" At what seemed like the last possible moment, they caught sight of him and pulled his "nearly drowned body" out of the water.

The next few days were much less eventful—filled with the breathtaking browns, blues, reds, and greens of the passing scenery. The last day of the trip loomed ahead, however, and Russell knew they would have to go over Lava Falls, known as the most dangerous drop along that stretch of the Colorado. When he realized what was ahead, he asked the guide to beach the raft so he could talk to his family and have a prayer together. "No matter what happens," he told them, "the rubber raft will remain on top of the water. If we cling with all our might to ropes secured to the raft, we can make it. Even if the raft should capsize, we will be all right if we hang tightly to the ropes." Russell was relieved when passing over Lava Falls proved to be much less eventful than the trip through the Horn Creek rapids had been earlier in the week.

The experience of nearly drowning stayed with him, so much so that more than forty years later he used it as President of the Church to teach a large audience in Seattle the lesson he had learned on the Colorado River:

"If anything good came from that experience, it was a powerful lesson for me," he reflected. "We are all, metaphorically speaking, on a rafting trip through life. Some of the trip is beautiful and peaceful, but at some point we all hit rapids. As we face the churning challenges of our lives, the greatest and only real safety comes as we hold on to the raft, which is the restored gospel of Jesus Christ. Clinging to others can help as we minister to each other, but *not* if it means letting go of the raft" (Nelson, "Lessons Life Has Taught Me").

"I thought maybe you needed me."

—Dr. Russell M. Nelson

I t was the evening of December 26, 1973, and the Nelsons were still disposing of all the wrapping paper, tinsel, decorations, and general hubbub that are part and parcel of celebrating the holidays with ten children and having them all at home on school break. Little but managing the chaos was on his mind when Russell turned on the television and was stunned to learn that President Harold B. Lee had died without much if any warning.

How could it be? President Lee was just seventy-four years old—by General Authority standards, he was a youngster. Everyone had "known" that he would serve as President of the Church for many years, if not decades. Now, suddenly, he was gone.

Russell was both surprised and not surprised at all. He was surprised that President Lee had passed suddenly and at such a young age. But his surprise was tempered by the vivid memory of what he had experienced in the operating room just following the complicated heart operation he had performed on then-Elder Spencer W. Kimball. Feeling that President Kimball might welcome his support, he left immediately for LDS Hospital, where he found the President and President Marion G. Romney in the board of directors' room. "I thought maybe you needed me," Russell said to President Kimball, who responded, "I surely do. Thanks for coming."

This was a tender and unusual time in the Church. Three Presidents of the Church—Presidents David O. McKay, Joseph Fielding Smith, and now Harold B. Lee—had passed away during the last three years. Now the presidential mantle would fall on a man

President Kimball on a wintertime walk.

almost no one had expected to advance to the center chair in the First Presidency. It was common knowledge that President Kimball had dealt with throat cancer that had resulted in the removal of one vocal cord and part of another, radiation treatment, heart disease that had led to open-heart surgery, and a recent illness that had hospitalized him just a month earlier.

"I began to sense a mood of anxiety, not only among President Kimball and the other Brethren," Russell recorded, "but in the whole community." In response, Dr. Nelson wrote President Kimball a letter, which the new President of the Church subsequently read to his Brethren in the temple at the time of his ordination and again at his

President Kimball addresses the Saints as their prophet.

first press conference as President. In part, the letter read: "Your surgeon wants you to know that your body is strong, your heart is better than it has been for years, and that by all of our finite ability to predict, you may consider this new assignment without undue anxiety about your health" (Condie, *Russell M. Nelson*, 158).

President Kimball was ordained and set apart as President of the Church on December 30, 1973, at the age of seventy-eight. He would live a dozen more years before passing away at the age of ninety. And though his health declined dramatically during his last few years, he was the President who energized the entire Church with the mandate to "lengthen your stride" and "quicken your pace."

"Who's looking for me?"

—Dr. Russell M. Nelson

Over time, Russell Nelson increasingly grew into the principle of revelation, as the Prophet Joseph Smith taught, and became increasingly responsive to the whisperings of the Spirit.

On one occasion, in an attempt to have some time together, he and Dantzel decided to take a few days off and combine them with medical meetings in Colorado Springs, Colorado. With the meetings concluded, in the middle of their third night away, Russell awoke with feelings of anxiety that had no apparent cause. Finally, he awakened Dantzel, described his unease, and asked if they could pack and go home immediately.

Within a matter of minutes, they were on their way to the airport, managed to get seats on the next flight home from Denver, and landed in Salt Lake City an hour after takeoff. When Russell called his secretary from the airport to ask who was looking for him, she responded with surprise in her voice, "How did you know? You're needed at the hospital for Elder Paul H. Dunn."

They hurried to the hospital to find that Elder Dunn had experienced heart-attack-like symptoms during the night, and a subsequent arteriogram

Dr. Nelson saved Elder Paul H. Dunn's life.

had confirmed that he had what amounted to a complete obstruction of the coronary arteries. As Dr. Nelson prepared to operate, President Kimball arrived to give Elder Dunn a blessing, and the surgical procedure began immediately.

Dr. Nelson had barely opened the patient's chest when Elder Dunn had a full-on heart attack. Russell was able to stabilize his circulation and perform the necessary bypasses. Elder Dunn recovered and in time was able to resume his full schedule.

Such experiences continued to help Russell Nelson refine his ability to discern promptings of the Spirit and know when to take action.

"Tell Sister Kimball we're going."

—President Spencer W. Kimball

In early 1976, Russell and Dantzel Nelson received an offer they could not—and did not want to—refuse. President Spencer W. Kimball invited them to join him and Sister Kimball, along with other General Authorities and their wives, to attend a series of nine area conferences over a period of three weeks in the beautiful, diverse South Pacific.

The experience did not disappoint. At every stop—in Tonga, Fiji, Tahiti, Samoa, Western Samoa, New Zealand, and multiple cities in Australia—the official party greeted the Saints, met with government officials, talked to the press, held devotionals, hugged youth and babies, and witnessed miracles.

In Apia, Samoa, government leaders, throngs of Saints, and a brass band greeted President Kimball when he and his party arrived. Part of the welcoming ceremony included a song with many verses, in their native Samoan, pleading for a temple. President Kimball's response was classic. "If I understand your Samoan well, I get the impression that you want a temple here," he said, prompting hearty laughter throughout the crowd. Then he said he would have more to say about it at the area conference the next day.

When President Kimball spoke the following day, he revived the issue of a temple and, nearly pounding the pulpit, said to the congregation, "You will not have a temple here in Samoa . . ." and then he paused for a moment before adding, "until you convert your genealogical information from memorized recollections to a written form that can be used in a temple. You also need to get more convert baptisms, for it takes a lot of people to run a temple. So, in essence, when you have done your part, the Lord will do His part and you shall have a temple here'" (Condie, *Russell M. Nelson,* 170). The next year President Kimball announced that they would build a temple in Apia.

While flying from Apia to Pago Pago in American Samoa, President Kimball, whose eighty-first birthday was just a few days away, suddenly became violently ill. By the time they reached the hotel, his temperature had soared to 104 degrees F. He assigned President N. Eldon Tanner and Brother Nelson to fill in for him on an interview on Samoan television and went to bed. But even still, it was a short night. The entourage was scheduled on a 5:00 a.m. flight to Auckland, which meant leaving the hotel at 3:30 a.m.

President Kimball slept on the four-hour flight, and he perspired—a clear sign that his temperature had fallen. As the plane descended, he awoke, began to straighten his tie, and turned to Sister Kimball, asking her to comb his hair for him. "Which hair do you want me to comb, Spencer?" she teased in return.

As they emerged from the plane, the prophet somehow managed to shake the hands of everyone in a long line waiting to greet him and then to stand in front of television cameras for nearly half an hour giving what amounted to a dissertation about the Church. "It was the finest presentation I have ever heard—thoroughly organized, comprehensive, and humbly and powerfully delivered," Russell said. "Brother Arthur Haycock and I looked at each other in utter amazement; we could hardly believe what we were seeing and hearing" (Condie, *Russell M. Nelson,* 171).

President Kimball then attended a luncheon with New Zealand Prime Minister Robert Muldoon. Once he got back to his hotel, his temperature again shot to 102 degrees F. As a doctor, Russell couldn't believe what he had just witnessed. "A man so ill had received the blessing of a two-hour remission, which allowed him to perform his

A Polynesian welcome.

Traveling to the South Pacific with President Kimball would prove to be but one of the Nelsons' experiences in that exotic part of the world.

duties faithfully and well, as though his spirit had the power to drive the illness, at least temporarily, from his body" (Condie, *Russell M. Nelson*, 172).

President Kimball and his party then drove the sixty-nine miles from Auckland to Hamilton, New Zealand, and President Kimball went again to bed. President Tanner handled a meeting with the Maori queen, and President Kimball told the party to please excuse them from the cultural event planned that evening. Only Arthur Haycock, assistant to the First Presidency, and Russell stayed behind with President and Sister Kimball to attend to their needs, and President Kimball fell into a deep sleep.

Just before 7:00 p.m., the President awoke suddenly, covered in perspiration, and asked Russell, who had been reading quietly in the room, what time the cultural event was to begin.

"At 7:00 p.m," he responded.

"What time is it now?"

"Almost 7:00 p.m."

"Tell Sister Kimball we're going."

The Kimballs dressed quickly and drove the short distance to the stadium at the Church College of New Zealand. As their car entered the stadium, a deafening roar went up from the crowd.

As soon as Russell took his seat next to Dantzel, she told him what had happened. When the official party reached the stadium, President Tanner welcomed the large Polynesian audience and explained that President Kimball had been fighting a serious illness and was, regrettably, too sick to attend. A young Polynesian man then walked to the podium to offer the invocation. As he prayed, he explained that they had been preparing for this event for six months, and then he petitioned the Lord: "We three thousand New Zealand youth have gathered here prepared to sing and to dance for thy prophet. Wilt thou heal him and deliver him here." As the prayer ended, the car carrying the Kimballs entered, and the stadium erupted in a spontaneous, deafening shout at the answer to their prayer (see *Teachings: Spencer W. Kimball*, 47–48).

New Zealand was the site of another miracle. Because there was no auditorium large enough to accommodate the fifteen thousand Saints and guests who wanted to hear the prophet speak, the area conference was scheduled for a large outdoor arena. But it was the rainy season in New Zealand, and Mother Nature threatened to spoil the event.

A photo from one of the Nelsons' South Pacific trips.

When it rained every day for the two weeks prior to the area conference, government officials called for a national day of fasting and prayer the Sunday before President Kimball's visit. Remarkably, this invitation was for Latter-day Saints and others alike.

The Sunday morning of the conference was bright, beautiful, and most of all, clear. Rain did not return until after the meeting concluded.

The three weeks Russell and Dantzel spent traveling in the South Pacific with the prophet and his wife and learning from them were life-changing. They counted the privilege of being with the prophet day in and day out on that trip as one of the greatest spiritual and mentoring experiences of their lives.

"He would come out of his bedroom at curfew time, look at me, and say, 'Did you know you are still here?'"

—David Webster, son-in-law

Russell Nelson had an intensely busy life as a surgeon whose expertise was in demand around the world. He also served in demanding leadership roles in the Church—stake president, general auxiliary president, and regional representative among them. And yet somehow his large family did not feel deprived of his attention. In fact, they felt they were his first priority. Much of the credit goes to Dantzel, who often managed the ever-increasing hubbub alone while helping their children not feel neglected.

President M. Russell Ballard, who was five years behind Russell Nelson through high school and college, later reflected: "How he was able to do everything he did with the heavy schedule he carried in his surgical and medical practice is a miracle. He is a miracle man when it comes to getting things done" (*Church News*/KSL Interview, January 9, 2018).

Years later, when she was a mother, fifth daughter Sylvia would explain: "I think my father's secret was that when he's at work, he's 100 percent at work. When he's home, he's 100 percent at home. When he's at church, he's 100 percent there. I think that's how he balanced things. I don't know—he seemed to do it effortlessly" (*Church News*/KSL Interview, January 10, 2018).

Russell taught his nine daughters and his son to ski and also water-ski, balancing them between his legs on those first runs down the mountain or on the lake. He read to them when they were young, and he taught them to ride bicycles and drive a car. During the more than twenty years there were only daughters in the family, he showed his girls how to mow the lawn and shovel snow from the sidewalks.

Even still, no one is quite sure how he did it all—and the truth is that he didn't do it all. When anyone asked him his secret for managing everything, his stock answer was, "Obviously, the credit goes to my wife." Dantzel had remarkable capacity and seemed born with a knack for managing the chaos inevitable in a large family. The reality was that he was gone from home a lot, and Dantzel gave a lot of private sacrifice for her husband's public success.

"When we were younger," says Sylvia, "Mother sewed all of our clothes, even our prom dresses. I vividly remember her hemming our dresses as we were walking up the stairs to greet our date. She would be saying, 'Walk slower, walk slower,' while still putting on the finishing touches. She was so talented and could do just about anything. She made having ten children look easy."

Rosalie added: "As a daughter growing up in a family of ten children, I always felt important and that my mother always had time for me. She had a way of making everyone feel special and loved" (Weaver, "Dantzel Nelson Succumbs").

After Dantzel's nine daughters became mothers, they would ask her how she had managed ten children. She would typically laugh and respond, "You just love them."

It was a team effort. For twenty years, Dantzel sang with the Mormon Tabernacle Choir, which meant she was gone from home every Sunday morning. "Daddy would take over and try to curl our hair and get everybody dressed," said Sylvia. "He's very prompt, though. He is never, ever late. He'd be out in the car waiting for us to go to church. If we weren't there when he had to go, we'd have to walk. We only needed to learn that lesson one time. He kept the home fires burning when Mother was gone. That's the kind of relationship they had. It was very sweet and very giving to each other."

Through it all, though, Russell gave credit where credit was due. "I pay tribute to Sister Nelson," he reflected years later, "this magnificent wife and mother who has always been supportive. When people have asked her how she managed with ten children with so little time available from her husband, she has responded with a twinkle in her eye, saying, 'When I married him, I didn't expect much, so I was never disappointed'" (Nelson, "Identity, Priority, and Blessings").

Both Russell and Dantzel were musical, and music was constantly emphasized in their home. One of the few things they scratched enough money together to buy early in their marriage was a used piano, which encouraged music at home. The children each learned to play musical instruments and sing. Russell had perfect

The Nelson family in handmade outfits.

pitch and played the organ and piano beautifully, and Dantzel's time in the Tabernacle Choir was a joy.

Years later, one Mother's Day all she "wanted was to hear her children and grandchildren share their talents in a musical program," Brenda remembered. "So that's what we did. She printed a program and was very proud of all those who participated" (Weaver, "Dantzel Nelson Succumbs"). One of Dantzel's last family activities before she died was attending a concert to hear her granddaughter Rachel perform on her flute.

Summer vacations were a must for the family, sometimes to a cabin near the Brighton ski resort not far from Salt Lake City and other years at a beach house in Newport Beach, California. And if

Singing sisters.

too much time had elapsed since the children had seen their father, Dantzel loaded them up in the car and took them down to the hospital. "That was always such a fun thing for us," Sylvia said. "A highlight growing up was to go have dinner with Daddy at the hospital. We thought, 'Wow, this is so cool. We get to eat hospital food with Daddy at the hospital'" (*Church News*/KSL Interview, January 10, 2018).

From time to time, as Russell traveled to medical conventions and on other professional assignments, he would take a daughter with him. Sometimes Dantzel would recommend he take someone whose recent behavior had been less than ideal. When he would question his wife about giving that particular daughter a privilege, she would inevitably respond, "Honey, it's not what she's been doing, it's who needs you the most."

Having a surgeon for a father had other side effects as well. "I didn't realize that a traffic jam was called a traffic jam until I was older," Sylvia admitted. "I thought it was a thrombosis. He would use medical terms for everyday things that were normal to us. I thought everybody knew that *thrombosis* was a traffic jam."

One day Elder Ezra Taft Benson asked Russell to come down to the Church Administration Building for a visit. Elder Benson owned a small cabin and several prime acres in Midway, in the beautiful Heber Valley about an hour's drive from Salt Lake City and within a few minutes of a major reservoir. He wondered if Russell and Dantzel would like to buy several acres to build a getaway for their growing family.

Russell and Dantzel jumped at the opportunity, and Dantzel oversaw the plans to build a vacation home with children in mind. She insisted that the "Pizza Hut"-type design included a balcony all the way around it so that children could run to their hearts' content and throw candy down to onlookers on holidays. She designed a fire pole dropping from floor to floor and a large circular driveway where children could ride their bikes and the family could hold Fourth of

Horseback riding with a granddaughter.

July parades and games. For children, and in time grandchildren and great-grandchildren, the Midway home became a place of frequent gatherings and family traditions. When Grandpa brought home Country Time lemonade and pink circus cookies, they knew they were heading to Deer Creek Reservoir to go water-skiing.

Once the oldest girls began to date, things at the Nelson home became even more chaotic. For more than two decades, their already full house became command central for the young men interested in the Nelson daughters.

Russell had his own way of dealing with his daughters' suitors. "I would be over at the Nelsons'," says David Webster, who married Sylvia, "and Sylvia's father would come out at about curfew time, look at me, and say, 'Did you know you were here?' If nothing happened after a few minutes, he'd come out again and say, 'Did you know you are *still* here?' If he had to come out a third time, he would hold out his hands and say, 'I have to operate on someone in the morning, and I need my sleep. I'm going to need these hands.' With that, we were out of there!"

The Midway vacation home under construction.

Dantzel throwing candy from the balcony at Midway.

Father and son each taking a turn sliding down the pole at Midway.

Children assemble for a bike parade at the Midway property.

Santa was a regular visitor at Nelson family Christmas parties.

As daughters began to marry and grandchildren started to arrive, the loving, supportive climate Russell and Dantzel created with their own children extended to family newcomers and the next generation.

"None of us measured up to our father-in-law," says David Webster. "At first we were always wondering, 'Are we okay?' But Sylvia's parents were both always so supportive. They've been complimentary even when we didn't deserve it. Both of them gave me something to strive for more than to feel any kind of intimidation" (*Church News*/KSL Interview, January 10, 2018).

One occasion, when a grandchild broke an expensive Lladro figurine during a family Christmas party, Dantzel signaled clearly what her priorities were. "I was very upset and angry with my daughter," Brenda Miles says, "and felt she needed to go apologize to her grandmother over what she had done." Rather than getting upset, Dantzel picked up the little girl and told her that "*things* like that don't really matter to her, but *people* like her do" (Weaver, "Dantzel Nelson Succumbs").

Grandson Stephen McKellar remembered the increasing chaos of their extended family. "There were always grandkids breaking things and making messes. But there was nothing a small child could do that ever seemed to bother my grandfather. That probably sounds crazy. But that's how he was" (*Church News*/KSL Interview, January 11, 2018). Russell typically responded to the noise and disruption of fussy children in Church meetings by saying, "That's the future of the Church we can hear. It sounds beautiful to me." And he would also say in response to noisy children, "Oh, that noise lets us know that we are in the right church!"

The longer he mingled with surgical colleagues, the more Russell came to realize how blessed he was. "Some of those men were always worried about their children because they couldn't afford their alcohol or drugs or all of the mischief they got into. I would think to myself, 'Wow, am I ever fortunate my children are so sweet and so bright and so good and such a bright part of my life. And I don't spend ten cents on what my colleagues are spending thousands of dollars on.'"

No doubt part of the reason was that Russell and Dantzel were true partners, equal partners. One picked up where the other left off. They wanted a large family, and when they were blessed with one, they learned how to care and love for those children a step at a time. As the years raced by and the family grew larger through marriages and the arrival of grandchildren and then great-grandchildren, the Nelsons found ways to stay connected.

"Our father is generous," said Sylvia. "He never misses a baby blessing, an ordination, a baptism, a wedding, or going to the hospital to see a new mom and her baby. Family has always been important to him, and he shows it by the effort he has always made to be with us as much as he can" (*Church News*/KSL Interview, January 10, 2018).

Very simply, family meant everything to him. "With every person there comes a new complement of love, and there is no limit to it," Elder Nelson summarized. "A newborn baby is the most helpless individual in all of life. When a colt is born, it can walk on its feeble legs. When an elephant is born, it can walk. But an infant can't do anything but cry. That very nature of dependency upon the father and mother allows you to serve them, and that service is what galvanizes the love. If they were self-sufficient, I don't think you could love them as much. Family is the supreme blessing in life."

"I didn't hear President Kimball invite everyone but Brother Nelson to learn Mandarin."

—Russell M. Nelson

As Russell Nelson headed to the regional representatives' seminar on September 29, 1978, he had no idea that his vision of the world and his experience in it was about to expand exponentially. As General President of the Sunday School, he, along with General Authorities, other General Officers, and regional representatives, heard President Kimball deliver a stirring message about taking the gospel to all the world—and particularly to areas yet untouched by the Church: Africa, India, Vietnam, Cambodia, Russia, Poland, and many other countries. In a special way, he singled out China.

"And what of China," asked President Kimball, "the third-largest country in the world? Nearly one billion of our Father's children live in China, one-fourth of the entire world's population. Six hundred and sixty million of them speak Mandarin Chinese. How many of us speak Mandarin Chinese? We must prepare while there is time to prepare to teach these people" (Kimball, "Uttermost Parts").

That evening Russell told Dantzel about the spiritual feast he had experienced that day and, in particular, the strong feelings he'd had when President Kimball began talking about China. "President Kimball told us there is nothing too hard for the Lord," he related to Dantzel, "but that we must do our part—to pray for the people of China, to start learning Mandarin, and to extend our own talents in whatever specialty we might have to the Chinese people. I didn't hear President Kimball invite everyone but Brother Nelson to learn Mandarin. So will you study Mandarin with me?"

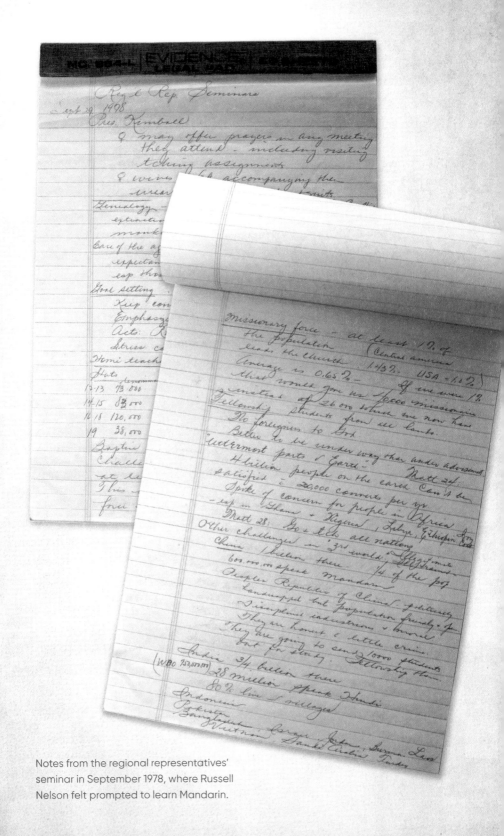

Notes from the regional representatives'
seminar in September 1978, where Russell
Nelson felt prompted to learn Mandarin.

Dantzel was instantly on board, and they hired tutors to help them. They could not possibly have foreseen, however, how taking this simple step would yield important benefits in a short period of time.

They had just begun to learn Mandarin when, a few months later, Dr. Nelson attended the annual meeting of the American Association of Thoracic Surgery in Boston. As was his normal practice, he sat up front. But as the meeting progressed, he became restless, and when the lights dimmed during a presentation, he stood and walked to the back of the room. After stretching for a few minutes, he spotted an empty chair and sat down. When the lights came back on, he found himself sitting next to a distinguished surgeon from China, Dr. Wu Yingkai, head of the Fu Wai Hospital in Beijing.

Russell began the conversation with a few words in Mandarin, which intrigued Dr. Wu, who then responded in perfect English. Russell quickly learned that the Chinese surgeon had been trained in thoracic surgery at Barnes Hospital in St. Louis and was now a high government official in China—roughly equivalent to being a member of the President's cabinet in the United States. In short order, Dr. Nelson invited Dr. Wu to visit Salt Lake City, and toward the end of 1979, Dr. Wu visited the University of Utah Medical School and delivered a lecture on surgery under acupuncture. In particular, Chinese surgeons were using acupuncture for thyroid surgery as well as operations on the extremities.

"Dr. Wu's lecture was fascinating because we would have never considered doing anything with acupuncture," remembered Dr. Nelson. "It would never work in our culture, where we are so interested in how fast someone can be put out. I watched the Chinese spend several hours working with their needles and electric current to get the patient to the point where they could operate."

Dr. Wu's visit to Salt Lake City was the beginning of a beautiful friendship, or, as it turned out, friendships. Dr. Nelson was at

Dantzel Nelson and Dr. Wu Yingkai at dinner in China. (Dr. Nelson is taking the photo.)

the airport to greet Dr. Wu Yingkai and his wife as they arrived and hosted them throughout their stay. Dr. Wu liked what he saw in Utah and shortly thereafter invited Dr. Nelson to be a visiting professor of surgery at Shandong Medical College in Jinan.

"Dantzel and I didn't learn to speak Mandarin very well," he explained, "but we learned enough that, when I was invited to go to China as a visiting professor to teach open-heart surgery, I was in a better position to accept the invitation."

When Dr. Nelson shared the letter of invitation to visit China with President Kimball, whom he still saw in regular postoperative appointments, the President responded, "Accept the invitation. This is what I have been telling everyone! Learn to serve the Chinese people."

As future trips to China unfolded, Dr. Nelson repeatedly inter-acted with Dr. Wu, even having dinner at the Wus' home within

Dantzel and Russell outside China's Forbidden City.

walking distance of Tiananmen Square in Beijing. They quickly developed a mutual professional respect that sustained their relationship.

The "chance" meeting with Dr. Wu that led to Dr. Nelson's first professional experience in China would launch a long and treasured exchange with, not to mention a great love for, the country and its people. And it all began with the way he responded to President Kimball's invitation at the regional representatives' seminar—to find a way to serve the Chinese people.

"I kept thinking, 'I have three lives depending on my finger.'"

—Dr. Russell M. Nelson

During a routine pregnancy checkup in the spring of 1980, Trudy Olmstead complained about a persistent cough that seemed to be getting worse. A chest X-ray revealed a large tumor filling most of her right lung, and subsequent tests indicated that it was an aggressive, fast-growing tumor that was "most likely" malignant, though the pathology was inconclusive. Doctors at the Santa Barbara, California, hospital where Trudy was admitted informed her and her husband, Rick, that she must abort the baby immediately so that treatment could begin.

Then the doctors decided to take a final ultrasound scan of the growing fetus. "I was awake during that scan," Trudy remembered, "and when I heard one of the doctors say, 'Oh, dear,' I wondered what they'd found now. But everything changed for me when the doctor said, 'You are carrying twins.' In that moment I said to myself, 'The Lord did not allow me to conceive twins only to abort them. We must fight for their lives'" (interview with author, November 3, 2018).

Nonetheless, doctors at the Santa Barbara hospital as well as specialists at both USC and UCLA continued to insist in the strongest terms that the only way to save Trudy's life was to abort the twins and begin treatment.

As the pressure to proceed with the abortions mounted, Rick began to insist that they find a Latter-day Saint doctor to review Trudy's situation and advise them. "My husband wouldn't back down," Trudy remembered. "He stood up to the doctors and even to family members who told him he should listen to the doctors and not threaten my life" (interview with author, November 3, 2018; see also Peggy Jean Huish Andersen autobiography, 228–38).

It was Rick's insistence on counseling with a Latter-day Saint doctor that triggered a prompting to Trudy's father, Dwayne N. Andersen. Just a few weeks earlier, he had been training in the Salt Lake Temple for his upcoming assignment as the first president of the Tokyo Japan Temple and while there had been introduced, coincidentally, to Dr. Russell M. Nelson. They had enjoyed a brief but cordial conversation. As Dwayne reflected on that encounter, he felt he could reach out to Dr. Nelson.

When Dwayne explained the situation, Dr. Nelson agreed to review the case. That afternoon, Dwayne gathered Trudy's medical records and pathology reports from the various California hospitals, flew to Salt Lake City, and appeared at the Nelsons' doorstep that evening around 10:00 p.m. Dr. Nelson took the records from Dwayne, told him that he would study them, and indicated he'd already talked to Trudy's doctor in California to gather more information and had arranged to meet with several colleagues early the next morning to review the case. Then, according to Trudy, Dr. Nelson looked Dwayne in the eye and said, "The Lord and I will discuss this tonight" (interview with author, November 3, 2018).

The next morning Dwayne went to LDS Hospital, where Dr. Nelson and his colleagues told him three things: first, his daughter's tumor was fast-growing and, because it was encroaching on the heart, life-threatening. They did not, however, believe it was malignant. "Your daughter does not have cancer," the doctors said. Second, they said, "Do not allow any doctor to touch those babies, because the Lord will decide if those babies live or die." And third, "The tumor needs to be removed as soon as possible." When Dr. Nelson explained the urgent need for surgery, one of the doctors in the room pointed to Russell and said, "This is the man to do it!" (Trudy

Andersen Olmstead interview with author, November 3, 2018; see also Dwayne N. Andersen autobiography, 150–53).

Eight days later, Trudy found herself lying on a gurney in a hallway outside an operating room at the LDS Hospital. "Dr. Nelson was in his scrubs when he talked to me before they wheeled me into the operating room," Trudy remembered. "I'll never forget him saying, 'The Lord and I will take care of you today.'

"When Dr. Nelson said that to me, every concern, every fear left," Trudy added. "In that moment, I knew I was doing the right thing and that I was in the hands of the Lord."

The operation proved to be complicated and more extensive than anticipated. "The tumor was so close to the heart that I did not have a clamp narrow enough to put a clamp on the artery and still have space for the cutting blade of the scissors," Dr. Nelson explained. "Therefore, the pulmonary artery had to be cut without being clamped. My only option was to put my finger in the artery to stop the blood and keep my finger there until I was able to suture the artery closed. All the time I kept thinking, 'I have three lives depending on my finger.'"

The operation, a total right pneumonectomy (removal of the right lung), saved Trudy's life and preserved the lives of healthy twin girls born five months later, on November 7, 1980: Heather and Nicole.

One evening while Trudy was still in the hospital, she heard a knock at her door and Dr. Nelson's voice asking if she was awake. When she replied that she was, he and Dantzel entered. "I wanted two important women in my life to meet," Dr. Nelson explained. As he told Dantzel about the operation he'd performed, Trudy began to realize just how blessed she was to be alive and to still have two babies growing inside her. She knew the Lord had worked a miracle with her.

In time, "Trudy's miracle babies" had a chance to meet the surgeon who had preserved their lives; by then he had been ordained

Trudy Olmstead with her healthy twin daughters.

an Apostle and called to the Quorum of the Twelve. Heather had just graduated from Utah State University when she first met Elder Nelson.

"He pulled out his journal recording the medical details of my mother's operation, and told me that my mother was an angel. That was powerful for me," Heather admitted. "To think that she was an angel here on earth really changed my relationship with my mother. Elder Nelson looked at me with those piercing blue eyes of his, and I believed him. I just really believed him. And I felt grateful that he was able to prayerfully take my mother's medical situation on to save her life and the lives of my sister and me" (interview with author, October 24, 2018).

Trudy's medical emergency proved lifesaving in another way as well. At the time of her diagnosis, she and Rick had been married for nine years but had not been sealed in the temple. "This entire episode falls in the category of being careful what you pray for," Trudy admitted. "For years I had told Heavenly Father I would do anything if he would just help me and my husband get to the temple. It was the

Heather (right) and Nicole on Nicole's wedding day in August 2015.

threat to my life and our little babies' that spurred him on" (interview with author, November 3, 2018).

In a matter of days, this was resolved. The Friday before Trudy's operation, she and her husband went to the Provo Temple to receive their endowment and were subsequently sealed, and their three children were sealed to them (see Trudy Andersen Olmstead interview with author, November 3, 2018).

As of this writing, Nicole is married with a daughter of her own. Heather is the head coach of BYU's nationally ranked women's volleyball team and was named the American Volleyball Coaches Association Coach of the Year in December 2018.

As for Dr. Nelson's part, he had become accustomed to saving lives, but never before three at once. "In retrospect, I can see how the Lord guided me to do that operation," he reflected. "He guided me through that treacherous interval when I had to close the right pulmonary artery with my finger in it. I've never done another like it before or since."

"Operative conditions in China were more primitive than in the United States, but Dr. Nelson never complained."

—Dr. Zhang Zhen-Xiang

At the invitation of Dr. Wu Yingkai, in September of 1980 Russell and Dantzel headed to China, where Russell had accepted a role as visiting professor of surgery at the Shandong Medical College in Jinan. This would be the first of many such trips.

Dr. Zhang Zhen-Xiang, head of the department of surgery in Jinan and a surgical colleague of Dr. Wu's, greeted them and served as their escort and interpreter throughout their visit. As they drove from the airport to the hotel, Dr. Zhang was surprised by Dantzel's pronunciation of *Beijing* and said it was the "first time I had ever heard a Westerner pronounce Chinese characters so beautifully with the proper musical inflection at the end of a word."

It was Dr. Wu, who had extended the invitation to Dr. Nelson to come to China, who chose to have him go to Jinan, the capital city of the Shandong province—significant because Dr. Wu, as minister of health for the entire country, could have invited him anywhere. "That turned out to be the hand of the Lord," Russell said, "because it led me to Dr. Zhang." His relationship with Dr. Zhang would, over time, bear important fruit.

Russell lectured and conducted operative clinics on cardiovascular surgery at the Shandong Medical College for nearly a month, and Dantzel stayed with him the entire time—a pattern they repeated on each successive trip.

At the time, Chinese surgeons at the medical school in Jinan were

Dr. Nelson's team with medical professionals outside the Shandong Medical College in Jinan, China.

performing operations that involved the heart, but they had yet to perform open-heart surgery. During this and subsequent trips, Dr. Zhang invited medical colleagues from throughout China to attend Dr. Nelson's lectures and operative clinics. Russell began each lecture in Mandarin and then shifted to English, relying on Dr. Zhang to interpret. Dr. Nelson also lectured at the medical school in Qing Dao, also in the Shandong Province, and, according to Dr. Zhang, after each lecture he "would listen attentively to all the questions raised from the audience and answer every one in detail. He showed great patience, respect, and courtesy for his Chinese colleagues" (Condie, *Russell M. Nelson*, 217).

Russell and Dantzel enjoyed their first trip to China immensely, along with their immersion in the Chinese culture. There was so much to like and respect. They stayed in housing at the hospital, and one morning their hosts arrived to pick them up, only to look through the window and find the couple kneeling. Not realizing they were in prayer, the Chinese hosts rushed in to see if they could help them find something.

Later, as Russell and Dantzel prepared to leave, their hosts gave them a farewell gift of moon cakes. "We biopsied them and found that our American taste buds didn't appreciate the flavor of the moon cakes," Russell said, "so we politely left them in our room. We had barely reached the car when someone came running after us calling, 'You forgot your moon cakes.' We had to wait until we were in Beijing to discard them, but you don't have to teach the Chinese people anything about honesty. It can be uncomfortable at times, because they are blunt. They'll tell you if you are too fat or if you look old. But you don't have to wonder about their honesty. We found it refreshing."

After the first trip to Jinan, Dr. Nelson invited Dr. Zhang and two other colleagues to Salt Lake City for an extended visit to observe Dr. Nelson and others performing open-heart surgery at the LDS Hospital. The Chinese always reciprocated, inviting Dr. Nelson back to China again and again. For several years, Dr. Nelson and Dr. Zhang exchanged positions every year. Dr. Zhang would come to Salt Lake City one year, and Dr. Nelson to Jinan the next.

When in Utah, Dr. Zhang typically had dinner at the Nelson home, played ping-pong with Russell and his son, Russ Jr., in the basement, and enjoyed a deepening friendship as well as the mutual respect of surgical colleagues.

"Dr. Nelson operated in the Shandong Hospital many times," said Dr. Zhang, "and during each operation he took the position of the first assistant in teaching the surgeons how best to perform their operations." This was to honor the Chinese surgeon so that he would not lose face by having someone teach him.

At the time, operative conditions in China were more primitive than in the United States. A word in Mandarin Russell quickly learned in the operating room was "mayo" (English phonetic spelling). Often

Sightseeing at the Great Wall of China.

when he asked for something he needed, the answer was "mayo"—meaning, they didn't have it. And when a bicycle with muddy tires came rolling into one of his operating rooms carrying needed supplies, he knew he wasn't in Salt Lake City anymore.

But "Dr. Nelson never complained," Dr. Zhang continued. "He never lost his patience when a surgical nurse misunderstood his request. He worked very hard and did an excellent job." In short, the "Chinese surgeons and nurses were very pleased because they had learned so much from this caring, patient American surgeon."

This prolonged and intimate association with his Chinese colleagues bore fruit of many kinds. Russell came to love the Chinese people and to understand the magnificence of their hearts; he was enamored with their culture and with the discipline they demonstrated as a people. And Dr. Nelson seized opportunities to share his fundamental beliefs beyond the operating room. "He once gave a lecture

145

on the grandeur of nature," Dr. Zhang explained, "teaching of the great Creator, and of prophets and apostles, and he was welcomed and very much respected wherever he went. To the Chinese, he had a Westerner's appearance, but his heart was very close to ours" (Condie, *Russell M. Nelson,* 217).

Russell's repeated associations with Dr. Zhang blossomed in a way he could never have foreseen. In early 1990, six years after his call to the Quorum of the Twelve, he received a letter from Dr. Zhang that caught him off guard. Dr. Zhang explained that he had lived under Japanese rule and Chinese rule, that he had lived in a Presbyterian environment, and that he had worked in a Presbyterian hospital. Then he said that he was now seventy years old and the only way of living that made sense to him was Russell Nelson's.

Dr. Zhang knew that he could not be taught the gospel in China, so he asked Elder Nelson, "If my wife and I move to Toronto to live near our daughter, would someone be able to teach us about your religion?" Yes, Elder Nelson assured him. That could be arranged!

Elder Nelson immediately contacted President Sidney A. Smith, president of the mission in Toronto, and asked him to send his best missionaries to meet with Dr. Zhang and his wife, which he did. In fairly short order, President Smith let Elder Nelson know that Dr. Zhang and his wife were ready for baptism. Elder Nelson approached his quorum president, Howard W. Hunter, and asked if he could receive an assignment the weekend of the baptism somewhere in the eastern United States so that he could also make it to Toronto to participate in this ordinance. President Hunter obliged, and, much to everyone's surprise in Toronto, on Easter Sunday at the appointed hour, Elder Nelson walked in unannounced but prepared to baptize his longtime friend Dr. Zhang Zhen-Xiang.

He subsequently ordained Dr. Zhang a priest in the Aaronic Priesthood, and Dr. Zhang had the privilege of baptizing his wife, Zhou Qingguo. Four months later, in August 1990, Elder Nelson

Dr. Nelson took Dr. Zhang (left) and his surgical colleagues to visit the Grand Canyon on one of their trips to Utah.

participated in the dedication of the Toronto Ontario Temple, where the highlight for him was seeing Brother and Sister Zhang in the temple. "I wept for him, and so did he," Elder Nelson admitted. And then, a year after the baptism almost to the day, Elder Nelson performed their sealing.

It all began when Russell accepted President Kimball's charge to learn Mandarin. "I often wondered," said Dr. Zhang, "'How can a man be so friendly, so kind, so loving, so generous, so hard working, so humble, so patient, so considerate and, in one word, so selfless?' After I visited Salt Lake City in 1980 and again in 1985, I gradually began to realize that it was his great faith in God that was motivating him" (Condie, *Russell M. Nelson*, 227).

147

"We are created in the image of God, and He gave each of us a great gift— the body that houses our eternal spirit."

—Dr. Russell M. Nelson

D r. Nelson's admiration and respect for the body consumed his interest throughout his life. He was fascinated with ailments that would heal on their own as opposed to those that would not. As a surgeon, when he diagnosed a patient's problem, he had to answer one pivotal question: would the problem improve over time on its own or would it become worse? A fractured rib will heal over time, but a deteriorating heart valve will not. So, in the case of the unhealthy heart valve, the surgeon's challenge is to put the patient in a position for the body to heal itself.

On the other hand, he marveled at all the body would do. "The body is an amazing gift," he declared. "When I was a young doctor, I tried to develop an artificial heart. So I bought some pumps, knowing the heart would need to pump blood, and I went into the laboratory and looked for a place to plug in my pumps. I couldn't run the pump without electricity. And then I realized that my own body has its own supply of electricity. If you've ever had an electrocardiogram done, your doctor has a graphic portrayal of the pattern of electric current as it goes through the heart. And we don't need to be plugged into the wall. That heart pumps enough blood to fill a 2,000-gallon tank every day. Whether we are awake or asleep, it does its work. And then I learned how the body regulates itself. Our body temperature is usually about 38 degrees Celsius—whether you're living in Alaska or Samoa, it's about the same. And it regulates countless ingredients in the body so that they are always in a regular range. The body can heal itself. If you get a cut, you know it will heal. If you break a leg, the probabilities are that it will heal. You have to hold the pieces together for a while, but think of that. If you could create a chair that could heal its own broken leg, you could use it in perpetuity. Every one of us has a gift from God of a body that in some circumstances can heal itself."

Unlike a broken chair, the body can mend itself.

When all was said and done, however, Dr. Nelson learned that the power to heal is a gift from God. In February 1978, Russell and a group of doctors he'd graduated with thirty years earlier made a quick trip to Manzanillo, Mexico. It was a chance to catch up, compare professional notes and experiences, and enjoy each other's company. While there, one of the physicians became violently ill, and the group of doctors at his side quickly diagnosed that he had massive bleeding into his stomach.

He was surrounded by doctors, but there in a remote fishing village many miles from the nearest hospital, they were powerless to help him. It was night, and no planes could fly. There was no equipment to make a transfusion possible. The decades of medical experience these doctors shared was basically immobilized.

Then the patient asked for a priesthood blessing. Those who held the Melchizedek Priesthood gathered around him as Russell pronounced a blessing in which the Spirit directed him to command the bleeding to stop and to promise the man that he would live and recover.

The bleeding did stop, he did survive, and he recovered to live many more years.

After years of experience in the operating room, including participating in miracles there, Dr. Nelson was also acutely aware of limits to his profession.

"Men can do very little of themselves to heal sick or broken bodies," he said. "With an education they can do a little more; with advanced medical degrees and training, a little more yet can be done. The real power to heal, however, is a gift from God. He has deigned that some of that power may be harnessed via the authority of his priesthood to benefit and bless mankind when all man can do for himself may not be sufficient" (Marvin K. Gardner, "Elder Russell M. Nelson").

"Thank you for the blessing.
Now you may do whatever you need to do
to make that blessing a reality."

—President Spencer W. Kimball

In May 1981, President Spencer W. Kimball had another issue with his heart, this one requiring a pacemaker. Once again, he turned to Dr. Nelson, who performed the procedure. The outcome was as they had hoped, and in fact, President Kimball left ten days later for Chile, where he broke ground for a temple in Santiago. But just a few weeks later, on a Saturday morning, Russell received a call from Dr. Ernest Wilkinson, President Kimball's primary-care physician, indicating that the pacemaker wasn't working. "That was a call I did not want to receive," Dr. Nelson admitted. "I told him to bring President Kimball to the hospital and I'd see him immediately."

Dr. Nelson had just completed a procedure and was still in his scrubs. Sure enough, he confirmed, President Kimball's pacemaker wasn't functioning and another procedure was necessary, which they should perform immediately. President Kimball agreed and then said to his surgeon, "Brother Nelson, give me a blessing."

Before scrubbing for this new procedure, Dr. Nelson pronounced a blessing in which he told the prophet that the pacemaker would work and that he would be able to resume his duties. Afterward, President Kimball said to Russell: "Thank you for the blessing. Now you may do whatever you need to do to make that blessing a reality."

During the procedure, Dr. Nelson found that, while the pacemaker itself looked good, there was blood under the plastic insulation of the wire that went from the pulse generator to the heart. He

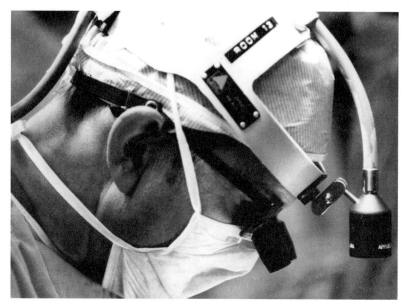

Concentrating in the operating room.

instantly knew there was a break in the insulation, replaced the defective wire, and reconnected it to the pacemaker. It worked perfectly.

"This episode was a great lesson to me," Dr. Nelson reflected. "I was reminded yet again that blessings are predicated on obedience to law. The patient can pray, the families can pray, I can pray, but if I make a mistake, all the prayers in the world won't compensate for an error. Because the law has to be fulfilled. You have to have a perfect repair, otherwise you'll have a poor outcome. So I learned absolute obedience to the laws of God. My students and those army surgical teams used to wonder why I was so particular about every step of the operation, but I learned that every step has to be perfect if the result is going to be perfect. There is a best way of doing every little maneuver in a complicated operation."

The practice of surgery taught Dr. Nelson that there can never be a blessing without "obedience to that law upon which it is predicated" (Doctrine and Covenants 130:21). Even for a prophet of God, the Lord would not break the law that governs electrical fields and insulation.

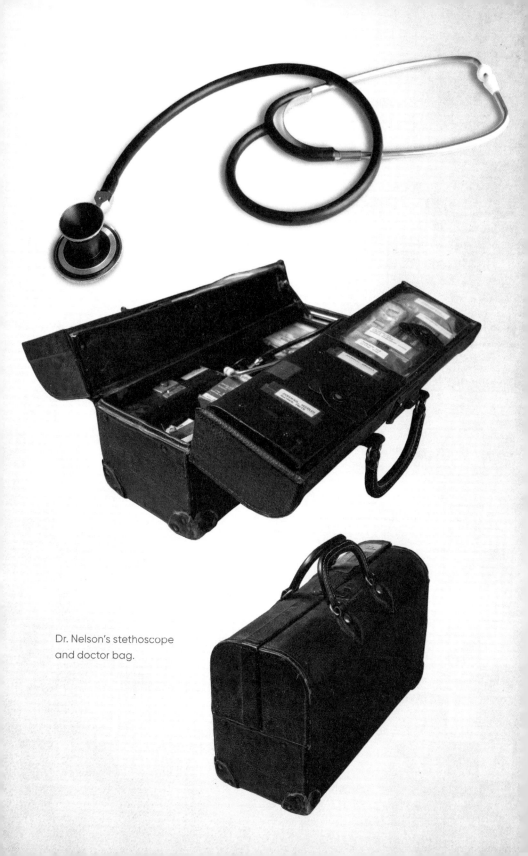

Dr. Nelson's stethoscope
and doctor bag.

"The same truth applies to what the Son of God had to go through in order to fulfill the law that would give us the privilege of eternal life and exaltation," Russell added. "The Savior had to fulfill the Atonement. He had to go through it, because that was the law upon which the blessings that would follow were predicated. A blessing comes through obedience to the law that governs that blessing."

PART THREE

THE QUORUM

OF THE

TWELVE

APOSTLES

1984 TO 2015

"Call Nelson and Oaks . . . in that order."

—President Spencer W. Kimball

On January 11, 1983, Elder LeGrand Richards of the Quorum of the Twelve passed away. With April general conference less than three months away, members looked forward to the calling of a new Apostle. The call of a man to fill a vacancy in the Quorum of the Twelve is the responsibility and prerogative of the President of the Church. Only he has the authority to receive revelation about whom the Lord has prepared and selected for that high and holy calling.

During the months preceding conference, President Kimball's health had become increasingly frail and his memory spotty. To the disappointment of many, the April 1983 general conference came and went without a call to the Twelve announced.

As the October 1983 general conference approached, speculation again mounted that this time, surely, the vacancy in the Twelve would be filled. But again, there was disappointment. No one was called. Conference came and went for a second time with an empty seat in the quorum.

Then on January 11, 1984, a year to the day after the passing of Elder Richards, Elder Mark E. Petersen of the Twelve passed away. Now there were two vacancies in the Twelve, and, if anything, the situation was more critical. President Kimball's health had deteriorated even further, and his mind was less dependable. To make matters worse, those privy to the situation knew President Kimball was in no condition to receive the revelation to extend such calls.

One of those persons was Dr. Nelson. The week before the April 1984 general conference, Russell's surgical nurse, Jan Curtis, mentioned how excited she was for the upcoming conference because two new Apostles would be called. Russell tried to gently tell her that it wasn't going to happen. "I was his doctor, and I knew it wasn't feasible, that President Kimball was not well or coherent enough to do it. I explained to her that calling an Apostle is the prerogative of the President of the Church and that President Kimball was simply in no condition to do that."

For months, President Gordon B. Hinckley, the only healthy member of the First Presidency at the time (President Marion G. Romney's health had also deteriorated), had left standing instructions with President Kimball's caregivers that if his mind ever cleared, they were to call him immediately, regardless of the hour. Month after month passed with no call. From time to time, President Hinckley looked in on President Kimball, but an opportunity to discuss such a spiritually sensitive topic as calls to the Twelve never presented itself.

Then, at about 2:30 a.m. on the Wednesday morning prior to the April 1984 general conference, the phone rang at President Hinckley's home. President Kimball was alert and would like to talk to him. President Hinckley rushed downtown to President Kimball's suite in the Hotel Utah, where the issue of vacancies in the Twelve was raised. President Kimball said simply, "Call Nelson and Oaks to the Quorum of the Twelve, in that order."

Two days later, on Friday morning, President Hinckley summoned Dr. Nelson from the regional representatives' seminar in process. He asked Russell just one question: "Is your life in order?" When he responded that it was, President Hinckley replied, "Good, because tomorrow we're presenting your name to be sustained as one of the Twelve Apostles" (Dew, *Go Forward with Faith,* 402). With that, President Hinckley embraced the stunned Russell M. Nelson, and both men wept. "You have permission to go home and tell your wife," President Hinckley said.

Reeling from the call, Russell drove straight home, anxious for the comfort of his wife. When he walked in the door, though, he was greeted by the eerie silence of an empty house—something unusual in the busy Nelson household. Dantzel was shopping. So he paced the floor and tried to sort through the questions, uncertainties, and overwhelming sense of inadequacy racing through his mind and heart.

This call meant the end of his life as Dr. Nelson. After decades of healing hearts by cutting into them, he would now try to heal them a different way. After daily appealing to the Lord to help him make the thousands of life-and-death decisions he'd made, he would now appeal to Him daily to help him be an instrument in His hands.

But there were a lot of unanswered questions: What about the operations he had already committed to do? What about a stint as a visiting professor in China he was supposed to undertake the following month? What did this mean for his family, and how would they respond? Was he spiritually ready for this? The immediate answer to that last question felt like a decided no, and yet he couldn't deny what he had felt when President Hinckley extended the call.

Finally, when Dantzel returned home, he said simply, "Honey, you'd better sit down." When he told her he had been called to fill a vacancy in the Quorum of the Twelve, her instant response brought him to the verge of tears: "I know of no one more worthy than you!"

"Of all the people who knew my imperfections," Russell said, "she knew them better than anybody. So for her to respond as she did meant everything to me. As she had done so many times before, she calmed my heart that day."

During the Saturday morning session of general conference, Russell Marion Nelson and Dallin Harris Oaks were sustained as members of the Quorum of the Twelve Apostles.

As Dr. Nelson, he had reached professional summits. Not only was he regarded the world over as an open-heart surgery pioneer, but his stature was validated by the positions he had occupied: director of the University of Utah thoracic surgery program, president of the

Utah State Medical Association, chair of the Division of Thoracic Surgery at LDS Hospital, president of the Society for Vascular Surgery, and a director of the American Board of Thoracic Surgery—which was roughly akin to being named to the Supreme Court of his profession.

But now, like Peter, James, John, and all of the original Twelve, both he and Elder Oaks were called directly from their professional pursuits into the Quorum of the Twelve. Like those early Apostles, they would now devote full-time service to the Lord and the building of His kingdom.

Neither man was permitted to tell anyone other than his wife, so Russell's large family heard the news at the same time the rest of the Church did. His daughter Emily, who was expecting a baby, called her father after the opening session: "Daddy, I was so shocked by the announcement that I think I am going into labor." That evening she gave birth to Russell and Dantzel's twenty-second grandchild. When Elder Nelson spoke for the first time in general conference the next morning, he told President Hinckley that he "should get credit at least for 'an assist'" with the delivery (Nelson, "Call to the Holy Apostleship").

In his remarks, Elder Nelson acknowledged the "personal inadequacy" he felt at the call. "That feeling is intensified," he said, "as I think of the incomparable power of Elders LeGrand Richards and Mark E. Petersen, whose absence we keenly sense. They were, to me, dear friends as well as esteemed leaders. Then, as I look about and see the strength of those more qualified and able than I, I truly am humbled by this calling."

He continued in his initial message as an Apostle by returning to a favorite topic: "While nominally I come to you from the science of surgery and its mother of medicine, in a truer sense, I have been forged from the stern discipline of law—not the laws of men . . . but the eternal and unchanging laws of our Divine Creator. The surgeon soon learns the incontrovertibility of divine law. He knows that hopes

Elder and Sister Nelson in 1984.

Elders Russell Marion Nelson and Dallin Harris Oaks at the time of their call to the Quorum of the Twelve Apostles.

and wishes are sometimes simply powerless sham. Desired blessings come only by obedience to divine law, and in no other way. . . . To this extent, there will be little difference for me in the activities of the past and those of the future. The endless laws of the Lord are the doctrines taught by His Apostles" (Nelson, "Call to the Holy Apostleship"). Elders Nelson and Oaks enjoyed the irony that in their initial messages, Elder Nelson spoke about law, and Elder Oaks, then serving as a justice on the Utah Supreme Court, spoke about the heart.

As President Hinckley concluded the April 1984 conference, he assured the Saints that these calls had been issued at the direction of President Kimball and under the direction of the Lord. "I want to give you my testimony that they were chosen and called by the spirit of prophecy and revelation," he affirmed. "While President Kimball is unable to stand at this pulpit and speak to us, we are on occasion able to converse with him, and he has given his authorization to that which has been done. We would not have proceeded without him"

(Hinckley, "Small Acts"; see also "President Hinckley Says Lord, Not Men, Called Pair").

On April 7, 1984, Russell M. Nelson was ordained an Apostle and set apart as a member of the Quorum of the Twelve Apostles. "In one short moment," he later said, "the focus of the last forty years in medicine and surgery was changed to devote the rest of my life in full-time service to my Lord and Savior, Jesus Christ" (Condie, *Russell M. Nelson*, 186).

He took his seat next to Elder Neal A. Maxwell, who, among others, took Elder Nelson under his wing. Not long thereafter, he sent Elder Maxwell a note expressing gratitude for "the privilege of sitting beside you, that your effective teaching and tutoring may continue infinitely" (Hafen, *Disciple's Life*, 165). Later, after they had been to a regional conference together, Elder Nelson thanked his seatmate for

Elder Nelson is greeted by Elder Bernard P. Brockbank.

helping him continue to grow. He had noticed "how much you have learned and are thereby able to teach [me]. . . . This . . . stimulates me to try to do better" (Hafen, *Disciple's Life*, 457).

As one of the newest members of the quorum, he was still on unfamiliar terrain and was grateful to those who helped him in his efforts to learn and become a more effective servant. He was just beginning to experience the unique brotherhood of the Twelve, described poignantly some years earlier by Elder Mark E. Petersen at the funeral of Elder Richard L. Evans: "In the Council of the Twelve, men are bound together in a great brotherhood which can hardly be equaled anywhere on earth. These men—these Twelve—have a special and distinctive calling from the Lord. They are called for one great purpose—to testify of Christ and teach His word. And this they do. One in their divine commission, one in a great effort to waken the world to its true opportunity to find peace and the abundant life, these men are united in heart and hand and soul. They *move* as one. They *work* as one. They *feel* as one. . . . [T]he Twelve know what it is to be devoted completely to the cause of Christ" ("Funeral Services for Elder Richard L. Evans").

> "I like the idea of an ordained Apostle in China."
>
> —President Gordon B. Hinckley

Not long after Elder Nelson's call to the Quorum of the Twelve Apostles, a medical colleague reported that at a recent professional meeting it had been announced that "Dr. Nelson was no longer practicing cardiac surgery because his church had made him a saint."

Amusing as this misinterpretation of his call was, with his ordination as an Apostle, Elder Nelson did what every other man called to the Twelve—both anciently and in this dispensation—has done: he straightway laid down his nets, so to speak, "forsook all, and followed Him," meaning of course the Lord (see Luke 5:1–11; Mark 1:17–18).

Nonetheless, it was all quite overwhelming. Just eighty-four men prior to Elder Nelson in this dispensation, beginning with Elder Thomas B. Marsh as number one, had received such a call and subsequently wrestled with the wide range of emotions and feelings that inevitably follow.

"After the initial shock was over," Elder Nelson reflected later, "I felt a huge gap between where I was spiritually and where I needed to be. I'd been a surgeon for thirty-five years and was to the point where I could perform those duties well. But I instantly felt aware of my weaknesses and shortcomings and wondered how I could possibly measure up to the spiritual standard of my Brethren in the Twelve."

Notwithstanding Elder Nelson's personal misgivings, his quorum president, President Ezra Taft Benson, welcomed him and Elder Oaks with open arms and expected them to participate. "President Benson was an apostle when I was in college," Elder Nelson reflected, "yet suddenly we were brothers, two of the Twelve together. But he

Elder Nelson shares a smile with President Hinckley at general conference.

couldn't have been more solicitous of my counsel in the council. I assumed there's nothing more appreciated than silence from a freshman. But he wouldn't have that. In fact, if I was silent on something, he would draw it out. He accepted all of us as colleagues without gradation" (Dew, *Ezra Taft Benson*, 430).

As Elder Nelson reflected on his life experiences, he could see ways in which the Lord had been preparing him for years, and some of those indicators were professional. One sign was the fact that Dr. Don Doty had just recently joined Dr. Nelson's practice. Seven years earlier, Russell and his surgical partners had tried to lure Dr. Doty, then a professor of surgery at the University of Iowa, to join their practice. They had nearly convinced him to make the move when President Hinckley, to whom Russell reported in his role as General President of the Sunday School, said he felt Dr. Doty should remain in

Iowa for a season. Doty was subsequently called as a stake president in Iowa.

But recently, Dr. Doty had inquired of Dr. Nelson if the earlier invitation to join his practice in Salt Lake City was still good. Assured that it was, Dr. Doty had just relocated to Utah. "Don is a master surgeon and a master Latter-day Saint," Elder Nelson affirmed. "He's now written the textbooks on how to do what we do. When President Hinckley asked who would care for my patients going forward, I told him that Dr. Don Doty, Dr. Conrad Jenson, and Dr. Kent Jones were all available and would give them better care than I could."

Sunday night after general conference, Elder Nelson went to his office and wrote a note to his receptionist indicating that he would make good on any appointments already scheduled but that she should not schedule any more. One major question remained, however. He was scheduled to spend May in China lecturing on the latest surgical techniques and conducting operative clinics. When he asked President Hinckley what he should do about that obligation, President Hinckley asked, "Have you made a commitment to them?" When Elder Nelson responded yes, President Hinckley replied, "If you've made a commitment, keep that commitment. But don't make any further ones. Plus," he added, "I like the idea of an ordained Apostle in China."

"President Hinckley's counsel about keeping commitments guided me during the transition period from my surgical career to full-time service to the Lord. And I've thought of it often in other circumstances as well. It is good counsel—if you've made a commitment, keep it."

"We would love to have your associate come, but we have no confidence in him. We want you to come."

−Dr. Zhang Zhen-Xiang

When Elder Nelson headed to China the month after his ordination, he was certain that would be his last professional assignment there. His medical career was now in his rearview mirror. In fact, when individuals continued to write him for a medical opinion, his response was typically, "When I accepted my current responsibility and my ministry as an Apostle, I left medicine behind and embraced my new role. I would encourage you to seek competent medical advice from those who still do that procedure" (*Church News*/KSL Interview, January 8, 2018).

But less than a year later, he received an urgent call from his friend Dr. Zhang, pleading for his help. A famous opera star in Beijing, Mr. Fang Rongxiang, was in full heart failure and in need of a quadruple coronary artery bypass graft operation. Mr. Fang, who was not only an acclaimed vocalist but an actor and acrobat as well, was a national hero, and Dr. Zhang was pulling out all the stops to save his life.

Elder Nelson explained that his call to the Twelve had ended his professional career but that he had an accomplished colleague in Salt Lake City, Dr. Conrad B. Jenson, who could perform the surgery if they would send Mr. Fang to Utah.

"You don't understand," Dr. Zhang explained. "He is too sick to even go down for x-rays. You've got to come here, and now."

Again, Elder Nelson deferred, saying, "Perhaps my colleague could come there, then."

Dr. Zhang persisted: "Oh, we would love to have your associate come, but we have no confidence in him. We want you to come." This, in Dr. Nelson's experience, was a perfect reflection of typical Chinese politeness combined with directness.

Recognizing that Dr. Zhang's gentle nature would never give way to such urgent pleadings unless the situation were dire, Elder Nelson sought the counsel of President Ezra Taft Benson, his quorum president. President Benson indicated they had best take this issue to President Hinckley. Ultimately, both Presidents Hinckley and Benson agreed that this was a beautiful opportunity to render important service in China, and they encouraged Elder Nelson to go.

He and Dantzel were scheduled to be in Europe at the time on a Church assignment, so he arranged for Dr. Jenson to precede him to China to do the preoperative tests and assist during the operation. From Europe, Dantzel flew west to Salt Lake City and Elder Nelson flew east to Beijing, reviewing his Mandarin and other operative notes all the way. When he landed at 3:10 a.m., a grateful delegation of Chinese medical professors, including Dr. Zhang, was there to welcome him to China.

The next day he and Dr. Jenson rehearsed in detail every step of the procedure they were about to perform. Then, the following morning, in an attitude of fasting and prayer, they performed a flawless, four-coronary bypass graft on China's most famous opera star.

Elder Nelson checks the pulse of Mr. Fang Rongxiang a year after his lifesaving surgery.

169

The following morning, Elder Nelson went early to Mr. Fang's hospital room to check on him and was horrified to see that the cardiopulmonary monitor—an oscilloscope—was dark. "Oh, no! Did my patient die and no one even call me?" he reacted with a flash of panic. His shock quickly subsided, though, when Mr. Fang called to him from across the room. The attending Chinese doctors had decided they didn't need the monitor any longer and had turned it off. And then when Mr. Fang had said he was hungry, they had fed him breakfast. "I would never have done either of those things," Elder Nelson admitted, "but it made all the sense in the world to them. He was doing well and he was hungry, so they fed him." Elder Nelson stayed until that afternoon and then, confident that Dr. Jenson and the Chinese doctors could handle anything that arose, caught a flight home. He was back in Salt Lake City in time to play the organ for the Brethren that Thursday in their temple meeting.

Before he left, however, he and Dr. Jenson—whose careful preparations for the surgery had impressed the Chinese surgeons and won them over—received a surprise visit from a group of grateful people: Mr. Fang's family and friends, the Chinese minister of health, the head of the Beijing Opera Company, and a delegation of physicians who came bearing gifts to express their gratitude.

After a distinguished record in thoracic surgery, Dr. Russell M. Nelson's career as a heart surgeon was now truly over. On March 4, 1985, in mainland China, he performed his last open-heart operation.

"It's the other way around, President Benson. How may I help you?"

—President Gordon B. Hinckley

O
n November 5, 1985, Elder and Sister Nelson arrived back in Salt Lake City after a trip to Portugal, only to be greeted at the airport by a Church Security officer who told Elder Nelson that President Kimball was in a dire condition and he was needed immediately at the prophet's bedside. One Church Security officer took Dantzel home while another raced Elder Nelson to President Kimball's room in the Hotel Utah. There he waited, with President Gordon B. Hinckley and Arthur Haycock, secretary to the President, until the Lord's prophet—Elder Nelson's mentor and treasured friend—slipped through the veil.

"I was sitting next to President Hinckley when he called President Ezra Taft Benson, the next in apostolic seniority, to tell him President Kimball was gone," Elder Nelson remembered. "President Benson expressed his deep sorrow and asked President Hinckley, in his typically gracious way, what he could do to help him. President Hinckley responded instantly, 'It's the other way around, President Benson. How may I help you?'

"In that moment, President Hinckley taught me a great lesson in Church government," Elder Nelson reflected. Upon the passing of President Kimball, the First Presidency was instantly dissolved, and presiding authority shifted automatically to the Quorum of the Twelve Apostles, presided over by President Benson.

Elder Nelson was subsequently among those privileged to pay tribute to President Kimball at his funeral. "When Sister Kimball

President Hinckley conducts President Spencer W. Kimball's funeral service.

asked that I speak at her husband's funeral, she made two very interesting qualifying statements to me. First, she said with a smile, 'No
one knew his heart better than you.' Second, 'You knew him at his
worst moments'" (Nelson, "Spencer W. Kimball").

He had also witnessed the deceased prophet at his finest—in
moments of sheer faith and courage. He struggled to find words to
do justice to the depth of his feelings about the man he had come to
know so well. "By his example," Elder Nelson said at the funeral, "he
became my great teacher." He then concluded his tribute with this
summation of the prophet's life:

"From one who knew his heart as well as any other man, from
one who knew him in his worst moments, I solemnly proclaim
that President Spencer W. Kimball taught as a prophet and testified as a prophet. He had the dignity of a prophet and the humility
of a prophet. He had the courage of a prophet and the kindness of a

prophet. He gave succor as a prophet, and he suffered as a prophet. He spoke as a prophet and was spoken to as a prophet. He revealed as a prophet and received revelation as a prophet. He blessed as a prophet and was blessed as a prophet. He loved as a prophet and was loved as a prophet. He lived as a prophet and died as a prophet, sealing with his life his testimony that God lives, that Jesus is the Christ, that His Church has been restored to the earth, that this work is true" (Nelson, "Spencer W. Kimball").

For Russell M. Nelson, the passing of President Spencer W. Kimball was poignant. President Kimball had trusted Dr. Nelson with his life. Dr. Nelson, in turn, had looked to President Kimball in moments of uncertainty and discouragement. And in a way that defied medical science, the prophet had emerged long enough from the fog of an increasingly feeble mind to receive the revelation that Russell M. Nelson and Dallin H. Oaks were to be ordained Apostles. For the rest of his life, Elder Nelson would cherish the hours he had spent with this prophet, seer, and revelator, and he would ever be grateful for the unparalleled influence President Kimball had had on his life.

"Who, me? Are you sure Dallin shouldn't do that? He's an attorney. I'm a heart surgeon. What do I know about opening countries?"

—Elder Russell M. Nelson

On Sunday, November 10, 1985, President Ezra Taft Benson was ordained and set apart as the thirteenth President of The Church of Jesus Christ of Latter-day Saints. Four days later, he and his counselors—President Gordon B. Hinckley and President Thomas S. Monson—came to the meeting of the First Presidency and Quorum of the Twelve in the Salt Lake Temple with new assignments for each Apostle in hand.

Beginning at the senior end of the circle and working around to those most recently called, they handed out new areas of responsibility and supervision. "By the time President Benson got to me," Elder Nelson recalled, "he said something that startled me: 'You are to be responsible for all of the affairs of the Church in Europe and Africa, with a special assignment to open up the nations in Eastern Europe that are now under the yoke of Communism for the preaching of the gospel.'" As first contact for all of Europe, he was succeeding Elders Thomas S. Monson and Neal A. Maxwell.

Elder Nelson's initial reaction may have been similar to Moses's when he was asked to lead the children of Israel out of Egypt: "Who, me?" Just nineteen months in the quorum, his immediate thought was, "Are you sure Dallin shouldn't do that? He's an attorney. I'm a heart surgeon. What do I know about opening countries?" "Thankfully," said Elder Nelson, "I may have thought it, but I didn't say it."

The assignment was Herculean in proportion. Europe was important to the Church. It was the homeland for many early converts who had immigrated to the United States and infused tremendous strength and stability into the Church during its fledgling, formative years.

But in 1985, more of Europe lay behind the Iron Curtain than not: Poland, Hungary, Czechoslovakia, Romania, Bulgaria, Albania, Macedonia, Yugoslavia, Estonia, Lithuania, Latvia, the German Democratic Republic, and all of the USSR. President Benson's assignment to Elder Nelson came roughly nineteen months before President Ronald Reagan would famously declare, on June 12, 1987, "Mr. Gorbachev, tear down this wall," and four years before the Berlin Wall would fall on November 9, 1989. There were more countries in Europe that had *not* recognized the Church than had. Further, this was during the politically frigid time referred to as the Cold War. "If a task ever seemed impossible to me," Elder Nelson admitted years later, "that was it" (Nelson, "The Lord Uses the Unlikely").

"I had spent much of my professional life opening hearts to perform lifesaving operations," he reflected, "but I had *no* experience that would lead me to believe I could open countries for the preaching of the gospel" (Nelson, "Becoming True Millennials"). And yet, a prophet had given him an assignment, and so he set out to do what seemed at the outset "utterly impossible."

It was difficult to know where to even begin. It took Elder Nelson several months to make initial contacts, lay groundwork, and map out an approach. Over the next several years, he would make dozens of trips to Eastern Europe and to the former Soviet Union, as well as an endless parade of trips to Washington, DC, to meet with ambassadors, diplomats, and anyone who could help open doors throughout Europe.

One country with which he already had both an affinity and first-hand experience was Russia. He had studied the language and been

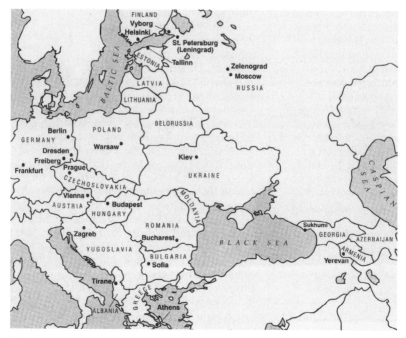

The countries of Eastern Europe in the late 1980s.

there to lecture professionally several times, and he already loved the Russian people. With Elder Hans B. Ringger of the Seventy, a Swiss General Authority then serving in the Europe Area Presidency, Elder Nelson traveled to Moscow on a fact-finding, bridge-building mission in the summer of 1987.

Elders Nelson and Ringger were, on the one hand, an unlikely pair—an American heart surgeon and a Swiss engineer and architect. On the other hand, they were quite different from leaders of other faith groups, and they often disarmed dignitaries with whom they met. They came asking only that the Church be recognized and allowed to function in those countries. "Other churches often asked for money from various governments," Elder Nelson explained. "We didn't ask for anything except permission. We always go through the front door and abide by the laws."

In Moscow in 1987, Elders Nelson and Ringger sought an

audience with Konstantin Kharchev, chief of the Council of Religious Affairs. He refused to see them, but he represented the first hoop through which they had to jump. So they stayed in the waiting room of his office all day until it was time for him to go home. When at day's end they were still there, an impatient Kharchev demanded to know what they wanted. Elder Nelson responded, "We just want to ask you a question. What would we need to do to get the Church we represent established in Russia?"

This was Communist Russia, and the Soviet Union was still intact. Kharchev couldn't have been less interested in the questions of these two church men, one of them an American, with whom he hadn't wanted to talk anyway. He did respond, however, that for a church to be legally registered it had to have twenty adult Russian citizens who were willing to sign a paper indicating they were members of that church, and they all had to be from the same political district. At the time, there were eleven political districts in Moscow alone.

Elders Nelson and Ringger asked if they could establish a reading room or visitors' center where citizens could come of their own volition and learn about the Church.

"No," Kharchev barked.

"You have given us a chicken-and-egg problem," Elder Nelson responded. "You say we can't receive recognition until we have members, but we can't get members if we can't have a reading room or visitors' center."

"That, sir, is your problem," answered Mr. Kharchev. "Good day."

The next day, Elder Nelson and Elder Ringger sat on a park bench near the Kremlin and reviewed their dilemma. They pondered, prayed, brainstormed possible solutions, and pondered some more. Could young adults from the nearby Nordic countries immigrate and help with the situation? Were there ways Scandinavian members could help? Were there other ways to introduce the gospel without using missionaries, reading rooms, or visitors' centers? "We finally decided we couldn't meet their requirements," Elder Nelson remembered, "and that was when the Lord stepped in."

Roughly a year later, on July 24, 1988, a Moscow resident named Igor Mikhailusenko was baptized while visiting the United States. This was followed by a Russian family from Leningrad—Yuri and Liudmila Terebenin and their daughter Anna—being baptized in Budapest. Then another Moscow resident, Olga Smolianova, was baptized while visiting Italy. A Russian man living in Vyborg, near the Finnish border, then became acquainted with a Finnish Latter-day Saint family, and he was baptized.

A few missionaries in the Finland Helsinki Mission began learning Russian and received permission to teach Russian tourists visiting Finland. Svetlana Artemova's experience demonstrates how actively the Lord helped reach Russian citizens with His word.

For some time, Svetlana had yearned to acquire a Bible in Russia, but ever since the Communist revolution in 1917, Bibles had been

The Kremlin in Moscow, Russia.

difficult for Russian citizens to come by. After pleading with her husband over an extended period of time, she made a trip to Helsinki in the fall of 1989 for the express purpose of obtaining a Bible in the Russian language.

During her stay, she visited a Helsinki park, and Svetlana stumbled on an object covered by a pile of leaves. Almost unbelievably, it was a Bible—and even more miraculous, it was a Bible in Russian! She was ecstatic and so thrilled that she couldn't help but share her delight with the first woman who walked by. That woman, Raija Kemppainen, just happened to be the wife of District President Jussi Kemppainen. Raija was fluent in Russian and English, as well as her native Finnish, and she asked Svetlana if she would like to have another book that would teach her even more about Jesus Christ. Svetlana was delighted at the prospect, and Raija—who with her husband, Jussi, had been praying to find ways to help take the gospel to Russia—quickly obtained a copy of the Book of Mormon in Russian for her new friend. Svetlana was soon baptized in Helsinki.

At this point in time, missionaries could enter Russia but could not stay permanently nor could they preach or baptize. But they could teach when invited to do so. Svetlana wanted missionaries to teach friends of hers in Leningrad and arranged for the elders to meet with one of them. When missionaries knocked on the woman's door, she was not home; but a neighbor, Sasha Teraskin, heard the knocking, opened his door, and invited the missionaries in. When they identified themselves as missionaries from The Church of Jesus Christ of Latter-day Saints, Sasha was moved to tears. Since meeting Church members in Warsaw,

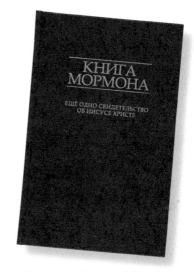

The Book of Mormon in Russian.

Poland, while on a recent trip there, he had been praying to know how to learn more about the Church. The missionaries taught him, and he was baptized.

And so it went. "Before too long," said Elder Nelson, "we had twenty members in Leningrad, and that is where it all started." He filled out the appropriate papers and took them to the office of religious affairs in Leningrad, seeking recognition for the Church. Three months later, nothing had happened, so Elder Nelson returned to that office and asked where the papers were that he had filed. "They're still in a drawer," an official admitted. "We don't know what to do with them. No one has ever asked for recognition for a church before."

That day, and on plenty of others, Elder Nelson's work felt like three steps forward and three and a half steps back. But on he pressed.

On one occasion, Elder Nelson was in the office of religious affairs in Leningrad with Yuri Terebenin, the first convert in that city. During their discussion, Elder Nelson invited the officials there to attend a meeting they were having that night with the small group of Saints living in Leningrad who had joined the Church elsewhere. Yuri panicked. He and his fellow Saints had tried hard to remain anonymous: "Elder Nelson, you don't do that. These are the police." Elder Nelson's response revealed the calm that so often characterized his demeanor: "Brother Terebenin, our Church is for everyone. We want them to come." Later, Elder Nelson commented, "They came, and I don't think I've ever seen a man so pale as Yuri Terebenin. But it's understandable. The Soviet Union was still under the yoke of Communism, and citizens felt threatened by the police."

There were still many more trips to take and meetings to arrange, many more luncheons to host with ambassadors and other Russian dignitaries visiting the United States, many more snubs from Soviet officials and setbacks with which to deal. But in June 1991, at a VIP dinner following the Tabernacle Choir's performance at the Bolshoi Theater in Moscow, Alexander Rutskoy, vice president of the

The Tabernacle Choir in Russia.

Republic of Russia, made the historic and unexpected announcement that The Church of Jesus Christ of Latter-day Saints had been granted full recognition in the entire Republic of Russia. Both Elder Nelson and Elder Dallin H. Oaks, who were at that concert and dinner,

were shocked, overjoyed, and overwhelmed by the Lord's goodness. After years of work, the breakthrough had finally come.

"It was an absolutely stunning moment," Elder Nelson recalled. "We had hoped it was coming, but we didn't expect it that night. That was a red-letter day. Many of us did all we could to bring this about, but make no mistake about it, it was the Lord who worked the miracle."

Alexander Rutskoy, vice president of the Republic of Russia, announces recognition of the Church.

Elder Gregory A. Schwitzer, who later served in the Europe East Area Presidency headquartered in Moscow, said in reflection about Elder Nelson's pioneering efforts in Russia: "It's important to understand his persistence. Russian government is a paragon of delay, bureaucracy, and creating barriers. Elder Nelson knew why he was doing what he was doing, and he knew that doors would open if he was politely persistent. He just kept at it. As a consequence, there's no deception about how the Church developed our missionary program in Russia. He took us through the front door" (*Church News/ KSL Interview*, January 8, 2018).

Some five years later, on October 7, 1996, Mikhail Gorbachev and his wife, Raisa, visited Salt Lake City. During a meeting, Elder Nelson was seated next to Gorbachev, and the former president of the Soviet Union asked Elder Nelson to explain the differences between the Russian Orthodox Church and The Church of Jesus Christ of Latter-day Saints. Among other things, Elder Nelson taught him about living prophets and then invited him and his wife to meet with President Gordon B. Hinckley and his counselors the next day. As he did so, he couldn't help but think about the ups and downs, the twists and turns, the disappointments and small breakthroughs that had characterized his experience with Russian dignitaries during the previous decade. But here, sitting in the Church Administration Building, was the man who had taken the dramatic step of tearing down the Berlin Wall. And Elder Nelson had the opportunity to introduce to him some of the basic tenets of the restored gospel.

Clearly, the Lord can do His own work, and Elder Nelson marveled at the privilege of being a small part of it.

"What is your greatest problem,
and how can we help you?"

—Elder Russell M. Nelson

S hortly after President Ezra Taft Benson extended the assignment
to open doors for the Church in Eastern Europe, Elder Nelson began working closely with Beverly Campbell, director of the Church's
new International Affairs office in Washington, DC. Her public re-
lations experience made Beverly adept at establishing relationships
with international dignitaries in the nation's capital.

Early on, she recommended that Elder Nelson focus on Hungary.
Congressman Tom Lantos, a Democrat from California (and the first
Holocaust survivor to serve in Congress), had a Latter-day Saint wife
and, because of it, an affinity for the Church. The congressman arranged for Elder Nelson and Elder Ringger to meet with Dr. Imre
Miklos, head of the State Office for Religious Affairs for Hungary.
"This was one of the only advance appointments I was ever able to
get," Elder Nelson recalled. "I was almost always in the position of
having to knock on doors and find out who I needed to talk to. But
thanks to this congressman, I was able to get an appointment with the
man I needed to talk to in Hungary."

The appointment did not begin well, however. At the outset, Dr.
Miklos asked if Elder Nelson knew David M. Kennedy.

"Oh, yes, he's a good friend of mine," he responded.

"Well, I hate him," Miklos replied.

Elder Nelson thought to himself, "No one who knows David
Kennedy hates him, but strike one!"

Then, as the conversation proceeded, the translators for Miklos and Elder Nelson began to spar with each other. Elder Nelson explained to his translator that they were there to make friends, not enemies. Nonetheless, tension now hung over the room like a shroud. Strike two.

Miklos remained aloof and cold. Finally, Elder Nelson said he could see it was time to leave, but before he did, he wanted to tell the diplomat about an experience he'd had the previous Sunday. "Late Sunday afternoon," he said, "I went to Mount Gellert, and there I prayed fervently that the Lord's Spirit would be poured out upon this beautiful land, its people, and their leaders, that they would prosper, that families would be happy and strong, and that peace would prevail in this nation. I wanted you to hear of this directly from me rather than indirectly from someone else."

The room suddenly grew quiet. "The Spirit of the Lord worked

Mount Gellert, where Elder Nelson invoked the Lord's blessings on the land of Hungary.

on that man," Elder Nelson related later. "He began to change his mind about us, and what was supposed to be a fifteen-minute meeting lasted an hour and fifteen minutes."

As they spoke, Elder Nelson indicated that it was his understanding that Hungary had one of the highest death rates from alcohol in Europe, and then he volunteered, "Our Church may be able to help you." When Miklos seemed skeptical, Elder Nelson reassured him by saying, "You don't have to take my word for it. You know the minister of religious affairs in the German Democratic Republic. He's been dealing with members of our Church for decades. Talk to him."

Miklos made the call, and when he heard the GDR officials refer to the twelfth article of faith, that The Church of Jesus Christ of Latter-day Saints always upholds and sustains the law of the land, his attitude shifted.

Miklos became an ally, and a year later, Elder Nelson went to Budapest to sign papers granting the Church official recognition in Hungary. He also connected the Church's Social Services department with officials in the Hungarian government to discuss ways to address the country's problem with alcohol. Elder Nelson and Miklos became good enough friends that when Miklos's wife suffered from heart disease some years later, he called Elder Nelson from Budapest seeking his professional advice about what to do.

On Easter Sunday, April 19, 1987, Elder Nelson dedicated Hungary for the preaching of the gospel, invoking an apostolic blessing that this would be the "dawning of a new era" (Condie, *Russell M. Nelson*, 262). He also declared there were young men in that congregation who would someday lead stakes of Zion. On June 4, 2006, Elders W. Craig Zwick and Bruce C. Hafen created the Budapest Stake, the first in Hungary, and were the ones to extend the call to the first stake president, Klinger Gabor. Then age thirty-seven, Brother Gabor had been in the congregation at the dedication of the country as an eighteen-year-old (see *Church News*/KSL Interview, January 5, 2018).

Elder Nelson's trips to Romania also produced opportunities to help. On his first trip there, also with Elder Ringger, he encountered the kind of suspicion an official representing an unknown American church often inspired. Believing they had an appointment with the chief of protocol of the State Office of Religious Affairs, Elders Nelson and Ringger were informed that their meeting had been postponed for two days, and they were turned away.

In two days, they were supposed to be in meetings in Turkey. But instead, they juggled their schedule and walked the streets of Bucharest, where they saw long lines of people hoping to buy a soup bone. The Romanian people appeared to be starving both spiritually and physically. They seemed to have nothing. The duo soon realized they were being followed. Repeatedly during those forty-eight hours, they were accosted by individuals wanting to exchange money on the black market. Prostitutes propositioned them. Everywhere they went, they were watched and tempted with illicit activities. Instead, they went to the circus, which was in town.

Thursday finally came, and when they reported back to the Office of Religious Affairs, officials asked why they hadn't gone to the American Embassy. "We didn't go to the Swiss Embassy, either," Elder Nelson responded, referring to Elder Ringger's nationality. "We had no business with them. We were here to see you."

"I don't know what would have happened if we'd gone to the American Embassy," Elder Nelson reflected later, "but in Romania and in other countries, it seemed to make a difference when I said that our business was not there. I frequently had to do that so that local officials understood I was not in their country as an American citizen first but as a representative of a worldwide church."

After the subsequent coup that deposed President Nicolae Ceaucescu, Elders Nelson and Ringger returned to Romania to meet with the head of religious affairs for the new government. This man was a pediatrician, and when the Brethren arrived at his office, his

Elder Hans B. Ringger.

waiting room was filled with crying babies and anxious mothers. "I came in with this pontifical message that we were from The Church of Jesus Christ of Latter-day Saints and were there to assist them with their work," Elder Nelson remembered.

The official responded with impatience: "If you really want to help me, you will leave my office immediately and get out of here."

Elder Nelson's reply most likely took the man by surprise: "I understand. I am a doctor, and I know what you are going through. But will you just tell me in one word how we can help you?"

The one word was "orphans."

"Sir, we will help you with your orphans," Elder Nelson responded. And he did.

It took Elder Nelson just one visit to a Romanian orphanage to understand how dire the situation was for a growing number of homeless children. "That visit had to be one of the most pitiful sights I'd ever seen," he recalled. "It was just awful."

Half-dressed children were strapped onto potty chairs all day long. Nobody talked to them, held them, or loved them. What Elder Nelson saw not only startled him, but the stark images of defenseless children, uncared for, lingered in his mind. He knew the Church could help.

Once back in Salt Lake City, he set in motion the process of calling humanitarian missionaries for Romania and rallied experts from Church Social Services and BYU to provide resources, know-how, and sheer labor to assist with the enormous challenge.

Dr. Wendy Watson, who began teaching at BYU as a professor of marriage and family therapy in January 1993, remembers how big the "Romanian orphan program" was at the time on campus. "I never realized until I married him that Russell was behind all of this," she later remembered (email to author, August 11, 2018).

Dr. Alvin Price and his wife, Barbara, as well as other professors and many students, traveled there to help in orphanages and assist with various kinds of humanitarian outreach. One such endeavor was a Special Olympics Games for disadvantaged children. Many Romanian citizens didn't even know that people with disabilities existed because the government kept them hidden from sight. The Special Olympics, as just one example of the wide-ranging efforts from BYU faculty and students, helped bring the disabled to the fore. A young Romanian girl in a wheelchair who'd been shot during the 1989 revolution carried the torch to light the Special Olympics flame. "Everyone in the stadium was crying," Dr. Price said. "When I saw the children coming into the stadium, I was absolutely overwhelmed. It was the biggest head rush I have ever had. My wife and I were hugging, crying, sobbing at the end of the track" ("Missionaries perform humanitarian service").

In another meeting in Bucharest, this one with Teofil Pop, the minister of justice, Elder Nelson asked again if there were ways the Church could help. This man needed help drafting a new constitution for the country. Elder Nelson contacted the Church's legal counsel for Europe and the Middle East, who subsequently worked with the man.

Elder Nelson's skill at diagnoses—in these cases diagnosing the source of a country's pain—repeatedly opened doors throughout Eastern Europe. "We were able to help with a constitution in one place, with orphans in another, with alcoholism in another," he reflected. "Everyone has pain somewhere, and our challenge is to find out where the pain is. Usually it's not physical pain but comes in the stress of living. The patient is always the expert. This is what we try to teach the missionaries. When you meet someone, find out how we can help them. The Church literally has the capacity to help people no matter what their problem is. The gospel exists to help people."

This approach helped Elder Nelson and Elder Ringger make friends for the Church in country after country. Beverly Campbell described what she observed: "From the time Elder Nelson received the assignment to open the doors to the Iron Curtain countries, he aggressively pursued every avenue in that regard. He was willing to go anywhere and meet anytime, at any inconvenience or danger to himself. I came to know a man whose judgment was so keen and whose ability to make correct decisions so uncanny, that there was no other explanation than that he had been chosen before the worlds were to be the Lord's servant in these countries for just 'such a time as this'" (Condie, *Russell M. Nelson*, 246–47).

Extended periods of time in Eastern Europe also helped Elder Nelson build relationships with the new members of the Church themselves. "You have to understand," said Elder Gregory A. Schwitzer, who earlier served as a mission president in Yekaterinburg, Russia, and then as a member of the Europe East Area Presidency, "that an Eastern European, partly because of almost a hundred years of Communism, has a natural kind of skepticism about people. But Elder Nelson melts their hearts. He's the perfect balance of kindness, confidence, caring, and integrity. They absolutely trust him. They love to have their pictures taken with him. They love to just be in his presence. He is Mr. Eastern Europe" (*Church News*/KSL Interview, January 8, 2018).

The intense schooling Elder Nelson received in these countries, where dignitaries were often resistant, obstinate, and unreceptive, would serve him well throughout his ministry. When Elder Mervyn B. Arnold served in the Brazil Area Presidency, he took Elder Nelson to meet with the mayor of São Paulo. "It was supposed to be a short visit," he remembered, "but the warmth and spirit of kindness that came from President Nelson completely consumed this man. The same thing happened with the governor of the state of São Paulo. That visit was supposed to go just a few minutes and it went on and on. It was as though he did not want Elder Nelson to leave" (*Church News*/ KSL Interview, January 11, 2018).

President James E. Faust observed: "Russell M. Nelson has an exceptional intuitive gift for knowing what to do and say with people in different countries. He is a natural diplomat" (Condie, *Russell M. Nelson,* 247).

That diplomacy usually began with a fundamental question: "How can we help?"

"The Lord likes effort."

—Elder Russell M. Nelson

For the better part of five years, Elder Nelson traipsed back and forth across the Atlantic Ocean seeking meetings with government officials and trying to further the Church's interests in Poland, Czechoslovakia, Yugoslavia, Bulgaria, Romania, Hungary, the German Democratic Republic, Turkey, Estonia, Ukraine, and the Soviet Union. And that didn't count the trips to Washington, DC, to meet with ambassadors and other dignitaries from the countries he supervised.

He was never wanted and rarely welcome. Many government leaders wouldn't even give appointments to a man who professed faith in God. Over time, he was both thwarted in his efforts and helped along the way; treated poorly in some circumstances and graciously in others; spied on by secret police and later greeted as friends by officials who got to know him; and treated suspiciously in some corners while being sought for medical consultation by others. Some trips seemed utterly futile, while on others, doors opened he could never have predicted or planned for.

His experiences in Czechoslovakia were representative of others. After a series of luncheons and meetings in Washington, DC, with various dignitaries from Czechoslovakia, Elders Nelson and Ringger had an initial meeting with Vladimir Janko, the vice minister and director of the secretariat for church affairs in the Czechoslovak Soviet Socialist Republic (CSSR). Mr. Janko had zero interest in dealing with these officials representing an "American church." If they were going to discuss matters of religion, he wanted to do so with a fellow Czech.

End of discussion, end of meeting. "He was tough," Elder Nelson said without elaboration.

The brethren excused themselves and went to the home of Olga and Jirí Snederfler, the devoted district president and his wife who had courageously provided leadership to the Czech Saints during years of Communist oppression. The Saints had met quietly, even secretly at times, in the Snederflers' humble apartment, which was adorned with twenty-three pictures of temples—temples that, at the time, they had no hope of attending. Their apartment, though, was filled with the Spirit.

Elder Nelson explained why they had come: Mr. Janko would deal only with a Czech citizen. "Jirí," he said, "we cannot ask you to do this because we realize it could cost you your life or at least a jail sentence." Even as they spoke, the previous president of Czechoslovakia, Vaclav Havel, was in prison for supporting freedom of religion, which many in that country still believed was inconsistent with the dogma of Communism.

Realizing full well what he was committing to, Jirí responded, "I will do it. It's for the Lord." As soon as he said these words, Olga began to cry but then quickly added, "We will do it for the Lord."

Jirí did as promised and met with Czech officials, which immediately landed him on a watch list. The government monitored him day and night. He and Olga gave up their privacy and at times were threatened with giving up everything they had for the Church.

After a period of time, Elder Nelson returned to Prague to try to further a dialogue with Janko, but this time Janko refused to even see him—despite having Czechoslovakian members with whom he could also deal. Elder Nelson had hit a brick wall, and the brick wall was Janko.

"So then the Lord intervened," he said. The subsequent velvet revolution, where not a single drop of blood was shed to overthrow Communism, resulted in new government leaders. Before long,

Elder Nelson with Olga and Jiri Snederfler.

Elders Nelson and Ringger, accompanied by President Snederfler, secured a meeting with Josef Hromadka, the new deputy prime minister of the Republic of Czechoslovakia.

Once again, Elder Nelson flew across the Atlantic. "This time I knew my way to the right office very well," Elder Nelson recounted. "I could have found it blindfolded at that point. Mr. Hromadka was willing to hear our story—that we were simply asking for legal recognition of the Church so that our people could worship in dignity." Hromadka responded that recognition would be forthcoming shortly, and he was true to his word.

The same day Mr. Hromadka promised that legal recognition would come soon, Elder Nelson, Elder Ringger, Brother and Sister Snederfler, and a few other Czechoslovakian Saints went to Mount Karlstein, where Elder John A. Widtsoe had dedicated the country on July 24, 1929. There Elder Nelson offered a prayer of gratitude for the Lord's intervention in behalf of the Saints there. After years of suppression and worshipping in secret, they would soon be able to worship openly.

In reasonably short order, the Church received recognition as a legal entity. And even better, when recognition came, it was indicated that the Church had been there since 1929—a literal godsend for the stalwart souls who had quietly kept the Church going throughout the Communist period. "So what the Lord did for us in Czechoslovakia," Elder Nelson summarized, "was to remove Vladimir Janko and give us a man we could talk to. I also felt that He honored the courage and faith of Jiří and Olga Snederfler."

When Elder Nelson posed the question he'd frequently asked of dignitaries—What could the Church do to help the people of Czechoslovakia?—he was inspired by Mr. Hromadka's response: "We don't need material goods or technology; we need a new spirit, we need moral values. We need the Judeo-Christian ethic back in our curriculum. Please help us to make this a time of spiritual renewal for our nation" (Condie, *Russell M. Nelson,* 254).

Often help from the Lord came in unexpected ways. The time came in Poland to open a mission there, but how do you open a mission without a mission president who can speak Polish? And where does one find such a person? This was on Elder Nelson's mind when, on October 27, 1989, he attended the inauguration of BYU President Rex E. Lee in Provo, Utah. At a reception celebrating President Lee's appointment, Elder Nelson just happened to meet Walter Whipple, a professor of Polish in the department of Germanic and Slavic Languages. Dr. Whipple had just returned to BYU after a teaching stint in Poland. Who became the first mission president in Poland? President Walter Whipple, who was also a professional organist and accomplished cellist. "The Lord doth provide," Elder Nelson summarized. "I've seen this over and over again. When we didn't know what in the world to do next, the Lord stepped in and handed the answer to us on a silver platter. We would have had to be blind not to see it."

Sofia, Bulgaria.

"Each of these countries was different," Elder Nelson later reflected. "But the message to me was the same: 'Work your heart out, Russ. Take the risks. Then when you can't go any further, I'll help you.'"

Opening up Bulgaria proved that point. Elder Nelson and Elder Ringger flew to Sofia, Bulgaria, on October 30, 1988, for appointments the next day. They arrived late at night in the middle of a snowstorm. Elder Nelson thought he'd made arrangements through an official at the U.S. Library of Congress with roots in Bulgaria to be met at the airport and then escorted to the appropriate meeting the next day. But no one showed up, so, using his familiarity with Russian to hail a taxi, they made it into the city.

Unfortunately, the taxi took them to the wrong hotel, and by the time they discovered the mistake their taxi had left and they were afoot, with no other taxis to be found at that hour. It was late, dark, and bitter cold, and clearly all of their plans had fallen through. So they trudged, dragging suitcases behind them, through the snow for several blocks until they found the right hotel.

Their initial frustration and disappointment only accelerated the next day when they learned that no appointments had been made for them and, in fact, it was unclear with whom they should even try to meet. Elder Nelson spent all day working with a bilingual telephone operator at the Sheraton Hotel trying to identify the appropriate official. It was all to no avail. They were at a dead end. All they could do was pray for help.

Finally, through a complex set of connections, they learned they needed to see Tsviatko Tsvetkov, the head of religious affairs in Bulgaria. Surprisingly, Mr. Tsvetkov had just returned to the city and was available. "But he was madder than a wet hen," Elder Nelson remembered. "He had been out of town, was behind in his work, and here he had two members of a church he'd never heard of in his office. His first words to us were, 'Nelson? Ringger? Mormons? I've never heard of you.'" Elder Nelson responded instinctively, "Well, Mr. Tsvetkov, we've never heard of you either. It's high time we got acquainted." That statement broke the tension and gave everyone a chance to laugh. As the meeting proceeded, Tsvetkov warmed somewhat.

Over the next eighteen months, Elder Nelson returned several times to Bulgaria, where he formed relationships with other officials, helped arrange for missionaries and senior couples to teach English, was interviewed by Bulgarian journalists, and eventually dedicated the country on February 13, 1990.

The message in Bulgaria as well as every other country was the same: "We are not here to do anything but bless the lives of your people," Elder Nelson summarized. "Our missionaries look at themselves as young and inexperienced in the ways of the world, and of course, initially they are. When they finally realize how helpful they can be, they become an entirely different brand of missionary. The gospel has the power to help people progress, grow, and deal with whatever challenges they're facing."

Elder Nelson delivered this truth over and over again between 1985 and the early 1990s. During a six-year period he went to the former USSR twenty-seven times and to other eastern bloc countries several dozen times.

What did that intensive season in Eastern Europe teach him? "That we're not alone," he said. "There are many people who had a hand in all that transpired in Europe during that era. I think much of the progress we made came because President Thomas S. Monson paved the way in East Germany and dedicated a temple there in 1985. That changed the whole landscape."

When later asked what he learned from the assignment to open the countries in Eastern Europe for the preaching of the gospel, particularly in light of the many stops and starts, failed meetings, and ups and downs, Elder Nelson replied simply: "The Lord likes effort. He could have said to Moses, 'I'll meet you halfway.' But Moses had to go all the way to the top of Mount Sinai. He required effort from Moses and Joshua and Joseph Smith and from all of the subsequent Presidents of the Church. He requires effort from bishops and stake Relief Society presidents and elders quorum presidents. There is always a test. Are you willing to do really hard things? Once you've shown you're willing to do your part, He will help you."

In 1990, Elder Nelson's assignments in the Twelve changed, and he was relieved of responsibility for Europe. On July 3, 1991, he and Elder Dallin H. Oaks, who succeeded him as first contact for Europe, went together to President Ezra Taft Benson's apartment to report that the Church was now established in every country in Eastern Europe. They also showed him certified copies of documents giving the Church full recognition in the Republic of Russia. It was deeply satisfying to Elder Nelson to be able to report this to the prophet who had given him the impossible assignment and to see his look of joy.

Later, Elder Nelson remembered further: "The President was thrilled. This had been something of a struggle for him, because on the one hand, he hated Communism. On the other hand, he was God's prophet to all the world. And he knew the gospel was the answer for people who had for so long been oppressed. I believe he was thrilled with our report."

As Elder Nelson reflected on what he had experienced during the previous several years, he couldn't help but remember President Spencer W. Kimball's landmark address to General Authorities and regional representatives in 1974, when the prophet spoke powerfully about reaching beyond the iron and bamboo curtains (see Kimball, "When the World Will Be Converted"). That had been followed with invitations to the members of the Church to pray for the doors of nations still closed to the Church to open. Since Elder Nelson's call to the Twelve, he had had a front-row seat to observe the gathering of Israel in action.

"When the Lord said He is able to do His own work, believe it. He wants us to grow. He wants us to learn. And testimonies don't come easily, either. You have to work for your testimony. My testimony is a lot stronger than it was a year ago—because I keep seeing how He guides us and leads us."

"We asked the Lord for help, and the Lord responded. There was no doubt in any of our minds that we had experienced a miracle."

—Elder Russell M. Nelson

In January 1988, Elder Nelson and Dantzel boarded the Concorde in New York for a quick three-hour and forty-five-minute flight to London's Heathrow International airport. Their first assignment in England was to speak to a large congregation, including missionaries from the London South Mission, that evening in Crawley, England.

About the time the plane should have begun its descent, the intercom crackled and the pilot announced that, unfortunately, Heathrow was socked in with fog and the plane was diverting to Manchester, 211 miles north of London. Elder Nelson's heart sank. There was no way he and Dantzel could get from Manchester back to Crawley to keep their appointment that night. He immediately sat back in his seat and offered a silent but fervent prayer that the way would open for them to honor their commitments and speak to the Saints who were assembling, even at that hour, in Crawley.

A few minutes later, the pilot came back on the intercom and announced that there was another change in plans. They didn't have enough fuel to make it to Manchester but had been cleared to land at Gatwick, another London area airport, for an emergency refueling stop. He added that no passengers would be allowed to disembark.

Gatwick was actually closer to Crawley than even Heathrow, so despite the announcement that passengers could not get off the plane there, Elder Nelson told Dantzel to gather her things because they were getting off. He then called a flight attendant, explained his dilemma, and asked if he and his wife could please deplane at Gatwick.

"No," she responded.

He gently continued with his appeal: "You don't understand. I have a thousand or more people gathered to hear me speak. I really must get off here."

The flight attendant persisted in saying no, and Elder Nelson insisted he really must get off the plane. Finally, the flight attendant summoned the pilot for reinforcements. Together they listed all the reasons the Nelsons could not get off the plane. There were no customs agents waiting to greet this flight. They would not be able to get their luggage from the cargo hold. And so on.

Elder Nelson had a response for each issue: "We will find customs agents to let us through," he assured them. "All of our luggage is carry-on and we have it with us." Finally, the pilot shrugged and told the crew to let them off.

Meanwhile, President Ed J. Pinegar, president of the London South Mission, and his wife, Pat, were waiting at Heathrow for the

Nelsons. With each new announcement about the change in flight, they too prayed silently and asked the Lord to intervene. When President Pinegar heard the flight had landed at Gatwick, he called the chapel where they were to speak. He didn't know if the Nelsons would be able to get off at Gatwick, but, hoping for the best, he arranged for a car to hurry to the airport to pick them up.

Not long after the Nelsons emerged from customs, a car arrived to get them, and they rushed off to the stake center. With all of the disruption, they were only fifteen minutes late to the meeting.

"A packed house witnessed a real miracle that night," Elder Nelson said. "We asked the Lord for help, and President and Sister Pinegar asked the Lord to help us, and the Lord responded. There was no doubt in any of our minds that we had experienced a miracle" (Pinegar, *What Every Future Missionary,* chapter 1).

"The Lord uses the unlikely to accomplish the impossible."

—Elder Russell M. Nelson

In late 1990, Elder Nelson received another assignment he felt ill suited for. The United States Internal Revenue Service in Washington, DC, had scheduled a hearing to explore the question of whether or not dollars spent to sustain missionaries in the field should be eligible for a tax exemption. Assigned to represent the Church, Elder Nelson couldn't help but wonder if one of his Brethren in the Twelve with a legal background—or one who had at least served a mission—wouldn't be a more logical choice. But it wasn't his nature to question assignments, so he attempted to prepare the best he could.

But the assignment weighed on him. He knew that the resolution of this issue, one way or the other, would affect every member of the Church in the United States supporting a missionary. He shared his concerns with President Monson as the two traveled to the German Democratic Republic. The crumbling of the Berlin Wall had made it possible to reorganize the stakes in Berlin and to unite Saints who had been divided by the wall for almost thirty years. President Monson and Elder Nelson both had deep ties with the GDR, and they relished this assignment in Berlin together.

After the meeting, in which new stakes were organized and stake presidencies called and set apart, President Monson surprised Elder Nelson by asking if he might give him a blessing in connection with his assignment with the IRS. "He promised me that I would know what to say and when to say it and reassured me that I was the person the Lord needed on this particular errand," Elder Nelson remembered.

With that, Elder Nelson flew to Washington, DC, and, at the appointed hour, appeared before key policy makers at the Internal Revenue Service. During the discussion, one person after another characterized missions for young Latter-day Saint men as a "rite of passage" and that, as such, funds to support a mission should not qualify as a deduction for charitable giving. The phrase "rite of passage" caught Elder Nelson's attention, and after hearing it repeated several times he asked for clarification.

"I am not sure I understand what you mean by a rite of passage," he said to the board of inquiry. "If a rite of passage is meant to indicate something that every young Latter-day Saint man must do, then I think you have a misunderstanding about that. I am a member of

Elder Nelson and President Thomas S. Monson, greeting each other here at the April 1994 general conference, enjoyed a long and treasured friendship.

the Quorum of the Twelve Apostles, and I did not serve a full-time mission."

His statement stunned the group, and the tenor of the hearing changed instantly. Learning that a senior leader in the Church had not served a mission invalidated the argument to the contrary, and the ruling went in favor of the Church.

He had felt like such an unlikely choice to represent the Church in this issue but proved to be the perfect spokesman. In the same way, he had felt completely out of his comfort zone as he began to make connections in Eastern Europe, but often his stature as a world-renowned surgeon softened hearts and opened doors.

His experience dealing with the IRS was but one of many personal experiences he'd had with the fundamental truth that the Lord is able to do His own work (2 Nephi 27:21), that He doesn't see things as man sees them, and that "man looketh on the outward appearance, but the Lord looketh on the heart" (1 Samuel 16:7).

Using his assignment to open the countries in Eastern Europe for the preaching of the gospel as an example, he told students at BYU–Idaho that "if ever a task seemed impossible, that was it. In the ensuing years, I tried my best. In each atheistic nation, I was never wanted and never welcome. . . . Each country presented different challenges for us. We did the very best we could, and then the Lord made up the difference. . . . I am an eye-witness—I am a part of that pattern: the Lord used the unlikely to accomplish the impossible" (Nelson, "The Lord Uses the Unlikely").

> "This is one way of our implementing the teachings of Jesus Christ, who taught that we are to love God and to love our neighbors."
>
> —Elder Russell M. Nelson

Despite the enormous time and energy Elder Nelson spent in Eastern Europe during the late 1980s, and the love he quickly felt for people in that part of the world—and particularly for those who had endured the yoke of Communism—his heart was never far from China. His extensive efforts to mentor open-heart surgeons in the People's Republic of China had won him many friends. He loved the Chinese people, felt a reverence for their culture and fundamental goodness, and welcomed any reason to return.

One such opportunity presented itself in February 1995. The year before, Vice Premier Li Lanqing had visited the Church's Polynesian Cultural Center in Laie, Hawaii. One result of that visit was an invitation to Elder Neal A. Maxwell and Elder Nelson to visit China.

Under typical Chinese protocol, Elders Maxwell and Nelson could not enter the country as official representatives of the Church. But because both men had established friendly relationships there, the government finally admitted them, with the proviso that the two could visit Beijing and that the "purpose of the trip was apostolic." The Chinese ambassador to the United States later told Beverly Campbell, the Church's Public Affairs director in Washington, DC, that "the good will of that trip had positive and unparalleled results" (Hafen, *Disciple's Life*, 476).

Elders Maxwell and Nelson met not only with Vice Premier Li, one of four prime ministers of the People's Republic of China, but

Elder Nelson meeting with Li Lanqing, vice premier of China.

also with President Qi Huaiyuan, president of the Chinese People's Association for Friendship with Foreign Countries (CPAFFC); Li Xiaolin, chief of American and Oceanian Affairs of CPAFFC; Zhang Xiaowen, the vice director of the State Education Commission; and finally, Vice Minister Yin Dakui of the Ministry of Public Health.

The Chinese keep records, and, in most meetings, they were well aware of Elder Nelson's efforts to train Chinese doctors in open-heart surgery. Because of that, they welcomed him and the entire delegation with open arms. Elder Nelson began most meetings by extending a simple greeting in Mandarin, which delighted their hosts. Then Elders Maxwell and Nelson employed one of Elder Nelson's favorite questions: How could they, and the Church they represented, best be of service to them? As one outcome of their meetings, they committed to send volunteers to teach English as a second language throughout the thirty-two universities currently in operation in the Chinese state educational system and to identify humanitarian aid that would be most useful. "This is one way of our implementing the teachings of Jesus Christ, who taught that we are to love God and to love our neighbors," Elder Nelson explained to leaders who knew little or nothing about the Savior.

Once again, Elder Nelson saw doors of understanding begin to open and relationships develop because of the question, "How can we help?" (see "Elders Maxwell, Nelson welcomed in China").

> "The Proclamation was a surprise to some who thought the doctrinal truths about marriage and family were well understood. Nevertheless, we felt the confirmation and we went to work."
>
> —Elder Dallin H. Oaks

___

One day in 1994, the Quorum of the Twelve Apostles spent a day in their council room in the Salt Lake Temple discussing issues surrounding the family. They considered everything from the increasingly ubiquitous nature of pornography to potential anti-family legislation of various kinds. This was not a new discussion, but that day the entire agenda revolved around this one vital topic.

The Twelve reviewed both doctrine and policies, considering those things that could not be changed—doctrine—and those things that possibly could be—policies. They discussed issues they saw coming, including an intensified societal push for gay marriage and transgender rights. "But that was not the end of what we saw," Elder Nelson explained. "We could see the efforts of various communities to do away with all standards and limitations on sexual activity. We saw the confusion of genders. We could see it all coming."

This extended discussion, along with others over a period of time, led to the conclusion that the Twelve should prepare a document, perhaps even a proclamation, outlining the Church's stand on the family to present to the First Presidency for consideration.

"It [the proclamation] was a surprise to some who thought the doctrinal truths about marriage and family were well understood without restatement," Elder Dallin H. Oaks would later detail in a general conference address. "Nevertheless, we felt the confirmation

Elder Nelson relished serving with his Brethren in the Twelve, pictured here at the October 1992 general conference (left to right): President Howard W. Hunter and Elders Boyd K. Packer, Marvin J. Ashton, L. Tom Perry, David B. Haight, James E. Faust, and Neal A. Maxwell.

and we went to work. Subjects were identified and discussed by members of the Quorum of the Twelve for nearly a year" (Oaks, "The Plan").

As an outgrowth of these discussions, a committee consisting of Elders James E. Faust, Neal A. Maxwell, and Russell M. Nelson was appointed to draft a document. Elder Faust, senior to the other two, suggested they each write a draft and then bring them together. Out of that initial merged document came a version for each member of the Twelve to review and revise. "Prayerfully we continually pleaded with the Lord for His inspiration on what we should say, and how we should say it," Elder Oaks explained. "We all learned 'line upon line, precept upon precept,' as the Lord has promised" (Oaks, "The Plan").

Finally a proposed text was presented to the First Presidency, who revised and refined it further. The document had just received approval from the combined First Presidency and Quorum of the Twelve when, in March 1995, President Howard W. Hunter passed away and President Gordon B. Hinckley became President of the Church. Though the senior Brethren encouraged him to read the proclamation at the April general conference, President Hinckley felt it was too early in his presidency to make a major policy statement, and he set it aside. But six months later, without informing anyone, he built his message in September 1995 for the general Relief Society meeting around "The Family: A Proclamation to the World," introducing it with these words:

"With so much of sophistry that is passed off as truth, with so much of deception concerning standards and values, with so much of allurement and enticement to take on the slow stain of the world, we have felt to warn and forewarn. In furtherance of this we of the First Presidency and Council of the Twelve Apostles now issue a proclamation to the Church and to the world as a declaration and reaffirmation of standards, doctrines, and practices relative to the family" (Hinckley, "Stand Strong").

While the document was received well by many Church members, the general reaction was almost ho-hum. Nothing in it seemed particularly earth-shattering. For many, the proclamation seemed to be little more than a restatement of well-understood, time-honored principles about marriage, family, and gender identity. In 1995, marriage between a man and a woman was a given. That gender was an "essential characteristic of individual premortal, mortal, and eternal identity" was regarded as uncontested fact. Few people of faith—or organized religions, for that matter—disputed the notion that the family was ordained of God.

"But we could see what was coming," said Elder Nelson some years later. "What seemed so obvious in 1995 is now a standard, really, for the entire world. Over the years, I've given copies of the

THE FAMILY

A PROCLAMATION TO THE WORLD

THE FIRST PRESIDENCY AND COUNCIL OF THE TWELVE APOSTLES OF THE CHURCH OF JESUS CHRIST OF LATTER-DAY SAINTS

WE, THE FIRST PRESIDENCY and the Council of the Twelve Apostles of The Church of Jesus Christ of Latter-day Saints, solemnly proclaim that marriage between a man and a woman is ordained of God and that the family is central to the Creator's plan for the eternal destiny of His children.

ALL HUMAN BEINGS—male and female—are created in the image of God. Each is a beloved spirit son or daughter of heavenly parents, and, as such, each has a divine nature and destiny. Gender is an essential characteristic of individual premortal, mortal, and eternal identity and purpose.

IN THE PREMORTAL REALM, spirit sons and daughters knew and worshipped God as their Eternal Father and accepted His plan by which His children could obtain a physical body and gain earthly experience to progress toward perfection and ultimately realize their divine destiny as heirs of eternal life. The divine plan of happiness enables family relationships to be perpetuated beyond the grave. Sacred ordinances and covenants available in holy temples make it possible for individuals to return to the presence of God and for families to be united eternally.

THE FIRST COMMANDMENT that God gave to Adam and Eve pertained to their potential for parenthood as husband and wife. We declare that God's commandment for His children to multiply and replenish the earth remains in force. We further declare that God has commanded that the sacred powers of procreation are to be employed only between man and woman, lawfully wedded as husband and wife.

WE DECLARE the means by which mortal life is created to be divinely appointed. We affirm the sanctity of life and of its importance in God's eternal plan.

HUSBAND AND WIFE have a solemn responsibility to love and care for each other and for their children. "Children are an heritage of the Lord" (Psalm 127:3). Parents have a sacred duty to rear their children in love and righteousness, to provide for their physical and spiritual needs, and to teach them to love and serve one another, observe the commandments of God, and be law-abiding citizens wherever they live. Husbands and wives—mothers and fathers—will be held accountable before God for the discharge of these obligations.

THE FAMILY is ordained of God. Marriage between man and woman is essential to His eternal plan. Children are entitled to birth within the bonds of matrimony, and to be reared by a father and a mother who honor marital vows with complete fidelity. Happiness in family life is most likely to be achieved when founded upon the teachings of the Lord Jesus Christ. Successful marriages and families are established and maintained on principles of faith, prayer, repentance, forgiveness, respect, love, compassion, work, and wholesome recreational activities. By divine design, fathers are to preside over their families in love and righteousness and are responsible to provide the necessities of life and protection for their families. Mothers are primarily responsible for the nurture of their children. In these sacred responsibilities, fathers and mothers are obligated to help one another as equal partners. Disability, death, or other circumstances may necessitate individual adaptation. Extended families should lend support when needed.

WE WARN that individuals who violate covenants of chastity, who abuse spouse or offspring, or who fail to fulfill family responsibilities will one day stand accountable before God. Further, we warn that the disintegration of the family will bring upon individuals, communities, and nations the calamities foretold by ancient and modern prophets.

WE CALL UPON responsible citizens and officers of government everywhere to promote those measures designed to maintain and strengthen the family as the fundamental unit of society.

This proclamation was read by President Gordon B. Hinckley as part of his message at the General Relief Society Meeting held September 23, 1995, in Salt Lake City, Utah.

proclamation to many governmental leaders not of our faith who've been grateful, telling them they were free to use it any way they might care to. I remember talking to a vice president in a Central American country, a woman in charge of health, education, and welfare—which of course concerns the family. She practically wept as she thanked me profusely for sharing this document."

As the years marched forward from 1995, and advocacy for various rights increased, particularly LGBTQ advocacy, the relevance and significance of the proclamation began to take shape. In a relative few years, dozens of countries, including the United States, legalized gay marriage. Transgender issues came to the fore, with celebrities and other influencers popularizing the notion that gender was a matter of choice rather than a divinely directed reality. Criticism of the Church's doctrinal position as well as policies associated with that doctrine came from both outside and inside the Church. Society increasingly hurled cries of bigotry toward anyone who opposed gay marriage on religious or moral grounds.

"There are those who label us bigots," said Elder Nelson, "but the bigots are those who don't allow us to feel as we feel but want us to allow them to feel as they feel. Our stand ultimately boils down to the law of chastity. The Ten Commandments are still valid. They've never been revoked. The commandment for a man to not even look at another woman in lust, for if he does he's already committed adultery in his heart, is not only in the Bible but in the Book of Mormon and Doctrine and Covenants as well. That powerful message is our stand. We cannot change it. We welcome people of different attitudes into the Church, but it is not our prerogative to change laws that God has decreed."

Elder Oaks signaled the importance of the family proclamation in this way: "Forty years ago, President Ezra Taft Benson taught that 'every generation has its tests and its chance to stand and prove itself.'

I believe our attitude toward and use of the family proclamation is one of those tests for this generation" (Oaks, "The Plan").

The Book of Mormon declares that seers have the spiritual capacity and endowment to see things others cannot see. As Ammon taught Limhi, "a seer is greater than a prophet," and the gift of seership is paramount among spiritual gifts: "For a gift which is greater can no man have, except he should possess the power of God, which no man can. . . . But a seer can know of things which are past, and also of things which are to come, and by them shall all things be revealed" (Mosiah 8:15–17).

Seership and the proclamation on the family are inextricably connected.

"I was her father, a medical doctor,
and an Apostle of the Lord Jesus Christ,
but I had to bow my head and acknowledge,
'Not my will but thine be done.'"

—Elder Russell M. Nelson

Emily was Russell and Dantzel's sixth daughter, born on January 15, 1958. While still an infant, she suddenly went into convulsions and then into a coma. Spinal meningitis was the diagnosis, and as the coma persisted into several days, the Nelsons pleaded with Heavenly Father to spare their little girl. Finally, emotionally and spiritually spent, Russell and Dantzel told Him they were deeply grateful to Him for sending that little spirit to them. They thanked Him "most sincerely," and then, weeping, told Him that if He needed her now more than they did, they were prepared to release her to Him for His care (see Nelson, *From Heart to Heart,* 243).

Not long after they offered this prayer of submission, Emily's fever broke and she slowly began to improve. "I suppose it will never be required of me to undergo a test such as Abraham had with Isaac," Russell wrote later of this experience, "but this came about as close as I may expect to come. Literally I had come to the point where I sensed that the Lord was asking me if I would be able to yield to His desire in calling her home" (Nelson, *From Heart to Heart,* 243, 245).

As it turned out, this was just the beginning of Elder Nelson's test regarding the health of his loved ones, including Emily's.

Emily grew to adulthood and married Bradley E. Wittwer, and the two proceeded to have four children. Then, while she was carrying her fifth child, Emily was diagnosed with inflammatory cancer of

Emily Nelson Wittwer with her family shortly before her death.

the breast. Elder Nelson realized immediately that the diagnosis was a death sentence, as inflammatory cancer of the breast is aggravated by the hormones of pregnancy much as gasoline ignites a fire.

The night of Emily's diagnosis, September 17, 1991, the family gathered in a family meeting. As Elder Nelson approached his daughter to give her a blessing, her first concern was for her unborn child: "Daddy, don't forget to bless my baby," she said.

Three days later, Emily underwent a mastectomy and shortly thereafter began an aggressive round of chemotheraphy. Her fifth child, Jordan, was born on December 6 with a mop of hair—a tender mercy, it seemed, and a sign that the chemo had not penetrated the membrane and affected the baby's blood system.

This was a grueling season, emotionally, for Elder Nelson. As Emily battled cancer, Dantzel was diagnosed with non-Hodgkins lymphoma. That, too, was a frightening diagnosis. With a wife and daughter both on chemo—sometimes in the same room at the Salt Lake Clinic, where they received their IV treatments together—Russell

re birthdays-

-Stephanie-

mberly-

HAPPY WEDDING ANNIVERSARY
HEIDI AND STEVE!

lson!

NELSON NEWS

❧ FEBRUARY 1995 ❧

EMILY NELSON WITTWER
January 15, 1958-January 29, 1995

Our precious little Emily was called home to heaven early Sunday morning, January 29, 1995, about 2:00 a.m. Her passing occurred just two weeks after her 37th birthday, and less than five days after returning from her trip to Florida.

She literally slept away, without struggle or other precipitating event. Her funeral is scheduled for Wednesday, February 1, at 12:00 noon, at the Murray Utah South Stake Center, 5735 South Fashion Boulevard.

We shall miss her greatly! Oh, how we shall miss her! We recognize the great blessing that she has been to us. This dear daughter nearly left us as a baby when she was afflicted with meningitis. She was spared to bless our lives, become a bride to Brad, and the mother of William, Wendy, Nelson, Preston, and Jordan.

Mother and Daddy feel a deep sense of gratitude for all members of the Wittwer family who have helped Emily to achieve all that she has accomplished in her short life. And we are especially grateful to our wonderful daughters and sons-in-law who have given so much to ease things for Emily, Brad, and children. Thank you, thank you very much!

Contributions for this issue were written before her demise occurred. Anxious to meet our goal by submitting articles by January 27, we made that deadline, but missed a more important one. That will explain the lack of news relating to this very wrenching experience in our lives.

We pray for the blessings of the Lord to be with each member of the family. We know that challenges will continue, but sorrows shared will make us strong, and happiness shared will bring us joy. We love you always!

Gratefully,
Mother and Daddy

Copies of the *Nelson News* at the time of Emily's death.

feared he was going to lose them both. "I tried to prepare myself for both of them to die," he admitted. "I had to deal with death, so I thought I'd better understand it."

As one way of coming to grips with his fear, and at the request of Deseret Book Company, he spent much of the summer of 1994 at a little house he owned next to the "Pizza-Hut property" in Midway, Utah, writing *The Gateway We Call Death*. "I could see," he said, "that you had to shift from a mortal perspective to an eternal one. The reality is that none of us can reach our highest potential and exaltation without passing through that gateway. The eternities ahead are going to be so much more glorious and so much more permanent than anything we have during this mortal experience." Mourning, he came to understand, was actually a commandment. We are to "live together in love, insomuch that thou shalt weep for the loss of them that die" (Doctrine and Covenants 42:45).

And yet, it was a shock when, on January 29, 1995, Emily died with a liver filled with cancer. Just thirty-seven, she left behind a husband and five children, the youngest of them a three-year-old.

"I saw her death coming," Elder Nelson reflected later. "No one knew more than I that hers was a fatal sentence; and yet, when Brad called me the night she died, I was stunned. A father is almost as bad as a husband. He is blind to reality. I knew it was coming and yet I kept thinking surely she would get better."

Elder Neil L. Andersen later quoted him as saying, "I was her father, a medical doctor, and an Apostle of the Lord Jesus Christ, but I had to bow my head and acknowledge, 'Not my will but thine be done'" (Andersen, "Prophet of God").

Elder Nelson's book about dying and eternal life.

217

In general conference just weeks after Emily's death, Elder Nelson told the Church that his "tears of sorrow have flowed along with wishes that I could have done more for our daughter. . . . If I had the power of resurrection, I would have been tempted to bring [her] back" (Nelson, "Children of the Covenant"). There was, however, nothing to do but somehow press on.

Granddaughter Katie Irion Owens vividly remembers seeing her grandfather at her Aunt Emily's funeral. "I watched him scoop up her children at the funeral and carry them out, just like he was going to scoop us up and carry us and help us come to terms with this. He really did such a tremendous job of helping us see the eternal perspective in everything" (*Church News*/KSL Interview, January 10, 2018).

Elder Nelson put his feelings in perspective when he wrote in the subsequent edition of the *Nelson News,* the monthly family newsletter: "Each of our contributions to the Nelson News this month will be difficult to compose. We are all mourning the loss of our dear Emily to the point that hardly anything else can find room on the stage of our minds."

He continued, adding words about his dear Dantzel: "I would like to pay special tribute to Mommy. She was a magnificent woman when I married her, but I didn't know how great she was until I see her handle the vicissitudes of life with such profound faith. She is truly a marvelous mother. I respect her, I honor her, and I love her" (*Nelson News,* February 1995).

To Elder Nelson's profound relief, Dantzel's cancer went into remission and, in time, she was pronounced cancer-free. But his greatest challenge yet lay ahead.

> "How many languages do I understand and speak? Honestly, I'm still working on English."
>
> —Elder Russell M. Nelson

On Sunday, May 18, 1997, more than eleven hundred people crowded themselves into an auditorium designed to seat eight hundred for the dedication of the new Missionary Training Center in São Paulo, Brazil. At the time, Elder Nelson had responsibility for supervising Brazil, with the resulting assignment to dedicate the new structure.

The room was filled with Church members and dignitaries, including the senate president of Brazil. At the time, the new MTC was one of the largest structures the Church had built outside the United States.

Elder Nelson gave remarks in English and then excused his translator, saying, in effect, "If you have faith sufficient and I do, I'm going to excuse my translator and we'll dedicate this building in the language that everyone understands."

According to Elder W. Craig Zwick, who was serving in the Brazil Area Presidency, Elder Nelson then dedicated the MTC in "perfect Portuguese. It was so historic and so significant that we placed a beautiful framed copy of the dedicatory prayer, in both Portuguese and English, on a column at the Brazilian MTC so that all missionaries could read and ponder its promises" (interview with author, November 6, 2018; see also *Church News*/KSL Interview, January 5, 2018).

Elder Nelson had long had a reputation for speaking multiple languages, and he had, in fact, studied or been tutored in quite a few. He took three years of high school French followed by premed Latin and Greek. For professional purposes, he studied Russian and Chinese. To aid his service in the Church, he studied Spanish, Portuguese, and German. On his own, he studied Hebrew, Bulgarian, Czech, and Romanian.

"I have files in my filing cabinet on all of these," Elder Nelson said. "How many do I understand and speak? Honestly, I'm still working on English. But I've studied or was tutored in a number of languages."

That he had an affinity, an "ear," for language was apparent, and his memory rarely let him down. So he was a quick study, picking up pronunciations quickly and understanding the roots of enough languages to be able to understand simple dialogue in many languages and converse modestly in others. His training in Russian and Chinese was largely medical in nature, while his exposure to Portuguese, Spanish, and German involved Church-related language more than anything else.

Most of all, he worked at the art and science of understanding languages and being able to converse in them, the dedication of the Brazilian MTC being a case in point. In advance of that event, he arranged for a native Brazilian to translate the dedicatory prayer he had written into Portuguese and then to record the prayer in Portuguese so that he could listen to it over and over again. He listened not only to make sure he understood all the words but to perfect his pronunciation and accent. And then he memorized the prayer. While it may have appeared to those there that he was speaking Portuguese, he was actually reciting memorized Portuguese—which he fully understood and which his acquaintance with the language allowed him to do.

"Don't pretend that I'm fluent in anything other than English," he insists. What is clear is that, when possible, he did his best to greet people in their native tongue and bear his closing testimony in their language. On occasion, as he did in Puerto Rico and the Dominican

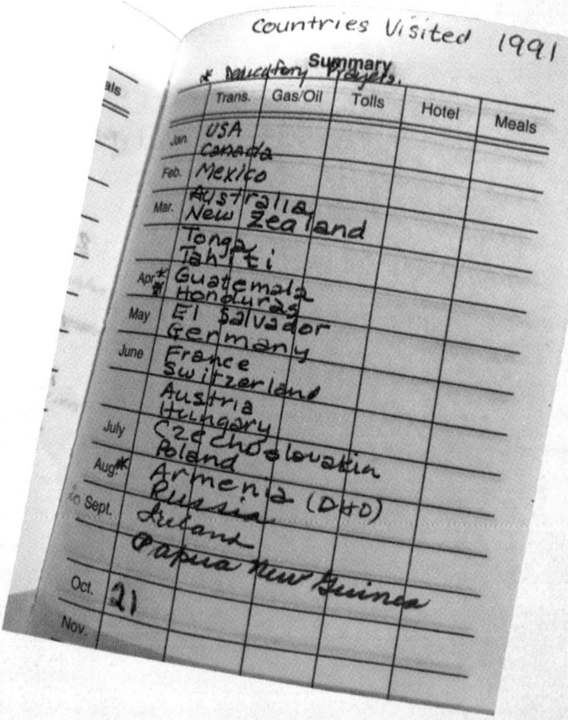

Travel Expense Record — APRIL 1991

Date	Trans.	Gas/Oil	Tolls	Hotel	Meals

Elder Nelson kept meticulous records of his travels.

Countries Visited 1991

Summary

	Trans.	Gas/Oil	Tolls	Hotel	Meals
Jan.	USA / Canada				
Feb.	Mexico				
Mar.	Australia / New Zealand / Tonga / Tahiti				
Apr.	Guatemala / Honduras				
May	El Salvador / Germany				
June	France / Switzerland / Austria / Hungary				
July	Czechoslovakia / Poland				
Aug.	Armenia (DHO) / Russia				
Sept.	Lebanon / Papua New Guinea				
Oct.	21				
Nov.					

Republic in September 2018 and then in five countries in South America in October of that year, he delivered entire messages in Spanish. Out of respect and love for the Saints wherever they lived, and with a desire to open their hearts to the truths of the gospel, he spoke as much of their language as possible whenever he could. The Lord provided the pattern, "for he speaketh unto men according to their language, unto their understanding" (2 Nephi 31:3).

"The fundamental principles of our religion *are* the testimony of the Apostles and Prophets, concerning Jesus Christ."

—The Prophet Joseph Smith

As the year 2000 approached, and thus the two-thousandth celebration of the birth of the Son of God, the First Presidency and Quorum of the Twelve discussed what, if anything, they should do to commemorate the turning of the century. With all the Y2K predictions of possible digital catastrophes and associated hoopla, these prophets, seers, and revelators felt that they, who had been called to bear witness of Jesus Christ throughout all the world, should do something different, something distinctive.

As they were deliberating about the opportunity in front of them, they were drawn to the statement from the Prophet Joseph Smith that "the fundamental principles of our religion *are* the testimony of the Apostles and Prophets, concerning Jesus Christ, that He died, was buried, and rose again the third day, and ascended into heaven; and all other things which pertain to our religion are only appendages to it" (*Teachings: Joseph Smith,* 49; emphasis added). The plural verb *are* caught their attention. "It was this very statement of the Prophet that provided the incentive for 15 prophets, seers, and revelators to issue and sign their testimony to commemorate the 2,000th anniversary of the Lord's birth," Elder Nelson said some years later in general conference (Nelson, "Drawing the Power of Jesus Christ").

"We realized we had never put forward in a combined way the testimony of all the living prophets and apostles concerning Jesus behalf of all who would ever live upon the earth.

We solemnly testify that His life, which is central to all human history, neither began in Bethlehem nor concluded on Calvary. He was the Firstborn of the Father, the Only Begotten Son in the flesh, the Redeemer of the world.

He rose from the grave to "become the firstfruits of them that slept" (1 Corinthians 15:20). As Risen Lord, He visited among those He had loved in life. He also ministered among His "other sheep" (John 10:16) in ancient America. In the modern world, He and His Father appeared to the boy Joseph Smith, ushering in the long-promised "dispensation of the fulness of times" (Ephesians 1:10).

see it together" (Isaiah 40:5). He will rule as King of Kings and reign as Lord of Lords, and every knee shall bend and every tongue shall speak in worship before Him. Each of us will stand to be judged of Him according to our works and the desires of our hearts.

We bear testimony, as His duly ordained Apostles—that Jesus is the Living Christ, the immortal Son of God. He is the great King Immanuel, who stands today on the right hand of His Father. He is the light, the life, and the hope of the world. His way is the path that leads to happiness in this life and eternal life in the world to come. God be thanked for the matchless gift of His divine Son.

THE FIRST PRESIDENCY

THE QUORUM OF THE TWELVE

January 1, 2000

Signatures of fifteen special witnesses of Christ.

Christ, and that doing so could be our commemorative action," he added.

They determined to do two things: first, to prepare a document entitled "The Living Christ" that each member of the First Presidency and Quorum of the Twelve could sign; and second, to film each of the fifteen bearing his testimony. Elder Nelson was assigned to oversee the project, which included shepherding the document through to completion, making sure each man was filmed at the location of his choosing, and then making the materials widely available.

"When it came to this document," he explained, "everyone served as editor in chief. There were fifteen editors in chief. And of course President Hinckley added his distinctive touches at the end of the process. Every Apostle then living had his hand in this process."

The document began, "As we commemorate the birth of Jesus Christ two millennia ago, we offer our testimony of the reality of His matchless life and the infinite virtue of His great atoning sacrifice. None other has had so profound an influence upon all who have lived and will yet live upon the earth." It was signed by Presidents Gordon B. Hinckley, Thomas S. Monson, and James E. Faust of the First Presidency, and by President Boyd K. Packer and Elders L. Tom Perry, David B. Haight, Neal A. Maxwell, Russell M. Nelson, Dallin H. Oaks, M. Russell Ballard, Joseph B. Wirthlin, Richard G. Scott, Robert D. Hales, Jeffrey R. Holland, and Henry B. Eyring of the Quorum of the Twelve Apostles.

Referring to "The Living Christ" as a "historic testimony," President Russell M. Nelson later said: "Many members have memorized its truths. Others barely know of its existence. As you seek to learn more about Jesus Christ, I urge you to study 'The Living Christ'" ("Drawing the Power of Jesus Christ").

> "Of all the changes I have ever faced, this month brought the most difficult one."
>
> —Elder Russell M. Nelson

Saturday, February 12, 2005, began as one of those rare and precious Saturdays when Elder Nelson was not traveling and could spend the day at home with Dantzel. They puttered around the house, enjoyed meals together, and relished a weekend without heavy pressures weighing on them.

Originally, they had planned to attend a BYU basketball game at the Marriott Center, but at the last minute they decided to stay home and watch the game on television so that they could alternate with a University of Utah game on a different channel. They were sitting on the sofa, holding hands, changing channels back and forth between the two games, when suddenly Dantzel slumped. Elder Nelson recognized instantly what had happened—she'd had a cardiac rhythm shift, and her heart had stopped—and he attempted to resuscitate her. For ten minutes, fifteen minutes, twenty, and much longer he worked, doing what he had done so many times with patients through the years.

At one point he grabbed the phone to make one call—to his long-time friend and cardiologist Dr. Robert Fowles, who it turned out was on an airplane returning to Salt Lake City. But he stopped for nothing else as he continued to do cardiopulmonary resuscitation far longer than medical science suggests would be useful. But to no avail. Her passing was instantaneous and without pain. It was also without any warning. Dantzel was gone.

The stunned Elder Nelson immediately began to try to reach the members of his large family. That night, though, it wasn't easy. At the moment their mother slipped through the veil, her children were located on four continents—Asia, North America, South America, and Europe, with some en route to a fifth, Africa. Two daughters with their husbands, Sylvia Webster and Rosalie Ringwood, were serving missions—in Brazil and Korea, respectively. Others were traveling or participating in Saturday evening activities. "I was all alone," he remembered. "I had ten children and I couldn't find any of them." It took several hours to reach his immediate family, and all the while he sobbed and then sobbed some more. At one point, overcome with grief, he nearly screamed out loud.

It was while he was still alone and still crying, however, that he received an unmistakable impression: "It wasn't audible, but it was very clear," he said. "The message was, 'I took her because of my love for her, and I thought you could take it, my boy.'"

Dantzel's passing *was* a gift for her. She had been experiencing health challenges and was just starting to struggle with her memory.

The night before she passed away, Dantzel went to hear a granddaughter perform.

Memories from sixty years together.

Shortly before her passing, she had said to Russell, "Daddy, I don't want to grow old." He had teased in response: "Too late, honey. You are already old." But aging or not, diminishing capacity or not, Elder Nelson could not fathom going forward without his beloved Dantzel.

Word spread, and finally family members and close friends began to arrive at his home. President Gordon B. Hinckley came to offer his condolences. He had just lost his wife, Marjorie, the year before and understood what Elder Nelson faced. Children and grandchildren boarded planes all over the world to get to Salt Lake City as soon as possible. Grandson Stephen McKellar remembered that poignant time: "When I flew home for my grandmother's funeral, there were so many of us around the country that were all flying home. I got to share a flight with my cousin Ricky who was in medical school in Wisconsin. We talked all the way home about what it meant to be a Nelson and to be having this Nelson experience" (*Church News*/KSL Interview, January 11, 2018).

During the ensuing days, visitors, cards, emails, and calls poured in from around the world. Dantzel and Russell Nelson's influence had reached millions, and they were beloved. Surgeons and physicians, the thousands of patients he had operated on and their families, Latter-day Saints they had met and loved everywhere they had traveled—so many reached out to express sympathy and support.

All of these expressions meant so much. But the grief of losing his wife was inexpressible. "Of all the challenges I have ever faced, this month brought the most difficult one," he wrote in the *Nelson News,* and he grappled to know how to go forward. He could scarcely remember life without Dantzel. Later that year they would have celebrated their sixtieth wedding anniversary. For nearly sixty years they had lived together, loved each other, and built a life together.

The timing of it all was ironic. Just six days earlier, Elder Nelson had spoken at a Church Educational System fireside originating from BYU's Marriott Center. Dantzel had been nursing a cold so had not accompanied him that night. He told the young adults about falling in love with the young Dantzel but then added that "to me, Sister Nelson now is even more beautiful." He continued, saying: "What is most important to Sister Nelson and me now? That we are husband and wife, wedded for time and all eternity. Our children are born in the covenant and are sealed to us forever."

He admitted that "we have tasted of life's successes and sorrows. We have dealt with disappointment, disease, and death among our children. But death cannot divide families sealed in the temple. That period of separation is only temporary." He put a fine point on it all with the statement, "Sister Nelson and I have learned that life is not a one-act play" (Weaver, "Dantzel Nelson Succumbs").

He meant every word of what he'd said, but now practicing what he had so recently preached created a stark reality: How was he to go on after a loss so penetrating and personal? "Because I was sealed to my wife, we were one," he said. "So when she died, half of me died also."

Elder Nelson understood the doctrine. He knew that this was simply the end of the second act in a three-act play. He had a deep testimony of the reality of the covenant that bound him and Dantzel as husband and wife forever. But those truths helped only so much when he walked into his home and no one was there, when he went from room to room and could almost hear his own heartbeat because she wasn't in the next room, poised to walk around the corner at any moment. The silence of being a widower was deafening. It was a season of deep grief. "I learned firsthand that the Lord loveth whom He chasteneth," he said. "Every man who has responsibility in this Church has had or will have a test, even as Abraham."

In addition, an entire—and very large—family reeled from the loss. "When my grandmother passed away, it was really hard to watch him without her," said granddaughter Katie Irion Owens. "He led with love, and because we watched him lead with love, we were

8/3?/10

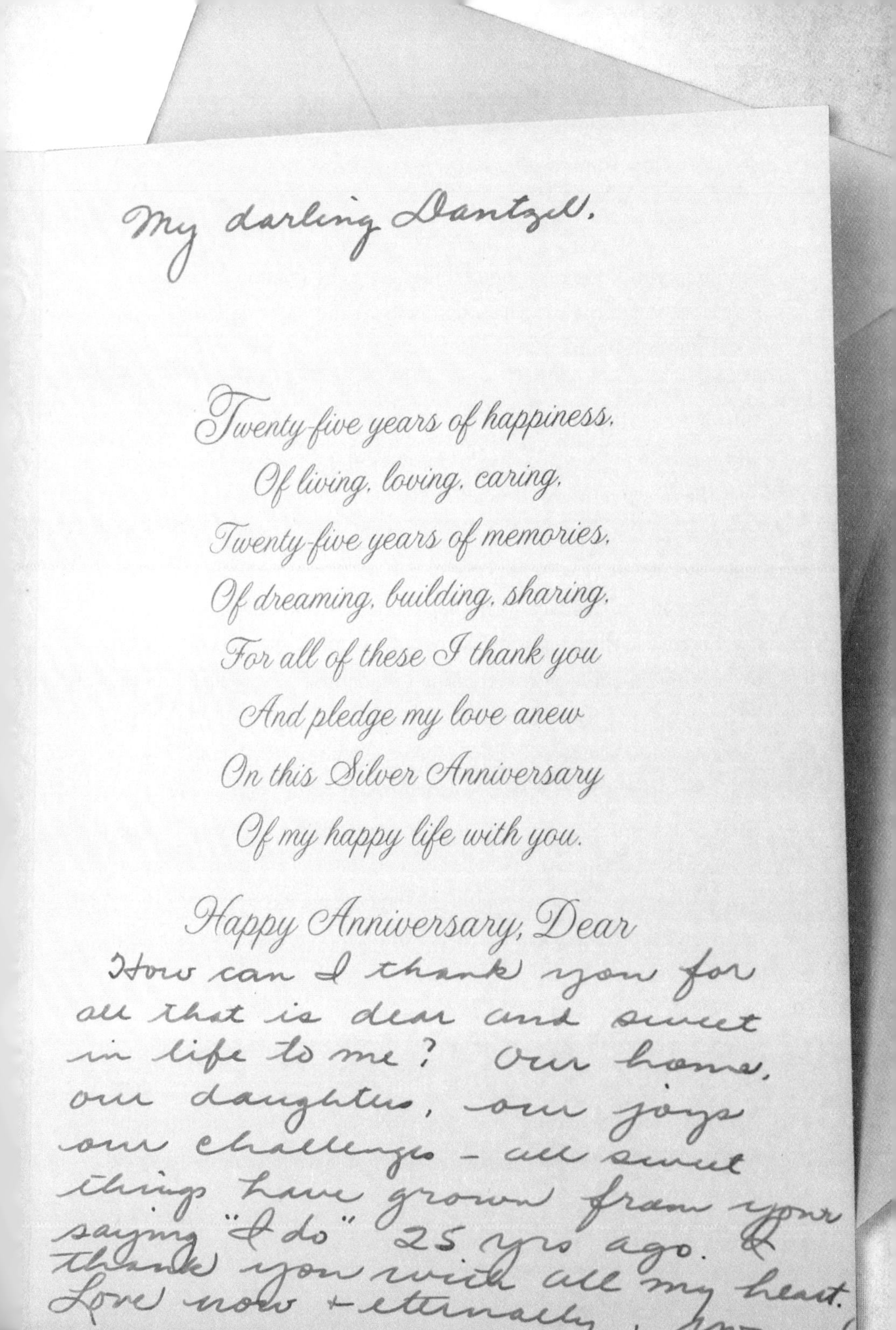

My darling Dantzel,

Twenty-five years of happiness,
Of living, loving, caring,
Twenty-five years of memories,
Of dreaming, building, sharing,
For all of these I thank you
And pledge my love anew
On this Silver Anniversary
Of my happy life with you.

Happy Anniversary, Dear

How can I thank you for all that is dear and sweet in life to me? Our home, our daughters, our joys our challenges — all sweet things have grown from your saying "I do" 25 yrs ago. I thank you with all my heart. Love now + eternally, yours!

One of many cards Elder Nelson gave to Dantzel over the years.

able to follow in his wake. But it was so hard" (*Church News*/KSL Interview, January 10, 2018).

After the funeral, Russ Jr. asked his father, simply, "How can we best help you?" He responded, "Just keep the commandments and stay close to your family. That will help me the most" (*Church News*/ KSL Interview, January 2018).

The month following Dantzel's death, Elder Nelson went to Curitiba, Brazil, to preside at the groundbreaking for a temple there. His son-in-law David Webster and daughter Sylvia were presiding over the mission there. "It would have been so easy for him to ask to be reassigned," remembered Sylvia. "He could easily have said, 'I've just lost my wife. The light is out in my eyes. I don't have a spouse to accompany me.' It was really a hard time for him. But he was amazing. He rose to the occasion. The people in our mission could feel his love for them, and they loved him all the more because he made the effort to be with them. It was healing for all of us to be together for those days" (*Church News*/KSL Interview, January 10, 2018).

Two months later, Elder Nelson attended a regional meeting in Paris, where the women wore flowers in his wife's memory. He was touched by their kindness but concerned that their focus was on the wrong thing. He did not want his grief to become a concern or preoccupation for others, particularly for Church members he was called to serve.

With questions on his mind about how to move forward with his life, he met with President Gordon B. Hinckley and asked the Church President if he had any counsel for him about remarrying. President Hinckley responded that it was entirely up to him, that different Brethren—as he well knew—had handled this difficult circumstance in different ways.

Elder Nelson pressed him with a second question: "Is it easier to assign me to serve if I have a wife?" Put that way, President Hinckley replied that it was easier to "be a part of the rule than the exception to the rule." With that counsel, Elder Nelson knew he should consider remarrying. At the moment, though, he couldn't fathom it. He adored Dantzel, was sealed to her for eternity, and had seen nearly six decades together with her—the lean years, when their young children slept on army cots; times of international acclaim, recognition, and travel; his call to the Twelve; and the death of a daughter. They had friends in literally every corner of the world. Everywhere he looked, everywhere he went, he saw Dantzel.

After so much history, and at the age of eighty—a vigorous eighty, but eighty nonetheless—how do you even contemplate starting over? After sixty years of marriage, how do you date? And how do you date as a member of the Twelve? But the loneliness was excruciating. At the moment, he was an exception to the rule, rather than the rule, and he didn't want anything to interfere with his ability to serve the Lord.

"Sign my name to it too."

—Wendy L. Watson

In the spring of 2005, Wendy Watson made a trip to southern Alberta to speak at a stake Relief Society conference in her hometown of Raymond, Alberta, Canada. One of her sisters, Kathy Card, from Edmonton, joined her. Following a session in the Cardston Alberta Temple, Wendy told her sister that she could feel a big change coming in her life but had no idea what it was. Maybe it was time to quit teaching at BYU. Maybe she should move. She just wasn't sure. But as they talked, she found herself saying something she'd never said to anyone before in her life: "Kathy, you can write it in your journal. There is a big change coming in my life."

The next morning, Wendy mentioned that she had awakened with a hymn in her mind and she didn't know what it was. When she hummed it for Kathy, her sister said, "Oh, don't you know, that's the hymn that Elder Nelson wrote new words to and that the Mormon Tabernacle Choir sang to accompany his general conference talk." Wendy responded, "Well, I don't know anything about that, but there's a big change coming in my life."

A few weeks later, in May 2005, Wendy and her friend Sheri Dew left for Europe on a trip that was part business and part vacation. Their first stop was Germany, where, among other things, they attended an endowment session at the Frankfurt Temple with Sisters Barbara Perry and Marie Hafen, whose husbands, Elders L. Tom Perry and Bruce C. Hafen, were serving in the Europe Area Presidency at the time. On the drive back from the temple, Wendy and Sister Perry sat in the backseat and chatted at length as Sister

Perry shared some of her experiences as Elder Perry's second wife. Wendy enjoyed Sister Perry's stories but didn't have even a fleeting thought about becoming the second wife of one of the Brethren.

From Germany, Wendy and Sheri went to Rome and met up with friends Sharon and Ralph Larsen, with whom they enjoyed the grandeur and majesty of the Eternal City. The crowds at the Vatican and Coliseum, the mob around Trevi Fountain (where Wendy and Sheri made sure they threw in the obligatory three coins for every woman interested in marriage), the lines for gelato—it was both education and sheer fun with good friends.

Elder Perry and his second wife, Sister Barbara Perry.

When the four arrived in Florence, they bumped into friends who happened to mention that the first stake in Rome was being created that very weekend by Elder Russell M. Nelson. They debated briefly about whether they should attempt to attend such an amazing historical event—the first stake in the shadow of the Vatican—but decided that a change in their itinerary at that point would cause a domino effect too major to overcome. So they soaked in the ambience of Florence. The iconic Ponte Vecchio, the Uffizi gallery, and of course Michelangelo's masterpiece—the *David:* it was all as eye-opening and enlightening as everyone said it would be. Surprisingly, however, both Wendy and Sheri became restless and decided to leave Florence earlier than they had expected to.

The foursome was scheduled to separate then anyway, so as Wendy and Sheri considered options, they decided to see if they could get last-minute tickets on a train from Florence over the Italian Alps to Zurich. Surprisingly, tickets were available, so they hurriedly packed, caught a cab to the train station, bought their tickets, and walked to the large yard filled with trains.

As they perused a large marquee identifying which trains were going to which cities—all in Italian—they heard someone from behind them say, "Sister Dew, may I help you?" When they turned around, they saw an adorable young woman, a returned missionary who had returned to Florence, where she had served much of her mission. She helped them identify the train headed to Zurich and casually mentioned that she was off to Rome to attend the creation of the first stake there. Wendy then left to check out platform number 8, which was where their train to Zurich would be.

Suddenly Sheri had an idea. She was almost certain that Elder Harold G. Hillam, then the Area President, and his wife, Carol, would be accompanying Elder Nelson to Rome. She had worked closely with Elder Hillam during her service in the Relief Society General Presidency, and she asked the young woman if she would be willing to walk up to the stand and hand a note to Elder Hillam. Sheri adored the Hillams and loved the idea of sending them a note. The returned sister missionary was game, so Sheri quickly jotted a note and handed it to her.

As they prepared to part, it occurred to Sheri that it would only be polite to send a note to Elder Nelson as well, though she did not know him as well as she did Elder Hillam. As she began to write a second note, Wendy suddenly reappeared from checking out the various train platforms. Sheri explained the note she had written to the Hillams and said that she was just finishing a second note, this one for Elder Nelson. "Sign my name to it too," Wendy said. Sheri signed both her and Wendy's names, the young woman took the notes and departed, and Sheri and Wendy boarded the train for Zurich. They wondered out loud if the young woman would actually deliver the

The note Sheri Dew sent to Elder Nelson with Wendy Watson's name added to it.

notes, but assumed they would never know.

However . . . they did find out that the young returned sister missionary did indeed deliver the notes to Elders Nelson and Hillam. And they found out in a most unexpected way.

Elder Nelson's wife, Dantzel, had passed away several months earlier. Knowing that he would be traveling alone to and from Europe, he asked his secretary to go to Deseret Book and get him a couple of books to read on the trip. On the flight over, he read one of those books: *Rock Solid Relationships,* by Wendy L. Watson.

When he read the note while sitting on the stand in Rome prior to the beginning of the stake conference and saw Wendy's name, it leaped off the page as all the other words faded away. He couldn't see anything except the name *Wendy Watson.* At the same time, Elder Nelson had a strong, immediate, and clear spiritual impression about her. Once home from Europe, he took the note with him to the Salt Lake Temple to seek confirmation about that impression. What he learned was that when it was time for him to consider remarriage, he needed to meet this woman.

It was a curious sequence of events. Wendy and Sheri weren't even supposed to be at the train station in Florence. And what are the odds that during the few seconds they were trying to identify the right train to board, a young Latter-day Saint woman would recognize Sheri and offer to help—and that she would just happen to be going to the location where Elder Russell M. Nelson was scheduled to preside at the creation of a stake? And that the thought would occur to Sheri to send a note. And that Wendy would ask for her name to be added to the note. And that she would then never remember saying that.

It was a stunning display of timing—the Lord's timing. And the rest, as they say, is history. The day came when Elder Nelson felt prompted to reach out to Wendy. As they became acquainted, it was clear that heaven was orchestrating their union. The Lord was their matchmaker, as Wendy would say ever after.

When Elder Nelson proposed, there was a lot they had yet to learn about each other. But as he said to Wendy, "There are plenty of things I do not know about you, but I do know revelation." As did she. Wendy had experienced three broken engagements in earlier years, and she wasn't interested in repeating the experience with an Apostle. Suffice it to say that both had sought clear direction on whether or not to even go on a first date—a date prompted by a note at a train station in Florence. That note, framed by Elder Nelson, sits prominently in his home office.

"When you love the Lord more than you love your spouse, your capacity to love will increase and you will increasingly love your spouse even more."

—Russell M. and Wendy W. Nelson

O n Thursday, April 6, 2006, President Gordon B. Hinckley performed the sealing of Elder Russell M. Nelson and Wendy L. Watson in the Salt Lake Temple. Following the sealing ceremony, the new Elder and Sister Nelson invited family and close friends to join them in an endowment session. Then, after a round of photographs, the new couple were off on their honeymoon. When they drove away, it was the first time they had been alone in a car together. "We were both excited, both scared, but both filled with faith," Wendy remembered.

They would quickly learn that just because, or maybe precisely because, the Lord had orchestrated their courtship and sealing, it did not mean marriage would be easy for them at first. Wendy knew, both from her own life experiences and also from her professional involvement with many couples, that when the Lord makes it clear that a certain course of action is directed or even ordained by God, it likely means there will come a time when you absolutely need to know that the decision or direction you've taken was inspired by Him.

Suffice it to say that marriage was not an easy transition for either of them. As a fifty-five-year-old, never-married woman, Wendy found that marriage to an eighty-one-year-old Apostle turned her life on a dime. She often quipped that he had turned her life upside down, to which he loved to retort, "No, actually, I turned it right side up."

Russell M. Nelson and Wendy Watson Nelson on their wedding day

Nonetheless, almost everything about the circumstances of her life changed instantly and dramatically. Her twenty-five-year career as a professor of marriage and family therapy was over, her clinical practice of thirty years ended.

She became part of an enormous family with many well-established traditions and practices. Beginning with Russell and Dantzel, then adding their children, then their children's spouses, then grandchildren and great-grandchildren, Wendy became the 113th person to come into the sprawling, constantly growing Nelson family.

Further, her schedule was now controlled almost entirely by her husband's. If he needed her to be with him on a plane traveling to some part of the world, that was where she would be. As just one example of many, in May 2008 Wendy was scheduled to speak at a multistake women's conference in eastern Canada—that is, until at the last minute President Monson invited Elder Nelson to accompany

The Nelson family.

Sister Nelson found herself suddenly swept up in a whirlwind of public activity.

him to the dedication of the Curitiba Brazil Temple on the same weekend. Wendy's plans changed instantly.

Yet, from the start, Elder Nelson said to Wendy what he had often said to Dantzel: "Mama knows best." For example, as the two of them would review an upcoming itinerary for an international trip, if Wendy felt hesitant about accompanying him on the trip, he honored it every time—which happened rarely but always later proved crucial for reasons unknown at the time.

For Elder Nelson, the changes accompanying a second marriage were also substantial. He had loved and been married to Dantzel longer than Wendy had been alive. Every pattern he had developed over sixty years—the way he communicated with his wife, their division of responsibilities, the frequency and way with which he interacted with his burgeoning family, and much more—was suddenly subject to change.

He and Wendy both had expectations for marriage, and those expectations didn't necessarily match. Additionally, there were

President and Sister Nelson speak at RootsTech 2017.

simply a lot of questions to answer. Did Wendy need to attend every baptism, ordination, endowment, and family party in the large Nelson family, or were there times when it was more considerate to give Elder Nelson's children time with him alone? What expectations did he have of her when they traveled on Church assignment? Were there unwritten laws about how a General Authority's wife should dress, act, and speak, and from whom did she learn them? How do you build a new relationship, a new marriage, onstage with the whole Church watching?

"To this point in my life, the most difficult thing I had faced was the death of my mother," Wendy explained. "She and I were very close. The beginning of our marriage, however, was more difficult and required more from me and more turning to the Lord than anything in my life. Almost from the beginning, everything I anticipated would be difficult for me and my husband turned out to be easy, but things I had never anticipated or things I thought would be easy turned out to be the most difficult challenges of my life. Those struggles turned me even more to the Lord, which in turn strengthened our marriage. To create the kind of marriage we wanted required a lot of work, sacrifice, forgiveness, and prayer from both of us in the beginning as we intertwined our lives to become one. And it was worth it!"

All in all, the first couple of years brought a new adventure, and often a new challenge, almost every day. It was a steep learning curve for both of them. The former marriage and family therapist found herself relying on what she had learned from her work with thousands of other couples. Most important, they turned to the Lord for His help. As Wendy would say, "Since the Lord was our matchmaker, I knew He would be our marriage and family therapist as well."

Elder and Sister Nelson also had important advantages they could build on. They knew the Lord had brought them together, and little by little, their faith in each other and in the Lord helped them build a relationship filled with love, wonderful communication, and joy-filled companionship. And in time, they were quite open with the fact that they were wild about each other.

Humor also helped. As just one example, Elder Nelson soon learned that his new wife's approach to cooking was creative. "A recipe for Wendy is just a suggestion," he explained. Given to experimenting with all manner of concoctions, she frequently placed dishes in front of him that weren't necessarily easy to identify. One night at dinner, he demonstrated his patented dry wit. Looking at the plate of food in front of him, he said, "Honey, if we were at a restaurant and wanted to order this, what would we call it?"

Wendy quickly learned that her husband was a man of action. "I have to be careful about asking him to do anything," she said, "because he wants to do it right now, even if it's in the middle of the night. If I say, 'Honey, could you put a hook on the back of the bathroom door,' he'll say, 'Well, let me do that right now.' He is a can-do, do-it-now man. He can't sleep unless things are done for the day." He also proved to be handy with a vacuum, and on Saturdays when he had the luxury of being home, or on Mondays, the Brethren's "day off," he would don plastic gloves and, to Wendy's joy and amazement, tell her the "cleaning lady" had arrived.

Another of her new husband's traits that Wendy found remarkable was the way he responded to her requests: " I quickly learned that if I began a sentence with something like, 'Would it be possible to . . . ?' Russell would interrupt me and say, 'Yes.' Then, after a pause, he would ask, 'What did I just agree to?' His quick 'yes' showed great trust in me from the beginning, which I believe is not only out of respect for his wife but an indication of the way he feels about the good judgment and instincts of women. I know he felt the same about Dantzel. After one of their children was almost hit by a car in the street outside their home, Dantzel went house-hunting that very day and called Russell to tell him they were moving. He supported her completely. When we were dating, I called him one morning while he was skiing and told him I thought I'd found our home. (He had previously told me to go find a home for us.) He sat right down in the snow and asked me to tell him about it. After I did, he said only, 'You sound really excited about it. I think we should buy it.' And we did so, sight unseen by him. To say that my husband is unusual in this way would be an understatement."

One aspect of Wendy's new life that could have been difficult, but wasn't, was interacting with the extended Nelson family. If they had hesitations about her, they did not show them. "I did not experience any of the resistance many second wives encounter," Wendy said. "Every member of the family made me feel welcome from day one. They could not have been more wonderful to me."

Further, neither Elder Nelson nor Wendy tried to turn her into Dantzel. On one of their first dates, Elder Nelson told her that he had already had the original Dantzel, and that now he needed the original Wendy. In turn, Wendy felt a great desire to honor Dantzel. On one of her first Mother's Days as Elder Nelson's wife, she suggested that they

Enjoying some leisure time together.

all meet at Dantzel's grave in the Salt Lake City Cemetery and invited everyone to share memories of their mother and grandmother.

"Wendy has really stepped up to the plate," said Sylvia. "I'm sure it's hard to walk into a family of more than two hundred people. But she has made an amazing effort. Our kids love and respect her. And she's so supportive of Daddy and what he needs today. It's very sweet to see her just love him and encourage him" (*Church News*/KSL Interview, January 10, 2018).

"Wendy brought a different element of joy into Grandfather's life," said Katie Irion Owens. "And she has been so great about helping our family stay connected. She reaches out to each of us individually. She does such a great job with relationships, just touching the one. We love her" (*Church News*/KSL Interview, January 10, 2018).

"One of the unique traits Wendy brings to our family is her ability to counsel and her ability to see right down to the heart of the problem and address it head-on," Russ Jr. added (*Church News*/KSL Interview, January 2018).

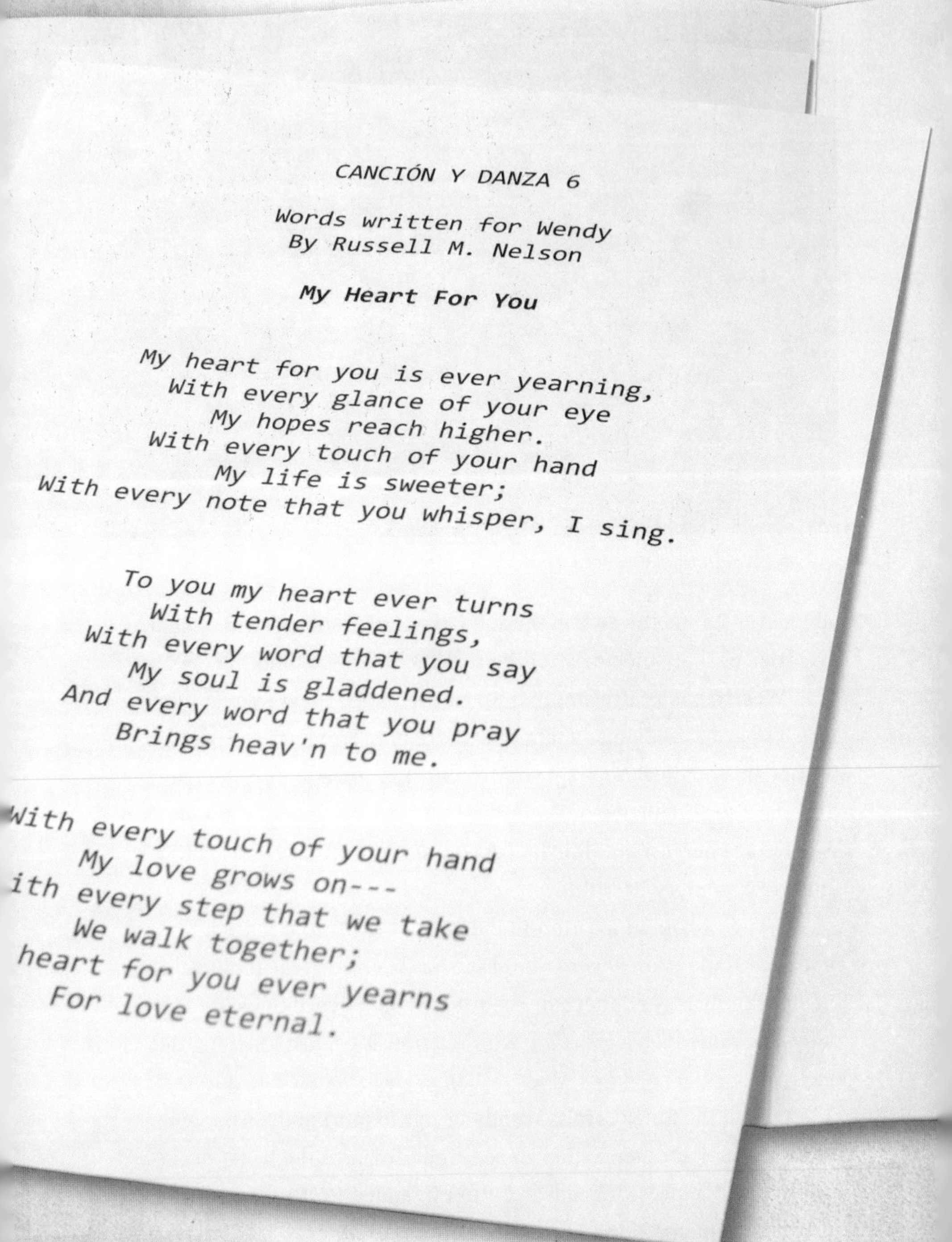

CANCIÓN Y DANZA 6

Words written for Wendy
By Russell M. Nelson

My Heart For You

My heart for you is ever yearning,
With every glance of your eye
My hopes reach higher.
With every touch of your hand
My life is sweeter;
With every note that you whisper, I sing.

To you my heart ever turns
With tender feelings,
With every word that you say
My soul is gladdened.
And every word that you pray
Brings heav'n to me.

With every touch of your hand
My love grows on---
With every step that we take
We walk together;
heart for you ever yearns
For love eternal.

Elder Nelson put words to a favorite song, expressing
his love for his wife Wendy.

A. Arthur Rubinstein

CANCIÓN Y DANZA 6
(Song and Dance No. 6)

Words written for Wendy by Russell M. Nelson

FEDERICO MOMPOU

Feb. 28, 2012

To My Angel Wife, Wendy

♥ ♥

A bud becomes a beautiful bloom
With both a flower and a marriage.
A couple starts as a bride and groom;
They slowly grow in love and courage.

My love for you is fairly bursting,
Like this new budding amaryllis.
You truly quench my love a thirsting
With your sweet, dazzling beauty and bliss.

I love you eternally!
Love,
Russell

Having a new wife did not change Elder Nelson's interactions with his large family. Monthly family birthday parties continued. Traditions around Christmas and July 4th, the weddings and ordinations of grandchildren, and the blessings and baptisms of great-grandchildren carried on just as they had before.

"Everyone in the family gets an individual card from Daddy for their birthday and wedding anniversary," explained Russ Jr. "With ten children and spouses and fifty-seven grandchildren and more than a hundred great-grandchildren, it's almost a full-time job to keep up with all of that calendaring, but he does it. And it's not a form letter. We receive individual cards with personal messages in his beautiful penmanship. He never forgets the individual, no matter how busy things get for him" (*Church News*/KSL Interview, January 2018).

The individual Elder Nelson was now most mindful of was his wife Wendy, however, often writing her poems and even on occasion setting those poems to music. He learned to play a very difficult piece of music in six flats that they both loved—it was "their song"—and then, while flying home from a weekend Church assignment, he wrote words to the music for her. The General Authority accompanying him was surprised to look over and see tears running down Elder Nelson's face as he worked intently on something. When he asked if he was okay, Elder Nelson responded simply, "I am writing a love poem for my sweetheart."

With each passing year, as they served together and grew closer to each other, the Nelsons' love for each other became stronger and sweeter. And in the spirit of practicing what you preach, something they had both preached through the years proved to be true in their case: when you love the Lord more than you love your spouse, your capacity to love will increase and you will increasingly love your spouse even more.

"I will go before your face. I will be on your right hand and on your left, and mine angels round about you, to bear you up."

—Doctrine and Covenants 84:88

May 29, 2009, began for the Nelsons in South Africa. Because of an unusual set of circumstances created by the irregularities of international travel, Elder and Sister Nelson had the chance to over-night at the Kruger Park game reserve. Their schedule allowed them time to enjoy the exotic animals there for a few hours the next morning before crossing an international border and pressing on to their next obligations in the afternoon.

The day began with sobering news—their dear friend Truman G. Madsen had just passed away. Elder Nelson's association with Truman and his wife, Ann, dated back to their days in Boston together, decades before; Wendy had served as a stake Relief Society president under Truman's direction as stake president. They both loved him dearly and immediately felt the impact of his loss.

Nevertheless, they drove across the border to Maputo, the capital of Mozambique, and after a humid afternoon of visiting with members in the city, they stopped at the welcome oasis of the mission home for dinner. There were six people dining together that evening—Elder William W. Parmley, the Africa Southeast Area President, and his wife, Shanna; the Mozambique Maputo Mission president, Blair J. Packard, and his wife, Cindy; and the Nelsons.

The three couples were enjoying dinner when, without warning, three large African men sauntered into the room. President Packard jumped up to confront the men and grabbed at the raincoat of the

The Nelsons and friends at the Kruger Park game reserve in South Africa.

ringleader, which revealed an AK-47 model M assault rifle that the man then pointed in President Packard's face. At about the same time, Sister Packard, who was standing because she had begun to clear the table, realized what was happening and said calmly, "This is a robbery!" She later remembered, "It took a minute to figure out who they were, but the feeling of evil they brought happened almost instantly" (interview with author, October 18, 2018).

As President Packard continued to confront the men, Cindy had the clear impression to "get help," and she tried to slip quietly into the kitchen and out the back door. The ringleader saw her attempt to escape, caught her and put her in a headlock from behind, dragged her outside, hit her on the side of the head with his fist, and threw her down hard. The fall broke her arm, but the man began to kick her

Mozambique mission home.

and then jerked her up and dragged her to a dark corner of the yard, where she yelled for help, hoping the neighbors to the back would hear the commotion. At one point she managed to break away, but the man caught her, threw her down again, put his knees in her back, and then pointed his gun at the back of her head and said, "You are going to die." At that moment, she had a clear impression to remind him that he hadn't come to kill her but to rob their home. In an instant she said, "Go take it all." That seemed to resonate with the intruder, and with that, he jerked her back up, put her in a headlock, and marched her inside, where he and his cohorts began to aggressively take phones, money, credit cards, wallets, a computer upstairs in the mission home—anything of value.

In all the mayhem, one robber went directly to Elder Nelson, put a gun to his head, announced that they were there to kill him and kidnap his wife, and then pulled the trigger. The gun made a clicking noise but didn't fire. The misfire infuriated the robber, who then backed up a couple of steps, got a run at Elder Nelson to use the full strength of his leg, and kicked him in the face with his heavy boot. The direct assault knocked Elder Nelson to the floor, where he lay almost lifeless, though his mind was spinning. He was certain he was about to die. "I thought to myself, 'I am going to pass out of this life and into the next, and this is going to be a very interesting experience,'" Elder Nelson remembered. "Most interesting of all is that I was calm."

Meanwhile, the third bandit walked around the table to where Sister Nelson was sitting and, shoving a pistol into her back, began rocking her chair in an attempt to pull her from it, saying, "You are coming with us. You are coming with us." With her eighty-four-year-old husband on the floor and a robber grabbing her from behind, Sister Nelson also felt a peace that surprised her. "I experienced first-hand exactly what the Lord means when He speaks of the peace that passeth understanding," Wendy said. "I wasn't panicked, I felt completely at peace."

Amidst all of the commotion, the Packards' nanny, Henriqueta, who was also in the home, managed to open the garage door. When Cindy Packard, broken arm and all, realized that Henriqueta had provided an escape route, she bolted out the door leading through the garage to the road in front of the mission home, where she continued to run, screaming, *"Ladrao, Ladrao!"* (Portuguese for *robber*).

It is unclear what was in the minds of the robbers at that point, but with one of their prey summoning help from neighbors, they appeared to change plans. One of them spotted the keys to the van the mission president had rented for the day and grabbed them. He motioned to his cohorts, and they left as suddenly as they had entered. Miraculously, Cindy's broken arm and Elder Nelson's bloody nose were the extent of the injuries. And the only things taken were items that could be replaced.

Although calm had prevailed during the attack, in its aftermath everyone realized how differently things could have turned out. The

Packards subsequently learned that there had been other robberies in the neighborhood around that time, and that some people had been killed.

"A man my age should have broken something during that kind of attack," Elder Nelson admitted. "The guy who came at me with his boot and let me have it with the full strength of his leg could have broken my neck. Yet all I got was a bloody nose. We felt protected. I honestly don't remember even feeling it when they knocked me to the ground. And the misfire on the gun, well, that had to be angels watching over us. Both Wendy and I know there were angels there to help us."

Sister Nelson could see the print of the boot on her husband's face, and she immediately began to attend to him. But by the next morning, he didn't look any the worse for wear. As she reflected on surviving the ambush, she marveled at both the courage of Cindy Packard and the undeniable presence of the Spirit and of angels. "We looked at each other and almost quoted the scripture together, that the Lord would go before our face and would send angels to bear us up. We know that is what happened to us that day in Mozambique."

The next morning, Wendy woke up with the thought to read Doctrine and Covenants 122. As a phrase from verse 5 leaped out, "if thou art in perils among robbers," she realized she had experienced only one of the harrowing experiences the Prophet Joseph Smith had endured. The words at the end of verse 7 then anchored her: "Know thou, my [daughter], that all these things shall give thee experience, and shall be for thy good." And verses 8 and 9 spoke to and calmed her heart: "The Son of Man hath descended below them all. Art thou greater than he? Therefore, hold on thy way. . . . Thy days are known, and thy years shall not be numbered less; therefore, fear not what man can do, for God shall be with you forever and ever." With those words, she knew what she needed to do going forward.

Despite the horror of the moment, Cindy Packard admitted that

Cindy Packard (arm in sling) with her husband, Blair, their nanny, Henriqueta, and her children, and a security guard.

she had never had a spiritual experience quite like that one: "I felt directed in a very specific way, telling me what to do almost moment by moment. When I look back on it, I think of it as one of the most spiritual experiences of my life" (email from Cindy Packard to Wendy Nelson, May 16, 2018; see also email from Cindy Packard to author, October 19, 2018).

From Wendy Nelson's perspective, Cindy Packard was nothing short of a heroine. "The next morning Cindy told me she woke up grieved at the thought that she had put us at risk by leaving the keys to the van in plain sight, thus allowing the robbers to get away. But instantly, the Spirit calmed and corrected her and let her know that if she had not left the keys where she did, I would have been kidnapped and my husband killed. This is a woman who was directed by the Spirit and, as a result, saved our lives."

The Saints in Mozambique were horrified about the attack.

"Elder Nelson was so sensitive about everyone's feelings," President Packard recalled. "He said, 'You know, these things have happened in other places in the world. This was not your fault.' He then invited everyone, including embassy personnel and others who had gathered at the mission home in the aftermath of the attack, to kneel as he offered a prayer inviting the Spirit to return to the mission home (interview with author, October 18, 2018).

There are those, however, who look back to that event and the district conference with members held the next day as a defining moment, a turning point for the Church in Mozambique. Many members became even more committed to their faith and their covenants. "Something changed," said Blair Packard. "It's as though the members saw what could happen if they didn't stand up and be a light to others, and they began to stand up more visibly for what they believed" (interview with author, October 18, 2018).

At the time of the Nelsons' visit, there were only districts in Mozambique. Nine years later, there were three full stakes, with the Church growing stronger. As far as the Nelsons were concerned, ever after they only thought or spoke of Mozambique as a place where they had experienced a miracle.

The Mozambique experience was not the first near-death experience for either Sister Nelson or her husband. Wendy should have died at an intersection in southern Alberta when a car ran a stop sign and T-boned her car. Miraculously, although her car was totaled, she survived the accident with no injuries.

Her husband's experience was even more dramatic. On November 12, 1976, Russell Nelson had boarded a commuter plane in Salt Lake City to fly the quick route to St. George, Utah, where he was to give the invocation at the inauguration of W. Rolfe Kerr as the president of Dixie College.

It was a short hop of less than an hour in a small, two-engine, propeller plane. Only four passengers were on board. The pilot had just announced that they were halfway to St. George when the engine on the right wing exploded, spewing oil all over the right side of the aircraft and then bursting into flames. In an attempt to douse the flames, the pilot turned the fuel off, causing the small plane to go suddenly into a free-fall death spiral.

The woman across the aisle from Russell began to scream hysterically. But Russell felt calm. "It was the most amazing thing," he said. "I thought, 'My wife and I are sealed. Our children are sealed to us. I've honored my covenants. I'll meet my ancestors and go on to a glorious resurrection.'"

He was, however, impressed with how quickly and comprehensively the mind can work. "It's true, your life *does* flash before you. I had a bright recollection and perfect remembrance of my whole life. One major thought was that all of the framed awards and honors on my wall, the various clothes I'd worn—tuxedos and uniforms and doctoral robes—didn't mean anything. What mattered was that I had my garments on and had been faithful to the covenants I'd made in the temple. I knew I was going to die, but I knew I would be fine."

Miraculously, the free fall extinguished the fire, and, in the nick of time, the pilot was able to start the left engine, regain control of the plane, and glide it to an emergency landing in a farmer's field not far from Delta, Utah. Everyone walked away from the incident unharmed. Another plane was dispatched, and Russell made it to St. George in time to give the invocation.

Twice, Elder Nelson's life had been seriously threatened. Both times he experienced the calm, the peace that passeth understanding.

Even more, he experienced firsthand what President Joseph Fielding Smith declared at the funeral of Elder Richard L. Evans: "No righteous man is ever taken before his time" ("Funeral Services for Elder Richard L. Evans"). Nor any righteous woman.

"We affectionately called this trip 'Pray, Eat, Fly.'"

—Wendy W. Nelson

Members of the Quorum of the Twelve don't determine their own schedules. They don't assign themselves to visit countries or sit on committees or create stakes. They accept assignments from the President of the quorum, and, little by little, over a period of many years, they have a wide range of experiences—visiting and ministering to members the world over, meeting dignitaries in behalf of the Church, reorganizing and creating stakes, and dedicating countries.

During his years as a member of the Twelve, Elder Nelson went to 134 countries, 31 of which he dedicated or participated in the dedication of. One highlight in that regard was a four-day whirlwind trip in September 2010 in which he dedicated six countries. Accompanied by Elder Erich and Sister Christiane Kopischke and Elder Johann Wondra, he and Wendy traveled first to Zagreb, where he dedicated Croatia, then flew on to Ljubljana, Slovenia, where he dedicated that country. The next day they flew to Podgorica, where, amidst the ruins of Duklja, he dedicated Montenegro, and then they pressed on to Sarajevo to dedicate Bosnia and Herzegovina. The next day took them to Pristina, where, in a Sacred Grove-like setting, he dedicated Kosovo. And finally, at sunrise on the fourth day, which was also his eighty-sixth birthday, he dedicated Macedonia on Mount Vodno. It was a remarkable four days on the Balkan Peninsula. "We affectionately called this trip 'Pray, Eat, Fly,'" said Wendy Nelson, "because that's all we did for four days—pray, eat when we could, and get on yet another airplane for the next country."

Participation in Dedication of Countries

(Listed in alphabetical order)
Elder Russell M. Nelson
1987-2017

1.	Armenia (Yerevan)	June 24, 1991	(Elder Oaks was voice)
2.	Australia (Sydney)	November 13, 1993	
3.	Belarus (Minsk)	May 11, 1993	
4.	Belize (Burrell Boom)	December 7, 1992	
5.	Bosnia-Herzegovina (Sarajevo)	September 8, 2010	
6.	Bulgaria (Sofia)	February 13, 1990	
7.	Congo (Brazzaville)	August 24, 1992	(Elder Scott was voice)
8.	Croatia (Zagreb)	September 6, 2010	
9.	Czechoslovakia (Karlstein)	February 6, 1990	(Prayer of gratitude)
10.	El Salvador (San Salvador)	April 7, 1990	(Accompanied by Elder Scott)
11.	Estonia (Tallinn)	April 25, 1990	
12.	Ethiopia (Addis Ababa)	Nov. 11, 2004	
13.	French Polynesia (Papeete)	May 8, 1994	
14.	Guatemala (G. City)	October 19, 1991	(Elder Ashton was voice)
15.	Honduras (Tegucigalpa)	June 1, 1991	
16.	Hungary (Budapest)	April 19, 1987	
17.	Kazakhstan (Almaty)	August 27, 2003	
18.	Kosovo (Pristina)	September 8, 2010	
19.	Kyrgyz Republic (Bishkek)	August 28, 2003	
20.	Macedonia (Skopje)	September 9, 2010	
21.	Malawi (Blantyre)	October 25, 2011	
22.	Montenegro (Podgorica)	September 7, 2010	
23.	Namibia (Windhoek)	August 22, 1992	
24.	New Zealand (Temple View)	November 8, 1993	(Elder Scott was voice)
25.	Nicaragua (Managua)	April 9, 1990	(Elder Scott was voice)
26.	Romania (Bucharest)	February 9, 1990	
27.	Russia (Leningrad)	April 26, 1990	
28.	Slovenia (Ljubljana)	September 6, 2010	
29.	Tanzania (Dar es Salaam)	November 18, 2003	
30.	Uzbekistan (Tashkent)	October 17, 2017	
31.	Zambia (Lusaka)	August 20, 1992	

COUNTRIES VISITED BY RUSSELL M. NELSON

as of Oct. 24, 2017

Country	Year of First Visit
Albania	2003
Andorra	1989
Argentina	1973
Armenia **	1991
Australia *	1976
Austria	1975
Bahama	1956
Balearic Islands	1973
Barbados	1994
Belarus *	1993
Belgium	1988
Belize *	1988
Benin	1992
Bolivia	1994
Bosnia-Herzegovina *	2010
Brazil	1975
Brunei	2010
Bulgaria *	1988
Canada	1934
Canary Islands	2004
Chile	1979
China, Peoples Republic of	1980
Colombia	1986
Congo **	1992
Cook Islands	1973
Costa Rica	1996
Croatia *	2010
Cuba	1972
Czechoslovakia ***	1975
Denmark	1981
Dominican Republic	1994
Ecuador	1988
Egypt	1980
El Salvador *	1990
England	1966
Estonia *	1990
Ethiopia *	2004
Fiji	1976
Finland	1966
France	1968
French Polynesia (inc. Tubuai, Takaroa) *	1994
French West Indies (Martinique)	1994
Georgia	20017
German Democratic Republic (DDR)	1977
Germany	1973
Ghana	1986
Greece	1968
Grenadines (Mayreau)	1994
Guatemala **	1978
Guam	2013
Honduras *	1988
Hungary *	1987
Iceland	1989
India	1966
Indonesia	2010
Ireland	1980
Israel	1968
Italy	1968
Ivory Coast (Côte d'Ivoire)	1992
Japan	1951
Jordan, Hashemite Kingdom of	1969
Kazakhstan *	2003
Kenya	1975
Korea (South)	1951
Kosovo *	2010
Kyrgyz Republic *	2003
Latvia	2017
Lithuania	2017
Liberia	1975
Liechtenstein	1989
Macau	1997
Malaysia	1966
Malawi *	1975
Macedonia *	2010
México	1938
Monaco	1969
Montenegro *	2010
Mozambique	2009
Namibia *	1992
Netherlands (Holland)	1969
Netherlands Antilles (St. Maarten)	1994
New Zealand	1976
Nicaragua **	1990
Nigeria	1975
Northern Ireland	1986
Norway	1981
Okinawa	2013
Pakistan	1992
Panamá	1996
Papua New Guinea	1991
Paraguay	1992
Peru	1973
Philippines	1987
Poland	1986
Portugal	1973
Puerto Rico	1974
Rhodesia (later-Zimbabwe)	1975
Romania *	1987
Russia ***	1976
Saint Kitts-Nevis	2004
Samoa	1973
Samoa, American	1973
Saudi Arabia	2004
Scotland	1975
Senegal	1975
Singapore	1966
Slovenia *	2010
Solomon Islands	1993
South Africa	1975
Spain	1973
Sri Lanka	2015
Sweden	1981
Switzerland	1973
Tahiti	1976
Taiwan (Republic of China)	1966
Tanzania *	1975
Thailand	1966
Togo	1986
Tonga	1973
Turkey	1980
Uganda	2001
Ukraine	1971
United Arab Emirates	1982
United States of America	1924
Uzbekistan *	2017
Uruguay	1975
Vanuatu	1993
Venezuela	1997
Virgin Islands	1974
Wake Island	1931
Wales	1986
Yugoslavia (Serbia, Croatia)	1980
Zaire (Dem Rep Congo)	1992
Zambia	1992
Total	**134**

Legend:
* (Dedicated the country)
** (Beside other Apostle who dedicated the country)
*** (Rededicated the country)

Participated in the dedication or rededication (*) of 31 countries

A list of the countries Russell M. Nelson has visited.

Sister Nelson added, "Even the selection of the sites of dedication showed the Lord's hand in those countries. One felt like its own Sacred Grove. Another was high on a mountaintop. Yet another was amidst Roman ruins that evoked a holy feeling. In each place, it felt that the Lord was accepting of our efforts and that the work was moving forward. It was beautiful to witness."

The pace was worth it to cover so much territory in such a short period of time and to open the blessings of the Lord to the people in six different nations. "When you dedicate a country, it is like unlocking a door," Elder Nelson explained. "Now the Lord can and does work His miracles in that land. It opens the door to the work of the Lord, which He does sometimes through missionaries, sometimes through humanitarian efforts, and sometimes through other means. But He does His work. We begin to become known, and people join the Church."

It was a privilege to receive an assignment to dedicate a nation or create a stake, as both were continued evidence of the gathering of Israel.

The pillow on which Elder Nelson knelt in each of the six countries he dedicated in September 2010.

"I am pleased to announce that effective immediately all worthy and able young men . . . will have the option of being recommended for missionary service beginning at the age of 18."

—President Thomas S. Monson

At the opening session of the October 2012 general conference, President Thomas S. Monson welcomed the Saints to conference in his patented upbeat, sunny style. He complimented the Mormon Tabernacle Choir, mentioned recent temple dedications in Kansas City, Brigham City, and Manaus, Brazil, in the heart of the Amazon, as well as the rededication of the remodeled Buenos Aires Argentina Temple. And then he announced two more temples to be built—one in Tucson, Arizona, and the other in Arequipa, Peru. As welcoming messages from the President of the Church go, it was standard fare.

And then President Monson dropped a bomb whose impact reverberated around the Church. "I am pleased to announce," he said, "that effective immediately all worthy and able young men who have graduated from high school or its equivalent . . . will have the option of being recommended for missionary service beginning at the age of 18." And if that remarkable announcement weren't newsworthy enough, he added that "worthy young women who have the desire to serve may be recommended for missionary service beginning at age 19" (Monson, "Welcome to Conference").

The reaction was immediate. Social media lit up with the news and feelings about the age change, and the topic trended on Twitter. Before the first session of conference concluded, bishops and stake presidents the world over were receiving texts and emails from young men and women in their wards and stakes asking for appointments. Even the typically staid Conference Center congregation buzzed with awe, where family members and teenage friends sitting side by side hugged and slapped each other on the back.

Immediately following the session, Elder Nelson, then serving as the chairman of the Missionary Executive Council (MEC), along with Elder Jeffrey R. Holland of the Quorum of the Twelve and Elder David F. Evans of the Seventy, both members of that council, held a press conference to provide additional detail and answer questions for members of the media. They explained that the Brethren had studied the possibility of lowering the age requirement for some time. Eighteen-year-olds from various countries where military and educational requirements demanded it had already been allowed on a case-by-case basis to enter the mission field at the younger age.

During the press conference, Elder Nelson explained that "young men and women should not begin their service before they are ready," but that "the response by the mission presidents [with younger missionaries] has been universal. Give me more eighteen-year-olds. They do well. They're sweeter. They're purer. They're smarter."

Elder Holland added that the Lord was clearly hastening His work. "The goodness of their lives," he said, referring to the youth of the Church, "inspires me to no end. It is obvious that the Lord loves them as well to entrust them with His precious gospel at such tender ages" (see "LDS Church announces historic changes").

Outside the Conference Center, journalists captured the shock, awe, and sheer excitement of members. Young men were excited; teenage girls saw a new door of opportunity. Parents, leaders, and youth alike had just had their worlds rocked in the most positive of ways. Sunday night at the traditional post-general conference Nelson family gathering, Elder and Sister Nelson were enthusiastically

Elder Nelson answers questions at a press conference following the announcement of the age change for missionaries.

Reactions to the announcement.

The Provo Missionary Training Center underwent significant expansion to accommodate the influx of new missionaries.

greeted by a teenage granddaughter who had already calculated how many days until her mission could begin.

The MEC had begun exploring the possibility of an age change for several reasons: many universities didn't like students interrupting their studies for a mission and were putting pressure on students not to leave campus once they entered as freshmen; military requirements in certain countries were tightening and precluding some youth from serving; and some young men weren't as pure at nineteen as they had been a year earlier and subsequently disqualified themselves from serving.

In one meeting, where the pros and cons of lowering the age requirement were aggressively explored, Elder Nelson cited the various reasons youth, particularly young men, were choosing not to serve and then drew on his medical background to characterize the situation: "We are losing the lifeblood of this Church," he said, "and in my world we'd call that a hemorrhage."

After a prolonged period of discussion, study, evaluation, and prayer by the MEC and then the Quorum of the Twelve, it was Elder Nelson's job as MEC chair to make a case for the change with the First Presidency. Further lengthy deliberation followed, but ultimately President Monson made the decision that the ages of missionaries should change. Just hours after he made the historic announcement, he said during the priesthood session that evening: "Within two short years, all of the full-time missionaries currently serving in this royal army of God will have concluded their full-time labors and will have returned to their homes and loved ones. Their replacements are found tonight. . . . Are you prepared to serve?" (Monson, "See Others").

Two years earlier, President Monson had called for more missionaries, and the numbers had increased somewhat: elders serving had increased by 6 percent, sisters by 12 percent, and senior couples by 18 percent. The age-change announcement, however, fulfilled the prophet's hopes on this score, and then some.

Within a year of the age change, the ranks of missionaries swelled from 58,000 to more than 80,000. By the following July, the Church opened fifty-eight missions to accommodate the influx of younger missionaries. The Provo Missionary Training Center bulged at the seams, and construction began on a major expansion. In the interim, the missionary department turned an apartment complex in Provo, Utah, into an adjunct MTC. Construction also began on an MTC in Accra, Ghana. In June 2013 a Church-owned high school in Mexico City, "Centro Escolar Benemérito de las Américas," was converted into the Church's second-largest Missionary Training Center, and a large number of North Americans assigned to Spanish-speaking missions in the Western Hemisphere began to be trained there.

Transitioning the Benemérito School into an MTC required great faith on the part of the Saints in Mexico City, and Elder Nelson and Elder Jeffrey R. Holland were dispatched to make the announcement.

"Instead of a few hundred being educated here at Benemérito, many thousands will be trained," Elder Nelson explained to those gathered. "Many of them will come from other countries. . . . This hallowed ground where we sit tonight will become more sacred with each passing year. Better, higher, and holier purposes will be served in the future, more than they ever have been before" (Nelson, Benemérito de las Américas address).

Afterward, Elder Nelson told an interviewer that "as we looked into the eyes of the faculty, there was a feeling of great faith, great support. Those dear leaders were 100 percent behind this. . . . For the students it was a twelve-Kleenex day. The tears flowed, and the hugging and crying and emotions of the students were very tender. . . . The students could see that they were leaving the school that day, but they would be coming back as missionaries. . . . To watch that transition from self-interest . . . [to] a greater appreciation of that land was emotional to watch" (Barbara Morgan Gardner, Interview).

The transition of the Benemérito School was indicative of widespread change in many things related to missionary work during the time Elder Nelson chaired the MEC. Seasonal initiatives at Easter and Christmas sponsored by the MEC—such as "Because of Him" and "Light the World"—encouraged members to spread the gospel and helped them do so by providing videos and other content easy to share online. Some of the videos ultimately had tens of millions of views in dozens of languages. For sister missionaries, new leadership opportunities as sister training leaders emerged. Certain missions began testing electronics as a way to spur missionary work and gave missionaries iPhones and iPads, including access to the internet, with all the challenges that entailed.

Change often creates growing pains, and these advancements in missionary work were no different. Some young men, swept up in the eighteen-year-old movement, went on missions before they were ready. Some sisters, caught up in a wave of "Why not serve since we

The Missionary Training Center in Mexico City.

can go so much earlier," were not adequately prepared. The number of missionaries not completing their missions increased. Access to technology and the web was too enticing for some missionaries. And there were naysayers who pointed out that though the number of missionaries had increased dramatically, the number of baptisms had not.

But when all was said and done, "we did not make this change because we expected more converts," Elder Nelson explained. "We did it to stop the hemorrhage and to save the lifeblood of the Church."

It was under Elder Nelson's leadership, said Elder W. Craig Zwick of the Seventy, then serving on the MEC, that electronic devices first went out to young missionaries. "He is the consummate teacher because he can identify with new material. He felt we could build them, teach them how important it was to keep their hearts and minds clean, and have them come back stronger" (*Church News*/KSL Interview, January 5, 2018).

Elder Gregory A. Schwitzer of the Seventy, also a member of the MEC at the time of this historic announcement, observed Elder Nelson's leadership style in various situations and settings. One day there was an open discussion in the MEC about the impact of recent changes, including both positives and negatives. Some General Authorities wondered out loud if they were sending missionaries out too young; others questioned giving them electronic devices. The attendees were respectful while probing tough questions that deserved discussion. "Elder Nelson listened quietly and then said: 'My brethren, remember why we made these decisions. We made them to save the next generation.' That statement has echoed in my mind," said Elder Schwitzer. "Elder Nelson was always focused on the missionary, the one who's out there knocking on doors, walking on rough streets, living in circumstances that aren't ideal. That's where his concern is. That's where his heart is. That's what I call a shepherd of the shepherds" (*Church News*/KSL Interview, January 8, 2018).

PART FOUR

PRESIDENT OF THE TWELVE, PRESIDENT OF THE CHURCH

———

2015 TO PRESENT

> "The worst thing I could have is a quorum full of 'yes men.'"
>
> —President Russell M. Nelson

A t the April 2015 general conference, Elder L. Tom Perry spoke with unusual power. The previous November he had accompanied President Henry B. Eyring and Bishop Gérald Caussé to Rome, where President Eyring had spoken at the colloquium on marriage and family at the Vatican. Elder Perry's subsequent testimony at general conference about the sanctity of marriage and family was strong, even booming. Social media chatter following conference was filled with speculation that, in light of President Monson's declining health and the increasing frailty of President Boyd K. Packer, Elder Perry might well become the next President of the Church.

But just days later, on April 24, Elder Perry shared the shocking news that he had just been diagnosed with advanced thyroid cancer that had spread to his lungs. The cancer was terminal, and it was just a matter of time before it took his life. Unfortunately, the time proved to be short. Little more than a month later, on May 30, he passed away at the age of ninety-two.

Elder Nelson spoke to Elder Perry for the last time by phone from Sofia, Bulgaria. He had

With Elder L. Tom Perry.

Elder and Sister Nelson had the privilege of attending the dedication of the Brigham City Temple on September 23, 2012, with his quorum president, President Boyd K. Packer, Elder Allan F. Packer, Donna Packer, Terri Packer, Barbara Perry, Elder L. Tom Perry, and Elder William R. Walker. Elder L. Whitney Clayton and his wife, Kathy, are in the back.

visited his ailing colleague, with whom he had served in the Quorum of the Twelve for thirty-one years, before leaving for Europe. Their final conversation was marked by expressions of love, Elder Perry's trademark enthusiasm and encouragement for the work, and optimism for their reunion at a future day on the other side of the veil. In terms of apostolic seniority, Elder Nelson now sat third, behind President Monson and President Packer.

Then, not quite five weeks later, the unexpected happened again. Without any advance warning, on the morning of Friday, July 3, President Packer's family summoned Elder Nelson and Elder Dallin H. Oaks to their father's home. Only days before, his doctor had told President Packer that, despite his weakening condition, he would

The Quorum of the Twelve Apostles in October 2015. Seated (left to right): Elders Russell M. Nelson, Dallin H. Oaks, M. Russell Ballard, Robert D. Hales, and Jeffrey R. Holland. Standing (left to right): Elders David A. Bednar, Quentin L. Cook, D. Todd Christofferson, Neil L. Andersen, Ronald A. Rasband, Gary E. Stevenson, and Dale G. Renlund.

likely live several more years. Then suddenly, Friday morning, he took a turn for the worse, and by 2:00 p.m. he was gone. In little more than a month, Elder Nelson had gone from sitting fourth in seniority to now becoming the new President of the Quorum of the Twelve Apostles.

"When a man is called to the Quorum of the Twelve Apostles," said Elder Nelson, "he is aware of where that road can lead, though none of us focus on that. We focus on the work to be done, and there is always plenty of work to be done."

He loved his Brethren of the Twelve as though they were his blood brothers. For more than thirty years he had learned from and sat in counsel with the likes of Elders Marvin J. Ashton, Bruce R. McConkie, James E. Faust, Neal A. Maxwell, and David B. Haight.

They had been his mentors, his colleagues, and his friends. And the quorum over which he now presided was filled with men of the same stellar caliber and spiritual strength: Dallin H. Oaks, M. Russell Ballard, Richard G. Scott, Robert D. Hales, Jeffrey R. Holland, David A. Bednar, Quentin L. Cook, D. Todd Christofferson, and Neil L. Andersen. What an unspeakable privilege it was to serve alongside each of them!

Despite his three decades as a member of the Twelve, President Nelson's view of the work to be done enlarged even further as President of the quorum. "It is a matter of duty," he explained. "As a member of the Twelve, you accept whatever assignments the President of the quorum gives you. Those might be working on the Missionary Executive Council, or Priesthood and Family Executive Council, and so forth. They might also include supervising the work in various areas of the world. You accept the assignments you receive and do the best you can with them."

As President of the Twelve, however, he was now responsible for leading the quorum and making those assignments. "With that you have two things in mind: what is best for the work and what is best for the man," President Nelson said. "Each member of the Twelve is an Apostle for the whole world, and in his years of experience he needs to learn about every part of the world, along with the people and languages and history. He needs to understand every part of Church administration. The President of the Twelve is responsible for making sure this happens for each Apostle, and he's also responsible for making every assignment to all of the Seventies. Being President of the Twelve is a huge responsibility."

With the passing of President Packer and Elder Perry, there were temporarily just ten men around the circle. And that number reduced again when, on September 22, 2015, Elder Richard G. Scott passed away. Then, in the October 2015 general conference, three new members of the Twelve were called: Elders Ronald A. Rasband, Gary E. Stevenson, and Dale G. Renlund.

The members of the Twelve found their new president to be open, inclusive, and intent on hearing from each man around the circle, including those most junior. If someone was conspicuously quiet on an issue, he would call on that colleague with: "We haven't heard from you yet. What do *you* think?" His rationale for wanting to hear equally from all was simple: "It takes the Lord a long time to school an Apostle. When that man is called to the

Russell M. Nelson shows a card Elder Richard G. Scott gave him after they served on an assignment together. The card was more than a thank-you note. It included a copy of an Elder Scott painting.

Twelve, the Lord has something unique He expects that man to contribute. We need to be sure we help that happen." To facilitate open discussion, President Nelson tried to create an environment in their meetings not always dominated by the clock or a pressing agenda.

"President Nelson is a wonderful listener," said Elder Jeffrey R. Holland. "That isn't a talent some of us have cultivated. We talk a lot. We're called on to speak all the time. We are witnesses. We are testifiers. But he has shown us how to be a wonderful listener."

Elder Holland recalled one discussion in the Quorum of the Twelve that was indicative of others. The conversation had gone around the room at length. Most had spoken their minds on the matter. Finally, Elder Holland said he would like to know how President Nelson felt about the discussion. "He said to us that he had been listening to the discussion and had feelings on the matter but that he wanted to think more about it before he offered his opinion. He wanted to think and listen to the Lord. And that's not a bad lesson for all of us. We are probably not learning much if we're doing all of the talking" (*Church News*/KSL Interview, January 9, 2018).

Through the years, and in many capacities, President Nelson had witnessed many leadership styles—surgeons who were so mean or condescending that to be in the operating room with them was terrifying if not plain miserable; businessmen who felt the way to drive a bottom line was by driving people and "beating them up" if necessary; teachers whose every word came across as a stern and sometimes punitive lecture, accompanied by the unspoken message, "It's my way or the highway," as they say.

"I just don't think that's the way you deal with people," President Nelson explained. "Everyone is a child of God and deserves to be treated that way. And by the time a man has been ordained an Apostle, what he needs is room to think, to pray, and to do the work he is uniquely prepared to do."

The new President of the Twelve welcomed, even encouraged, candor. "The worst thing I could have is a quorum full of 'yes men,'" he said. "The members of the Twelve are brilliant, every one of them. Absolutely brilliant. I wanted to hear what they each had to say." Because the quorum could not move forward on any initiative or take anything forward to the First Presidency without all being in agreement, he was eager to get everything on the table. When members of the Twelve disagreed with others' points of view, President Nelson would say, "Good, let's hear what you have to say."

"When like-minded men who are all dedicated and committed to the same cause have a difference of opinion, that just means we need more information," President Nelson explained. "We don't need to debate it longer at that point, we need to go back and study it more and gather more information, because we don't yet have enough information to agree."

Meeting room in the Church Administration Building where the Quorum of the Twelve and other General Authorities and General Officers meet.

"President Nelson has a very good sense of when something deserves more discussion and when we should just choose among alternatives and get on with the Lord's work," said Elder Dallin H. Oaks. "He's also a good delegator, an extremely good delegator, better than most leaders I've seen. I've formed a conclusion that it's because he was a surgeon, and it was necessary for him to delegate to others the preparation of the patient." Elder Oaks added, "He is very good at thinking through what the impact of a decision will be on youth, children, women, leaders, men, those trying to find their way back. He is not confrontive in his strategy for solving problems or getting things resolved. He is very inclined to allow time for things to work out" (*Church News*/KSL Interview, January 10, 2018).

These were skills he had acquired over time. Elder W. Craig Zwick remembered reporting to Elder Nelson as his first contact when he became the Area President in Brazil. At the time, the Church was having major challenges obtaining visas for missionaries called to serve there. "I asked Elder Nelson for a blessing, and he said the Lord was in charge and we will not stop assigning missionaries to Brazil. I learned very early his depth of faith and his willingness to let whoever was on the ground do the best they could. He shepherded us through in a masterful way" (conversation with author, November 6, 2018; see also *Church News*/KSL Interview, January 5, 2018).

Elder Neil L. Andersen recalled his first opportunity to travel on a weekend stake conference assignment with Elder Nelson. It was June 1993, he had just been called to the First Quorum of the Seventy, and they were assigned to call a new stake presidency in the Pocatello Highland Stake, next door to the high school Elder Andersen had attended as a boy.

After they interviewed all the candidates, Elder Nelson asked the

Elder Nelson's mentorship of Elder Andersen began in the early 1990s. Here the two enjoy a moment in those days with their wives, Dantzel and Kathy.

new Seventy if he would like to take a walk. "On that walk of thirty minutes, he taught me about revelation and how the Lord would communicate with me in the coming years as I served as an instrument in His hands in calling new stake presidents. These teachings have stayed prominently with me for the past twenty-five years."

Elder Andersen soaked in his mentor's teachings while also noticing Elder Nelson's attention to individuals. "I was amazed not only at Elder Nelson's teachings but his personal concern for everyone he met. On that Saturday we may have interviewed thirty to forty men. That evening and the next day before and after the meetings, he referred to each of them by name, and mostly by first name." Elder Andersen asked him how he could remember the names so well, and Elder Nelson responded, "Neil, why wouldn't I remember them? I want to know them and keep them in my memory. It is really a matter of concentration. If you want to remember them, you will."

"I have never been able to duplicate the intelligence I observed in Elder Nelson," Elder Andersen summarized, "but his teaching has made me much more attentive to people I meet" (Andersen, Facebook post).

Those who worked under Elder Nelson's mentorship, in whatever capacity, found him to be a man of superb judgment but someone who never judged them. And that openness and inclusive, collaborative style tended to bring out the best in those serving under his direction.

When asked what he considered his approach to leadership to be, President Nelson said, boiling down the challenge, "If you're a leader and servant in the Lord's Church, then you had better do your best to lead in the Lord's way."

The Susquehanna River.

> "Of all the priesthood assignments I've received in my life, the opportunity to dedicate the Priesthood Restoration Site was perhaps the most important."
>
> —President Russell M. Nelson

The Susquehanna River and its riverbanks have remained largely untouched since the late 1820s, when Joseph and Emma Smith moved to the area of Harmony, Pennsylvania, hoping to escape the persecution they had experienced in Palmyra, New York. Emma was born and raised nearby, and her parents and other family members still lived there. Isaac Hale sold the young couple 13.5 acres, and they moved into a small, three-room frame home Emma's brother Jesse had built.

The events that then transpired would forever secure for the Susquehanna and its surrounds a sacred place in the history of the Church. Joseph translated most of the Book of Mormon there, with Oliver Cowdery as his scribe. In the process, in response to a question the Book of Mormon prompted about authority, in May 1829 Joseph and Oliver retired to a grove of maple trees not far from Joseph and Emma's home. As the two men prayed, they heard the voice of the Lord speaking to them, and then "the veil was parted and the angel of God came down clothed with glory, and delivered the anxiously looked for message, and the keys of the Gospel of repentance" (Cowdery, "Dear Brother," 14–16).

That messenger was the resurrected being John the Baptist, who explained that he was acting under the direction of Peter, James, and John, who held the keys of the higher priesthood. With the laying on of hands, John the Baptist then bestowed priesthood authority upon Joseph Smith and Oliver Cowdery. In doing so, he conferred "the keys of the ministering of angels, and of the gospel of repentance, and of baptism by immersion for the remission of sins" (Doctrine and Covenants 13:1). Then followed the first baptisms in this dispensation when Joseph baptized Oliver, and Oliver did the same for Joseph in the nearby Susquehanna River.

Not many days thereafter, the Prophet Joseph and Oliver were taught again by heavenly messengers when Peter, James, and John appeared and conferred upon them the Melchizedek Priesthood. With this, Joseph Smith now had the keys to organize the Church, send forth missionaries, and ordain other priesthood leaders.

Other than the Sacred Grove in upstate New York, perhaps no other location was as central to the Restoration of the gospel of Jesus Christ as the area in and around Harmony, Pennsylvania. These pivotal events paved the way for the reorganization of the Lord's Church.

On September 19, 2015, President and Sister Nelson traveled to the greater Harmony area to dedicate the renovated Priesthood Restoration Site. As they prepared for the trip, President Nelson told his wife that of all the priesthood assignments he had received in his life, the opportunity to dedicate the Priesthood Restoration site was perhaps the most important.

They arrived at the site and were joined by Elder Steven E. Snow of the Seventy, Church Historian and Recorder, and his wife, Phyllis, along with Bishop Gary E. Stevenson and his wife, Lesa. As they began to experience all that was there, that feeling of the importance of the site only intensified. The Nelsons visited the restored cabin where Joseph and Emma had lived and where much of the Book of Mormon had been translated. They walked through the woods along a new trail system that connected the visitors' center to the historic area—a grove of sugar maple trees on the north end of the Hale farm property—where Church historians believe the priesthood restoration

President and Sister Nelson at the Priesthood Restoration Site.

occurred. They expected the experience to be unforgettable, and it was that and more.

"You cannot walk on those grounds and not feel something," Sister Nelson marveled. "For me, the reality of the priesthood and priesthood keys was palpable. The feeling in those sacred maple woods where the Aaronic and Melchizedek Priesthoods were restored was right there with the Sacred Grove for me. I told my husband, 'There is another sacred grove. It is a sacred maple grove. That is very holy ground.'"

President Nelson was struck yet again by all that the Prophet Joseph accomplished in his young life. "I had of course always marveled at the profound nature of the Book of Mormon, but I had not fully appreciated the humble circumstances, the cramped and unfavorable conditions Joseph dealt with during translation. You look at all of the accomplishments of Joseph Smith, and they are almost unbelievable. They are astounding. And then add to that the fact that

President and Sister Nelson with other Church leaders and their wives on the bank of the Susquehanna River.

The restored cabin where Joseph and Emma lived.

President and Sister Nelson at the grave of Joseph and Emma's infant son.

he didn't have a moment of peace from the time he had that First Vision. Even his own in-laws made life tough for him. His father-in-law wanted to see the plates, so Joseph had to hide them from him every night. It is remarkable to contemplate it all."

Adding to the unique burdens the young Prophet and his wife carried, Emma had given birth on June 15, 1828, to a son who lived only a few hours. And she was then near death herself. For some weeks, Joseph devoted most of his energy to caring for her. It was she who insisted that, despite her condition, Joseph travel back to Manchester, New York, to find out what had happened to the first 116 pages of Book of Mormon manuscript he had loaned Martin Harris. When Joseph discovered they were gone, he was inconsolable. His mother, Lucy, described "sobs and groans and the most bitter lamentations" filling the home and recorded that Joseph paced "backwards and forwards weeping and grieving like a tender infant until about sunset." Through it all, Joseph cried out, "Of what rebuke am I not worthy from the Angel of the most high?" (see Nelson, "Historic

A replica of the desk where much of the Book of Mormon was translated.

Site"). When Emma later learned about the lost 116 pages, the grief, added to her already frail state, almost killed her.

In the dedicatory service, President Nelson attempted to put the importance of all that occurred in Harmony in perspective. "Harmony provided Joseph with spiritual solitude and protection, allowing him to focus on the translation of the Book of Mormon," he said. "Through this period, the Lord tutored Joseph in his divine role as prophet, seer, and revelator. Receiving the priesthood empowered Joseph Smith to function fully as the prophet of this last dispensation. Here he worked during a remarkable and formative season of translation, revelation, and restoration" (Nelson, "Historic Site").

President and Sister Nelson left the Harmony area with strengthened testimonies about the reality of the Restoration and the heaven-directed process of the coming forth of the Book of Mormon. And they felt an even greater reverence for the priesthood keys that heavenly messengers returned to the earth—the same keys that had passed in an unbroken line from Joseph Smith to President Thomas S. Monson, the very keys that gave prophets, seers, and revelators in The Church of Jesus Christ of Latter-day Saints authority to administer the Church in the name of God the Father and His Son Jesus Christ.

"Men provide for the present. But women shape the future."

—President Russell M. Nelson

In his first general conference address as President of the Quorum of the Twelve, in October 2015, President Nelson spoke directly to the sisters of the Church, reminding them of who they were in the Lord's eyes and how crucial they were in the work of the Lord. For many women, his message was a clarion call, even a game changer in the way a senior leader viewed their significance in building the kingdom of God.

In "A Plea to My Sisters," he minced no words about what the Lord expected from His covenant daughters: "We need your impressions, your insights, and your inspiration. We need you to speak up and speak out in ward and stake councils," he urged, continuing: "We need women who have a bedrock understanding of the doctrine of Christ and who will use that understanding to teach and help raise a sin-resistant generation. We need women who can detect deception in all of its forms. . . . We need women who have the courage and vision of Mother Eve." And he declared, simply, "We

President Nelson urged women to develop a bedrock understanding of the doctrine of Christ.

brethren cannot duplicate your unique influence" (Nelson, "Plea to My Sisters").

The impetus for what many women regarded as a landmark message to and about them was straightforward: "Men provide for the present," he said, "but women shape the future. I wanted to try to help the sisters of the Church understand how distinctive, how irreplaceable they are in the Lord's work."

In his address, President Nelson referred to a prophecy President Spencer W. Kimball had made thirty-nine years earlier that "much of the major growth that is coming to the Church in the last days will come because many of the good women of the world . . . will be drawn to the Church in large numbers. This will happen to the degree that the women of the Church reflect righteousness and articulateness in their lives and to the degree that the women of the Church are seen as distinct and different—in happy ways—from the women of the world" (*Teachings: Spencer W. Kimball*, 222–23). President Nelson then declared without reservation that the women living today were the ones President Kimball foresaw—that they would be the ones to fulfill prophecy.

No one who had known President Nelson through the years was the least bit surprised by his message. "I never heard him refer to my grandmother as anything other than an angel mother," grandson Stephen McKellar said (*Church News*/KSL Interview, January 11, 2018). David Webster said that every time his father-in-law received a medical award or was asked why he chose medicine, "he would say, 'Because I couldn't choose to be a mother.' He believed that, and he lived that way. His respect for women has shone through everything he's done" (*Church News*/KSL Interview, January 10, 2018).

One evening, while speaking with some energy on a topic he deeply cared about to a Spanish-speaking congregation in South America, President Nelson said, "As *the mother* of ten children, I can tell you that . . ." and then finished the sentence. The translator, assuming he had simply misspoken, translated him saying "as the father of ten children." But Sister Nelson heard the Freudian slip and took some delight in making note of it. "When Russell says he chose medicine because he couldn't choose motherhood, he means it," she said. "He has deep personal feelings about how vital women are. One of the first things I learned about him was how deeply he respects womanhood and motherhood and how crucial he believes women are to the Church."

His actions spoke as persuasively as did his words. In May 2015 then-Elder Nelson and Sister Nelson traveled to the Europe East Area, beginning in Moscow. Susan Porter, wife of Elder Bruce D. Porter, the Area President, was struck by the way Elder Nelson handled a member devotional in Moscow.

Prior to the meeting, he asked Elder and Sister Porter, along with Elder Donald L. and Sister Diane Hallstrom, who were accompanying them, to each speak. When Sister Porter asked how long he would like her to take, he answered that she should take as long as she needed. To preserve as much time for Elder Nelson as possible, however, the Porters and Hallstroms kept their remarks short. Then, Sister Nelson got up and gave a marvelous message for twenty minutes. "I glanced over at Elder Nelson, who was as relaxed as could be and soaking up every word that Wendy had to say as he looked at the congregation with love," Sister Porter remembered.

Elder Nelson then took the remainder of the time. "He greeted the Saints in Russian, spoke from his heart, and bore a pure testimony. When he concluded I felt I had witnessed something very significant. I prayed that the Russian Saints were paying attention. The soon-to-be President of the Quorum of the Twelve had spoken with his actions about the importance of the witness of women in this, The Church of Jesus Christ of Latter-day Saints. This pattern continued throughout the trip" (email from Susan Porter to author, August 13, 2018).

One of the other memorable moments on that trip occurred the next morning when the Nelsons and Porters, along with Russia Vladivostok Mission President Gregory S. Brinton, his wife, Sally, and their son Sam drove by van to Lake Baikal, the largest, deepest rift lake in the world. This lake, according to the Buryat people, was visited by the Savior after His Resurrection, and for that reason, Elder Porter thought the Nelsons might enjoy the rare opportunity to visit its shores and experience its surroundings. The Nelsons marveled at the feeling surrounding the lake, which has more fresh water than the five Great Lakes of the United States and Canada combined. That sacred feeling continued as they walked briefly through a lakeside marketplace.

Visiting Lake Baikal in Russia. Left to right: Susan Porter, Elder Bruce Porter, Gregory Brinton, Sally Brinton, Wendy Nelson, President Nelson, and Sam Brinton.

Then Sam Brinton, who had just returned from serving in the Russia Yekaterinburg Mission, struck up a conversation with a woman named Valentina who was selling fish in the market. Valentina was so taken with this bright young man that she asked to meet his mother. Much to her surprise, Sam walked her to the van where the rest of the party were waiting. "I want to meet this young man's mother," she explained in her native Russian. "He is so polite, intelligent, and kind. I want to meet his *mother*!" (see Nelson, "Becoming True Millennials"; also email from Wendy Watson Nelson to author, August 11, 2018).

Valentina's reaction illustrated President Nelson's deeply held belief that women have such irreplaceable impact on children and youth that they literally shape the future.

He had experienced firsthand the mothering of his own mother, of his wife Dantzel, who mothered their large family masterfully, and of Wendy, whom he saw mother not only members of their family but friends, wives of General Authorities and mission presidents in need of encouragement, and countless others. And he had had the inevitable schooling that came as the father of nine daughters and a daughter-in-law who is loved like a daughter. He had watched them follow in their mother's footsteps and have tremendous influence in their families, in the Church, and far beyond. "How I adore my daughters!" he said. "They shape the future of the world, those girls. They know how to build faith, how to have fun, how to teach, how to make a home. They can do it all. They are mothers in the loftiest sense of the word. Mothers shape the destiny of the future."

With twenty-six granddaughters, many of them now mothers in their own right, and sixty-four great-granddaughters (and counting), he could only imagine that the influence of the women he was closest to—those in his own family—would do nothing but continue to multiply.

To them and to each covenant daughter, President Nelson issued a plea: "I plead with my sisters of The Church of Jesus Christ of Latter-day Saints to step forward! Take your rightful and needful place in your home, in your community, and in the kingdom of God— more than you ever have before. I plead with you to fulfill President Kimball's prophecy. And I promise you in the name of Jesus Christ that as you do so, the Holy Ghost will magnify your influence in an unprecedented way!" ("Plea to My Sisters").

President Nelson and his son, Russell Jr., are used to being outnumbered by women in family gatherings, as in this Mother's Day photo. Left to right: Russell Jr., Gloria Irion, Sylvia Webster, Laurie Marsh, President Nelson and Wendy, Marjorie Lowder, granddaughter Olivia Nelson, daughter-in-law Britney Nelson, Brenda Miles, Rosalie Ringwood, and Wendy Maxfield.

"Brother Nelson, we are not sealed to anyone. Can you help us?"

—Laural Ann and Gay Lynn Hatfield

During the late 1950s, while he was in the early days of his surgical career, Dr. Nelson had attempted to save the lives of two little girls from the same family—Laural Ann and Gay Lynn Hatfield, the daughters of Jimmy and Ruth. Both girls had died. It was a traumatic series of events for all involved.

Understandably, the parents were grief-stricken, but they were also spiritually shattered. Not only did they lose two daughters, they lost their faith in God. And, from their point of view, it was their surgeon's fault. He should have been able to save their girls' lives.

For decades they had been angry at Russell M. Nelson for failing them, and that anger festered and blossomed into a deep resentment that led them away from the Church. The Hatfields weren't shy about expressing their anger, even hatred, toward Dr. Nelson. That anger only intensified when Dr. Nelson became Elder Nelson, called to serve in the Quorum of the Twelve Apostles.

Elder Nelson was well aware of this hostility, and it grieved him. Not only had the death of those two girls hurt him deeply at the time, but he was devastated that he'd had a part in the Hatfields' disaffection from the Church. He felt personally responsible for their inactivity as well as the invective they spewed anytime someone mentioned his or the Church's name. Repeatedly through the years, he had attempted to establish contact with Jimmy and Ruth—usually working through local priesthood leaders to help him. But to no avail. One stake president after another had told him that the Hatfields literally hated him.

And they always refused to see him. For a man whose basic nature is to avoid contention and resolve differences quickly, the situation gnawed at Elder Nelson. It was a heartache that had haunted him for years.

Then, one night in 2015—nearly sixty years after the first failed operation—Elder Nelson was awakened in the middle of the night by those two Hatfield daughters from the other side of the veil. He did not see or hear them with his physical senses, but he felt their presence and, spiritually, could hear their pleadings. They had one short but clear message for him: "Brother Nelson, we are not sealed to anyone! Can you help us?" (Nelson, "Price of Priesthood Power").

The next morning he told Wendy about the vivid experience he'd

The Hatfield family and friends gather outside the Payson Utah Temple. Jimmy Hatfield is at President Nelson's left.

had during the night, and, with renewed determination, he again tried to contact the Hatfields. This time, he learned through the stake president and bishop where Jimmy and his son Shawn lived that Ruth Hatfield had passed away. Much to his surprise, the father and son agreed to meet with him.

The Hatfields lived in a small community south of Provo, Utah. Out of convenience for them, Elder Nelson arranged to meet with Jimmy and Shawn, along with their stake president and bishop, on June 26, 2015, during the seminar for newly called mission presidents held annually at the Provo Missionary Training Center.

The feeling was strained as Elder Nelson entered the room. The Hatfields weren't going to make this visit pleasant for the General Authority they had hated for years. Elder Nelson began the conversation and during the first few minutes felt he was getting nowhere. Finally, he knelt in front of the eighty-eight-year-old Jimmy Hatfield. He told him about the thinning of the veil he'd experienced a few weeks earlier and of Laural Ann and Gay Lynn's pleadings to be sealed to their parents. He then said, "Jimmy, I would be honored to be the one that seals your wife to you and your children to you and your wife."

As Elder Nelson quietly spoke to Jimmy, the Spirit flooded the room. Jimmy Hatfield was now listening, and it became clear that Elder Nelson's words were resonating with this father's tender heart. Elder Nelson told him what would be required for him to prepare to be ready and worthy to enter the temple, and then said, "You're eighty-eight and I'm ninety, so that means you'd better hurry." After a few moments, Jimmy responded, "All right, I'll do it."

Elder Nelson then turned to Jimmy's son and said, "Shawn, this family is going to be sealed. Will you be sealed with them?" and he responded, "Yes, I will."

The Hatfield men were true to their word. With the help of their priesthood leaders, home teachers, and ward mission leader—as well as young missionaries and a senior missionary couple—they took the necessary steps to enter the temple to receive their own endowments.

During the intervening months, President Nelson had become President of the Quorum of the Twelve, and on November 24, 2015, he had the "profound privilege" of sealing Ruth and Jimmy Hatfield and then their four children to them in the Payson Utah Temple. President and Sister Nelson, the Hatfields, and countless friends and family wept that day as many hearts, including Hatfield hearts on both sides of the veil, were healed. For the first time in decades, President Nelson no longer felt the anguish of knowing he was hated by the Hatfield family.

He subsequently spoke about this experience in general conference: "On reflection, I have marveled at Jimmy and Shawn and what they were willing to do," he said. "They have become heroes to me. If I could have the wish of my heart, it would be that each man and young man in this Church would demonstrate the courage, strength, and humility of this father and son. They were willing to forgive and let go of old hurts and habits. . . . Each was willing to become a man who worthily bears the priesthood 'after the holiest order of God'" ("Price of Priesthood Power").

Elder Gregory A. Schwitzer was sitting on the stand and looking into the faces of the Hatfield family as President Nelson spoke. "I could see their emotion. Afterwards, President Nelson went down from the stand, and they were the first people he made contact with. He was still caring about his patients" (*Church News*/KSL Interview, January 8, 2018).

Finally, after nearly six decades, President Nelson had been able to help heal Hatfield hearts. In the process, his own heart was healed.

"We were amazed when I was warmly welcomed as an 'old friend of China' and reunited with surgeons I had taught thirty-five years earlier."

—President Russell M. Nelson

In November 2015, President and Sister Nelson traveled to China on a visit that included a return to his old stomping grounds at the Shandong University School of Medicine in Jinan. What he saw there both surprised and delighted him. The Jinan of the early eighties had boasted one traffic light. Now there were freeways, parking terraces, high-rise buildings, and infrastructure improvements everywhere. During his visits twenty-five years earlier, he had walked the dusty city streets at night and used his modest Mandarin vocabulary to talk to the children. Today he returned to a far more modern city and a greatly improved medical center.

It was a wonderful walk down memory lane. "We were amazed when I was warmly welcomed and reunited with surgeons I had taught thirty-five years earlier," he reported. A highlight of the visit was meeting with the son and grandson of Mr. Fang Rongxiang, the opera star whose life he had saved in 1985. Mr. Fang's relatives traveled to Jinan to present President Nelson with a framed remembrance of that lifesaving operation.

He was also able to contact via Facetime his dear friend and colleague Dr. Zhang, who was once again living in China, in Qingdao, on the eastern side of the Shandong province. The two old colleagues and friends reminisced about their years of experiences there at the medical school. And then, when the head of the delegation greeting

President Nelson is honored by the son and grandson of Fang Rongxiang, the opera star whose life he saved.

them in Jinan gave President Nelson the title of "Old Friend of China," it was the proverbial icing on the cake for him.

"The Chinese revere their seniors; they honor the elderly. So to be called an Old Friend of China is about the highest compliment you can get from them," President Nelson explained.

This trip yielded other significant moments as well. In both Shanghai and Beijing, the Chinese government allowed President Nelson to meet with Chinese Church members and even speak to them. "It was a first to have an expatriate, let alone a General Authority, speak to Chinese members," he explained. "It was a high privilege for me."

Sister Nelson also had the opportunity to speak to the local Chinese Latter-day Saints in their sacrament meeting in what was a new and unforgettable experience: "What makes these Chinese members so irresistible? They have open, light-filled faces with eyes so clear and filled with light that they look deeply into your eyes, your soul. Something happens to me when I look at them. I just want to stare—to help me remember them, perhaps, from our premortal experiences together.

"Our Chinese members have made so many sacrifices," she continued. "That is one of the keys. They love keeping the commandments. Actually, they are thrilled to keep the commandments because they know they are from God. They know the Church is led by God and His worthy leaders. Based on my interactions with them before the meeting, I was prepared to have the feeling in that sacrament meeting be special, but I never expected that room to feel like a temple. And it did."

During this trip, President Nelson could not help but think about President Spencer W. Kimball. In the notes he had taken in the 1978 regional representatives' seminar that prompted him to begin to learn Mandarin, he had written, in all caps: "WHEN WE ARE READY, THE LORD WILL USE US." He had tried to make himself ready, and now, almost forty years later, he owed his love for China and its people to the urgings of a prophet.

"At that point, we knew that whatever the Brethren had in mind in that interview was now off the table, because the only member of the Quorum of the Twelve for whom any of this explanation would mean anything was seated across from us."

—Susan Porter

On December 28, 2016, Elder Bruce D. Porter of the Seventy passed away at the age of sixty-four. Eight days later, President and Sister Nelson attended his funeral, where President Nelson was the concluding speaker.

His long and watchful care over Elder Porter and his wife, Susan, had begun more than twenty years earlier, when in February 1995 he had invited them to his office for a get-acquainted visit. Bruce Porter's background fascinated Elder Nelson. Bruce had received graduate degrees in Russian studies and political science from Harvard, followed by a career spent studying Soviet foreign policy. At the time, he had recently joined the political science faculty at BYU.

Bruce Porter's expertise on Russia coupled with Elder Nelson's extensive experience in Eastern Europe and the former USSR made for a lively conversation that first meeting. Among other things, he asked the Porters how their health was. Bruce explained that he had a congenital kidney defect that had been surgically corrected after his mission. But he acknowledged that doctors had told him his kidneys would continue to decline until they failed, and there was nothing the doctors could do about it. Elder Nelson asked for Bruce's creatinine clearance number. "At that point," Susan remembered, "we knew

Elder Bruce Porter and his wife, Susan.

that whatever the Brethren had in mind in that interview was now off the table, because the only member of the Quorum of the Twelve for whom any of this explanation would mean anything was seated across from us" (email from Susan Porter to author, August 13, 2018).

Susan was struck by how focused Elder Nelson was on the two of them. "He exuded a calmness that was contagious," she said. Following the interview, he took them on what he described as a "cook's tour" of the building and introduced them to President Monson, President Packer, and Elder Hales. They drove home marveling about this once-in-a-lifetime experience. Their time with Elder Nelson seemed all the more remarkable when they later learned that his daughter Emily had recently passed away. "I was overwhelmed that in his grief he had been able to give us his all," Susan said.

Much to their surprise, just a few weeks later, and five days before the April 1995 general conference, President Gordon B. Hinckley called Bruce Porter to the Second Quorum of the Seventy and assigned him to serve as the second counselor in the Europe East Area Presidency, headquartered then in Frankfurt, Germany.

"From this moment on," Susan recalled, "Elder Russell M. Nelson became a support to Bruce. He watched over him and was ever mindful of his health."

The Porters moved to Europe, and "Bruce was in heaven!" Susan remembered. He relished playing a role in helping take the gospel to the lands of Eastern Europe. Twenty months later, however, his kidneys failed, and, leaving three of their four children in Frankfurt, Susan flew back to Salt Lake City with a very ill husband. "Elder Russell M. Nelson was there to greet us at the airport," Susan said. "He was compassionate, he was kind, and he was dignified."

Over the next thirteen years, Elder Porter served in various assignments at Church headquarters while he endured two failed kidney transplants, twelve years of dialysis, and multiple operations. "For every medical procedure, Elder Nelson made sure that Bruce had the best doctors and that they were giving him the best treatment," Susan recounted. "He gave Bruce several blessings that brought power into our lives. The Lord was very generous with us."

In 2010 the Porters' son David donated a kidney to his father, freeing him from the restrictions of dialysis and totally changing the daily routine in Susan and Bruce's home. They were now grilling salmon for dinner together rather than being ruled by the dialysis machine for hours each day. In consultation with his doctors and Elder Nelson, in 2014 Bruce was cleared to receive an assignment to go back to serve in the Europe East Area Presidency. "Bruce was overjoyed," Susan remembered. "Elder Nelson gave me instructions to watch over him and keep him well." And off they went.

The Porters were thrilled when Elder and Sister Nelson visited their area in May 2015 and had unforgettable experiences with them in Moscow, Novosibirsk, and Irkutsk, which was five time zones east of Moscow.

Because no Apostle had ever before visited Irkutsk, some of the 207 members who attended sacrament meeting Sunday morning in a large room in a local hotel rode all night by bus from Ulan Ude to attend. "He bore testimony," Susan recalled. "He encouraged them. He lifted them and he loved them. At the end of his remarks he pronounced an apostolic blessing on them." It was a stunning spiritual experience.

"Elder Nelson was dignified, fully present, kind and considerate, and gentle" throughout the trip, Susan said. "He never seemed rushed or occupied with a schedule to meet or an agenda to satisfy."

Whenever they boarded a plane, Elder Nelson quickly grabbed the Porters' luggage and lifted the cases into the overhead bins. "I would give anything to have a picture of us boarding a small plane from the runway. Elder Nelson grabbed both of our carry-ons and ran up the stairs before we could say, 'Wait!'" Susan remembered. "His security officer carried Elder and Sister Nelson's suitcases, and up we went, with an Apostle almost thirty years our senior having carried our luggage for us. Elder Nelson was always solicitous of Bruce's energy and health, not wanting to overtax him."

Elder and Sister Porter relished their time with the Nelsons as well as every day, every week they had in Russia. They couldn't have been happier. But their time there was short. In November 2016, Elder Porter suddenly fell gravely ill. He was helping mash potatoes and stir gravy in preparation for a Thanksgiving dinner in Moscow with their fellow American families who were serving for the Church when he admitted to Susan that he felt weak and tired. Three days later, when he felt short of breath, they went to the hospital, and that night his health literally collapsed. As soon as it became clear that Elder Porter's condition would not improve, the Porters were flown home by a medical transport, and Elder Porter was taken directly to the hospital.

"This continued President Nelson's ministry of love to Bruce," Susan remembered. "We had heard how President Nelson watched over the General Authorities who were in the hospital. This time his ministry focused on us. For the next two weeks, President Nelson and Elder Hallstrom visited every few days. Upon arriving at the hospital, President Nelson would wait until it was an appropriate time and then walk to Bruce's side, hold his hand, and gaze into his eyes. He would stand silently as I imagined that he was trying to feel the Lord's Spirit and direction. If Bruce was awake, he would speak to him with gentleness and love. He listened intently even when Bruce's speech may have been hard to understand. Then he would step aside and speak to me about the situation."

Ultimately, "President Nelson gave Bruce a blessing and invoked our Heavenly Father's blessing and His will. He expressed gratitude for Bruce's service in Eastern Europe.

"A crowning blessing for us," Susan concluded, "was President Nelson's gracious desire to speak at Bruce's funeral. His words were a healing balm to our wounded souls" (email from Susan Porter to author, August 13, 2018).

In his message at Elder Porter's funeral, President Nelson referred to a stalwart Russian couple the Nelsons and Porters both knew—Viacheslav and Galina Efimov, early Russian converts who were called to preside over the Yekaterinburg Mission just a few years after their baptism. President Efimov had passed away suddenly, and Galina told President Nelson that she felt they were still doing missionary work together, just on different sides of the veil. President Nelson then spoke directly to Susan, expressing his faith that this would be the case with her and her husband—they would continue to serve and help gather Israel, but on different sides of the veil for a season.

"You could have given me diamonds or rubies, but nothing is more precious to me than this additional knowledge about the Lord Jesus Christ."

—African Tribal King

n the April 2017 general conference, President Thomas S. Monson spoke only briefly to the general membership of the Church, but his message was clear: Read the Book of Mormon. "I implore each of us to prayerfully study and ponder the Book of Mormon each day," he said with as much energy as his weakening voice could muster. There was a promise for all who did, he said: "As we do so, we will be in a position to hear the voice of the Spirit, to resist temptation, to overcome doubt and fear, and to receive heaven's help in our lives" (Monson, "Power of the Book of Mormon").

Six months later, at the October general conference, President Nelson picked up the baton from President Monson, explaining what the prophet's words had meant to him and what he'd done about them. During the intervening time, he had asked various groups— beginning with his Brethren in the Quorum of the Twelve and going on to include missionaries in Chile and mission presidents and their wives serving in South America—to consider three questions: First, what would your life be like without the Book of Mormon? Second, what would you not know? And third, what would you not have?

The answers he received ran the gamut, such as:

• "Without the Book of Mormon, I would be confused about

the conflicting teachings and opinions about so many things. I would be just like I was before I found the Church."

- "I would not know about the role the Holy Ghost can play in my life."
- "I would not know that there is continuing progress after this life. Because of the Book of Mormon, I know that there really is life after death. That is the ultimate goal for which we are working."

In addition to initiating discussions about the power of the Book of Mormon in one setting after another, President Nelson took President Monson's challenge personally, reading a new copy of the Book of Mormon from cover to cover. In the process, he made lists about what the Book of Mormon is, what it affirms, what it refutes, what it fulfills, what it clarifies, and what it reveals. "Looking at the Book of Mormon through these lenses has been an insightful and inspiring exercise!" he told the general conference audience. "I recommend it to each of you" (Nelson, "The Book of Mormon: What Would Your Life Be Like without It?").

The Book of Mormon and its power to change lives was not a new theme for him. When asked how he obtained his testimony of the Book of Mormon, he couldn't identify anything dramatic. "I just knew it was true," he said, "and that living by it would make a difference in my life." That was why he told the army nurse who asked why he was different from other surgeons that, if he was different, it was because he knew the Book of Mormon was true.

In 1986 he had been invited to lecture at a university in Accra, Ghana. Prior to the lecture, he met an African tribal king who spoke to Elder Nelson through his linguist. After the lecture, the king sought out Elder Nelson and asked him directly, in perfect English, "Just who are you?"

Elder Nelson answered, "I am an ordained Apostle of Jesus Christ."

At that answer, the king asked, "What can you teach me about Jesus Christ?"

Elder Nelson replied, "May I ask what you already know about Him?"

The king's response let Elder Nelson know that the king was a serious student of the Bible and that he loved the Lord.

Elder Nelson then asked the king if he knew that Jesus Christ had appeared to and taught the people of ancient America. As Elder Nelson expected, the king did not know about that. Elder Nelson then explained that after the Savior's Crucifixion and Resurrection, He came to the people of ancient America, taught His gospel, organized His Church, and asked His disciples to keep a record of His ministry there. The Book of Mormon, he explained, contains a record of that ministry.

Elder Nelson turned to the mission president accompanying him and asked if he had an extra copy of the Book of Mormon with him, which he did. Elder Nelson opened it to 3 Nephi 11 and, with the king, read the Savior's sermon to the Nephites. When he handed the book to the king, the man responded, "You could have given me diamonds or rubies, but nothing is more precious to me than this additional knowledge about the Lord Jesus Christ" (see Nelson, "The Book of Mormon: What Would Your Life Be Like without It?").

Elder Nelson believed in the power of the Book of Mormon to change lives; he referenced it whenever possible and taught about its power again and again, including in spontaneous moments. One beautiful winter morning when Utah's deep powder snow was perfect for experienced skiers, he and Elder W. Craig Zwick headed to a nearby resort for a day on the slopes. As they hopped on the four-person chairlift for their umpteenth ride up the mountain, a young man skied up and got on with them. They remarked how wonderful it was that Monday morning to be out in the fresh Utah snow, and the young man responded, "Yes, but my life is in a shambles." Elder Zwick

President Nelson's personal copy of the Book of Mormon.

remembered, "I felt like saying, 'This is your lucky day,' and about then the man realized he was on the chairlift with President Nelson and gasped.

"In about four minutes," Elder Zwick related, "President Nelson taught that young man the importance of the Book of Mormon and promised that if he would read it every day, his problems wouldn't go away but they would be alleviated. That is how clearly he taught" (*Church News*/KSL Interview, January 5, 2018).

Whenever and wherever an opportunity presented itself, President Nelson taught what he believed about the Book of Mormon—that "as you prayerfully study the Book of Mormon every day, you will make better decisions—every day. I promise that as you ponder what you study, the windows of heaven will open, and you will receive answers to your own questions and direction for your own life. I promise that as you daily immerse yourself in the Book of Mormon, you can be immunized against the evils of the day" (Nelson, "The Book of Mormon: What Would Your Life Be Like without It?")

> "How kind of the Lord to impress upon President Russell M. Nelson right at the end of this morning's session to quickly leave the building, skip his lunch, and hurry to the bedside of Elder Hales."
>
> —Elder Neil L. Andersen

T he Sunday morning session of the October 2017 general conference was well under way when President Nelson had a clear impression—actually, a repeat of an impression he had had the night before: as soon as the morning session ended, he should forgo lunch and slip up to LDS Hospital to see Elder Robert D. Hales, who had been hospitalized for several days after a recent cardiac arrest. The impression surprised him. Just the day before, between the Saturday afternoon and priesthood sessions of conference, he had stopped to check on Elder Hales. They had had "a wonderful visit, the best we'd had for a long time," President Nelson said. "Bob was showing signs of improvement and breathing on his own for the first time during this illness." But later that night, President Nelson began to wonder if he should go see his longtime friend and colleague again on Sunday, and then the same impression came over him

President Nelson greets Elder Robert D. Hales at general conference.

315

Elder Nelson with President Boyd K. Packer.

and persisted throughout the morning session. So, as the session concluded, a Church Security officer rushed President Nelson to Elder Hales's bedside at LDS Hospital.

"As soon as I looked at him," President Nelson recalled, "I knew he was *in extremis*. He was struggling for air and was not responsive. I had the privilege of being with Mary and their two sons when Bob departed."

Elder Hales had suffered with a succession of serious illnesses for nearly twenty years, and Russell Nelson had visited him in the hospital and at home countless times. "Bob was a real fighter," he said. "He had been ill for twenty years, fighting all the time to stay alive."

President M. Russell Ballard and other members of the Twelve had seen Elder Nelson attend to their brother and colleague. "Before a quorum meeting, he would feel Bob's pulse, look him in the eye, and get a report as to what happened overnight. He was a physician filled with love for those whom he could serve," said President Ballard (*Church News*/KSL Interview, January 9, 2018).

Elder Hales passed away ten minutes after his quorum president arrived for his final visit. Not wanting to "spoil the conference" with the news of her husband's passing, Mary Hales encouraged President Nelson to let the afternoon session pass without mention of what had taken place. "Mary, we can't do that," he told her. "We have to share it. Your husband belonged to the Church and to the world, and members everywhere will want to know and share in your sadness."

The announcement of Elder Hales's passing was made at the outset of the afternoon session, and during his concluding remarks, Elder Neil L. Andersen said, "How kind of the Lord to impress upon President Russell M. Nelson right at the end of this morning's session to quickly leave the building, skip his lunch, and hurry to the bedside of Elder Hales, where he could arrive and be there, his quorum president, with the angelic Mary Hales as Elder Hales graduated from mortality" (Andersen, "Voice of the Lord").

Hurrying to the bedside of his Brethen was nothing new for President Nelson. He had been watching over the health of his colleagues, and many of their family members, from the time he was called as a General Authority. Elder Dallin H. Oaks once referred to him as "the urim and thummim for the quorum in matters of health" (Condie, *Russell M. Nelson,* 207).

Hundreds of times he had made hospital and home visits to check on General Authorities and their family members and to consult with their physicians. He frequently visited President Ezra Taft Benson, Elder Bruce R. McConkie, Elder Marvin J. Ashton, and President Howard W. Hunter when they were hospitalized for periods of time.

The week after President Henry B. Eyring was named first counselor to President Thomas S. Monson, he had several episodes in which he either blacked out or felt he was going to. Elder Nelson suggested he be wired and continuously monitored for abnormal heart function, and twenty-four hours later his doctors diagnosed the problem and solved it by inserting a pacemaker (see Eaton and Eyring, *I Will Lead You Along*, 445, 467).

On other occasions, Elder Nelson actually stood in the operating room while procedures were performed on his Brethren.

When Elder M. Russell Ballard underwent heart surgery for five coronary bypasses in 1995, he awoke to learn that Elder Nelson had "stood over the surgeon" throughout the entire operation. "It just endeared him to me all the more," Elder Ballard said. "Who better to have his eyes on your heart than my dear friend who knew exactly what should happen" (*Church News*/KSL Interview, January 9, 2018). Elder Nelson was also in the operating room when President Howard W. Hunter, Elder Hales, and Elder David B. Haight had heart surgery.

When Elder Neal A. Maxwell was confined in the hospital's sterile room for chemotherapy treatments, Elder Nelson visited there frequently. As he watched Elder Maxwell struggle with his disease, he saw him develop "an objectivity . . . that most patients don't have in looking at his own circumstances. Most people focus more subjectively on 'I'm miserable, I'm hurting. . . . But Brother Maxwell sees himself going through this period of testing and trying," and never losing "sight of his place in the work of the Lord" (Hafen, *Disciple's Life*, 557).

Most of President Nelson's visits and assistance were private. But in the October 2007 general conference, Church members around the world looked on as Elder Joseph B. Wirthlin began to tremble while delivering his address. With each few seconds, his trembling increased and his voice became shakier and weaker as he seemed to struggle for air. For the viewing audience, it was unnerving. As the minutes passed, it looked as though Elder Wirthlin could not possibly complete his message.

Then, suddenly, Elder Nelson stood behind him, putting one hand on the Apostle's shoulder and grabbing his belt with the other.

Offering a steadying hand to Elder Joseph B. Wirthlin.

He remained there for the last five minutes of Elder Wirthlin's talk, stabilizing him as he finished his address. "Thank you," Elder Wirthlin whispered as Elder Nelson helped him back to his seat. (Elder Wirthlin had served as a counselor to Russell Nelson when he was called as a stake president, and then again in the General Sunday School Presidency.)

As Elder Jeffrey R. Holland faced double hip-replacement surgery, President Nelson—then his quorum president—asked if he might give him a priesthood blessing. He chose the quorum's Thursday meeting in the Salt Lake Temple as the time and place so that all of the Twelve could participate. "I was moved to tears under his hands," Elder Holland recalled. "It was not Dr. Nelson who would have known anything and everything about whatever was going on with a few bones and joints. It was Apostle Nelson, Elder Nelson, Prophet, Seer, and Revelator Nelson. The language of that blessing wasn't a medical opinion. It was faith and power in the priesthood. It moved me to tears. I could hardly receive it. And that's not a comment

An educational auditorium at the Intermountain Medical Center in Salt Lake City, Utah, bears President Nelson's name.

about me, it's a comment about him" (*Church News*/KSL Interview, January 9, 2018).

Elder Nelson's call to the Twelve complemented perfectly his professional training as a healer because both satisfied the two great commandments—to love God and neighbor. It was natural for him to watch over the health of his Brethren. As he himself had stated, "One loves best who serves best" (Nelson, "Call to the Holy Apostleship").

> "I have to confess that for a few moments,
> I got hung up on the line, 'Where can I run?'"
>
> —Wendy Watson Nelson

Tuesday, January 2, 2018, began as a tender but memorable day. Wendy Nelson had the joy of speaking at the funeral of her dear friend Allie Derrick, wife of Elder Royden G. Derrick, who had just passed away at the age of one hundred. Because meetings at the Church Office Building had yet to begin after the holidays, President Nelson accompanied her, and then they went to the temple together. A trip to Costco rounded out the day, and, after working on a few time-sensitive projects for the new year, they turned in early.

As it turned out, they had no idea what awaited them in the new year. When the phone rang at 11:01 p.m., it woke them from a sound sleep. Brook Hales, secretary to the First Presidency, was on the line. President Thomas S. Monson had just passed away. Though the Nelsons knew that President Monson was frail, the news still sent a shock wave through both of them. It was a call they'd hoped would never come.

They made a few phone calls and talked for quite a while. When they finally turned out the lights, sleep did not come. "As I stared into the dark of night and tried to think about the future," Wendy admitted, "the hymn that came to my mind was, 'Where Can I Turn for Peace?' And I have to confess that for a few moments, I got hung up on the line, 'Where can I run?'"

The next few days went by in a whir. President Monson was honored in a beautiful service befitting his decades-long, extraordinary contribution to the kingdom of God and then laid to rest. President

Russell M. Nelson speaking at President Thomas S. Monson's funeral.

Nelson was ordained President of the Church and called counselors to serve at his side, and the new First Presidency was introduced to the world through an announcement meeting broadcast worldwide, followed by a press conference. The Nelsons had new security issues to deal with. As high as their visibility had been, it now hit an apex among members of the Church. President and Sister Nelson were having new experiences, and wrestling with new emotions and new expectations, every day.

One of Wendy Nelson's experiences was, for her, spiritually penetrating and deeply reassuring. Two days after President Monson passed away, the Lord gave her, in her words, a "most unique, most distinctive experience with my husband to let *me* know that the mantle of prophet was upon him. It was a never-to-be-forgotten experience. It was so vivid, so clear, and so real."

Every detail of that experience was seared into her heart and mind. And then, two days later, much like the Prophet Joseph and his experience with the Angel Moroni, she had the same experience again. "That experience, repeated twice, is too sacred for me to share over the pulpit," she subsequently told many audiences around the world, "but it is one I can never forget or deny. Because of those experiences, I could take any witness stand in any nation on earth to testify that I *know* that President Russell Marion Nelson has been called by God to be the living prophet of the Lord on the earth today."

Sister Nelson observed other changes. During their twelve years

For years, President Nelson has always kept a small journal with him to record daily information and events.

of marriage, she had become accustomed to seeing her husband awakened during the night with ideas for general conference messages or projects with which he was wrestling. "But since he became President of the Church," she said, "the nighttime messages to him have increased exponentially."

One Saturday morning in January, she witnessed—and experienced—something unusual. She woke up early and had the distinct impression she should leave the room. It was two more hours before her husband emerged from the bedroom. When he did, he said: "Wendy, you won't believe what has been happening for the past two hours since you left. The Lord gave me detailed instructions about a process I am to follow on a crucial matter." He did not share the tutoring he'd received but just told her that it had occurred.

"I am a witness," she says, "sometimes by being absent, and sometimes by being present, that the Lord indeed instructs His prophet." She came to see, early on, that she was uniquely positioned to be a witness to the fact that the Lord was working in her husband's life.

With all of the changes that had occurred, Sister Nelson wondered how she would feel at the April general conference when her husband was sustained by the membership of the Church in a solemn assembly. She was prepared to feel anxious but instead had a much different experience. "I felt something I didn't expect to feel," she said, "and that was an overwhelming feeling of peace, a peace that surpassed my understanding. I couldn't believe the palpable, sustaining, encircling peace that overcame me. Actually, even more than being encircled in peace, it felt as though I was immersed in peace."

During the early weeks in her husband's tenure as President of the Church, there were days when the demands and pressures seemed unmanageable, too overwhelming to comprehend. But Sister Nelson began to find joy in her sure knowledge that her husband was exactly where he was supposed to be.

When asked in a private setting what, more than anything else, she wanted the world to understand about her husband, she responded without hesitation, "That he receives revelation." After a pause, she added, "And as loving as you think he is, he is even more loving."

After further reflection, she added something else: "My husband is exquisitely honoring of the agency of others. He is the epitome of the words in the hymn 'Know This, That Every Soul Is Free' [*Hymns*, no. 240]. These lyrics say it all: 'He'll call, persuade, direct aright, And bless with wisdom, love, and light, In nameless ways be good and kind, But never force the human mind.' That is Russell M. Nelson."

President and Sister Nelson on January 16, 2018, following the press conference announcing his ordination.

In various congregations she shared a statement Elder Bruce R. McConkie made about President Spencer W. Kimball, but substituted her husband's name: "Premortally, [Russell Marion Nelson] knew and worshipped the Lord Jehovah. He was a friend of Adam and Enoch. He took counsel from Noah and Abraham. He sat in meetings with Isaiah and Nephi. He served in the heavenly kingdom with Joseph Smith and Brigham Young." She then added her witness: "I know that before the foundations of this earth, my husband was foreordained to be the prophet of the Lord—at this precise time on the earth."

This sure knowledge sustained both President and Sister Nelson as they embarked on a journey only sixteen other couples in this dispensation could possibly understand.

"Words are inadequate to tell you what
it felt like to have my Brethren . . . place their
hands upon my head to ordain and set me
apart as President of the Church. It was
a sacred and humbling experience."

—President Russell M. Nelson

O n Sunday, January 14, 2018, President Russell M. Nelson was
ordained the seventeenth President of The Church of Jesus
Christ of Latter-day Saints. Elder Gary E. Stevenson described the
meeting of the Quorum of the Twelve Apostles in the Salt Lake
Temple where this took place: "The Brethren were seated by seniority in a semicircle of 13 chairs and raised their hands first to sustain
the organization of a First Presidency and then to sustain President
Russell Marion Nelson as President of The Church of Jesus Christ of
Latter-day Saints. This sustaining was followed by the Quorum of
the Twelve gathering in a circle and placing hands upon the head of
President Nelson to ordain and set him apart, with the next most-
senior Apostle acting as voice."

Elder Stevenson continued: "This was a deeply sacred experience,
with an outpouring of the Spirit. I offer to you my absolute witness
that the will of the Lord, for which we fervently prayed, was powerfully manifest in the activities and events of that day" (Stevenson,
"Heart of a Prophet").

Two days later, on January 16, 2018, President Nelson and his
counselors—Presidents Dallin H. Oaks and Henry B. Eyring—were
introduced first to Church members in a brief announcement meeting originating from a room overlooking the Salt Lake Temple, and

The Brethren gather on Tuesday, January 16, 2018, to announce the reorganization of the First Presidency with Russell M. Nelson as President, Dallin H. Oaks as First Counselor, and Henry B. Eyring as Second Counselor.

subsequently to the world through a press conference. In the announcement meeting, President Nelson admitted that words were "inadequate to tell you what it felt like to have my Brethren . . . place their hands upon my head to ordain and set me apart as President of the Church. It was a sacred and humbling experience."

He pledged that the First Presidency would work hand in hand with the Quorum of the Twelve to discern the will of the Lord and to lead His Church. And he signaled to each member of the Church what he hoped he or she would focus on: "Keep on the covenant path. Your commitment to follow the Savior by making covenants with Him, and then keeping those covenants, will open the door to every spiritual blessing and privilege available to men, women, and children." He also addressed those not currently participating in the Church: "If you have stepped off the path, may I invite you with all the hope in

The congregation at the Conference Center sustains the prophet at the solemn assembly.

my heart to please come back. Whatever your concerns, whatever your challenges, there's a place for you in this, the Lord's Church."

The press made a big issue of President Nelson's age, that at ninety-three he was the second-oldest man to assume leadership of the Church, and some journalists focused predictably on contemporary issues confronting the Church, such as the question of being opposed to same-sex marriage while extending a hand of fellowship to those with LGBTQ orientation; the desire of some Latter-day Saint women to be ordained to the priesthood; the discrepancy between a global Church with the preponderance of General Authorities still being Caucasian Americans; and the Church's increasingly strained relationship with the Boy Scouts, to name a few.

But President Nelson launched his presidency with the optimism and vigor characteristic of his life and of the sixteen men who had preceded him in office. "Begin with the end in mind," he counseled Church members in this first brief message to them—a pattern he had followed his entire life. And the end he hoped each member had in mind was qualifying for and being regularly in the temple—the site of his first message to members worldwide.

Cards, letters, emails, texts, and press coverage around the world welcomed the new Church President, and countless individuals sent commendations. One prominent Catholic scholar and friend voiced a sentiment repeated by many others. In an email to Elder Jeffrey R. Holland, he recalled that then-Elder Nelson had been the first General Authority he'd met and had shaped his early positive impressions about the Church. He then added, "Russell Nelson is as fine a man as God ever created" (email from Jeffrey R. Holland to Russell M. Nelson, January 6, 2018).

"I've watched the Lord place the mantle on Russell M. Nelson," said Elder Holland. "I've been able to watch him from the day I came into the circle of the Quorum of the Twelve. I've seen the Lord magnify him and bless him and shape him for this hour. He gave the Lord a wonderful package of raw material to work with, but I have seen the Lord bless him and mold him into becoming the prophet of the Lord" (*Church News*/KSL Interview, January 9, 2018).

During the solemn assembly held during the opening session of the April 2018 general conference, members of the Church worldwide had the privilege of sustaining President Russell M. Nelson as President of the Church. A few days later, in a devotional address at BYU, Elder Neil L. Andersen described the power of that experience: "The entire Church is speaking about general conference," he said. "I will never forget the sustaining of President Russell M. Nelson. I anticipated that it would be a spiritual experience, but the rush of power and peace that permeated the LDS Conference Center was palpable to me. . . . The closing session, with the announcement of the temples and the singing of 'Let Us All Press On,' moved my soul" (Andersen, "Holier Approach to Ministering").

The Church was moving forward.

"Have I felt the loneliness of leadership?
No. I have not felt lonely at all. I have great
counselors, and when we pray about
something and are unified, we move
forward. I literally have not felt the
loneliness of leadership."

—President Russell M. Nelson

President Gordon B. Hinckley served almost fourteen years in the First Presidency before becoming President of the Church, and President Thomas S. Monson more than thirty-two years. As counselors, they learned how the First Presidency functions and understood the distinctions between that council and the Quorum of the Twelve Apostles. The seventeenth President of the Church did not enjoy that luxury.

"I had served in the Quorum of the Twelve for almost thirty-four years," President Nelson said, "so I wasn't totally uninformed, but the First Presidency is different from the Quorum of the Twelve."

One major difference involved working directly with the Presiding Bishopric on matters related to temples, meetinghouses, the expansive welfare program and humanitarian arm of the Church, and all the temporal affairs of the Church. The Church does business—it buys mission homes, builds buildings, leases vehicles, and hires a host of professional services—in more than 185 countries in the world and, by any measure, is an enormous operation. Though the Twelve are to "regulate" the affairs of the Church in all the world (Doctrine and Covenants 107:33), the Bishopric executes on all temporal affairs. "They are the ones who do the buying and the selling, the hiring and

The First Presidency of The Church of Jesus Christ of Latter-day Saints. Left to right: Presidents Dallin H. Oaks, Russell M. Nelson, and Henry B. Eyring.

firing," explained President Nelson. "It was a steep learning curve for President Oaks and myself, who had not had previous experience with this. Thankfully, President Eyring had had more than ten years' experience, which helped us come up to speed."

There were other differences as well. The new President found himself dealing with legal issues that come before the First Presidency, making decisions involving large sums of money, and handling the sensitive and deeply personal issues involving cancellations of sealings and restoration of blessings. But in all except the latter, he had the benefit of his counselors' wisdom.

From day one, the new First Presidency found themselves in sync and working together hand in glove. President Nelson's background in medicine, science, and research, combined with President Oaks's legal background and President Eyring's training as a professor of business at both Harvard and Stanford—not to mention the more than ninety combined years the three had served in the

The First Presidency is heavily involved in temporal affairs as well as spiritual matters.

Quorum of the Twelve or First Presidency—made for rich, informed, enlightening discussions and deliberations.

President Nelson found their diversity of experience supportive and sustaining. "I've been asked if I have experienced the loneliness of leadership since becoming President of the Church. No, I haven't," he said. "I have not felt lonely at all. I have great counselors, and when we pray about something and are unified, we move forward. I literally have not felt the loneliness of leadership."

Wendy Nelson acknowledged, though, that as of 11:01 p.m. on January 2, 2018, the burdens on her husband increased exponentially. "I watch his shoulders get wider and wider. We go to sleep earlier than we ever have now, both of us. This is taxing, it is wearing, it is intense," she admitted. "On the other hand," she quickly added, "I have never seen my husband as happy as he is now. So I see both. I see the increased burdens he carries, and I also watch him being unleashed to do his best work. So he's the happiest I've ever seen him. He is doing what he was born to do!"

"I have the best job in the world," President Nelson said, pushing aside the suggestion that he carries heavy burdens. "I get to approve temples and make other determinations that will bless people's lives and move the work forward. And I have the privilege of feeling the love that the Lord has for His children—for *all* of His children. Could there be anything better than that?"

"It is in the nature of mortality that there must be opposition in all things, beginning with the law of gravity."

—President Dallin H. Oaks

Some days as President of the Church were long, intense, and complex. The simple decisions in Church administration all get made by others; only the difficult ones escalate to the top. Concerns about lawsuits, the Church's position on sensitive social issues, calls for the Church to end one-on-one bishop's interviews with youth, LGBTQ advocacy, the claim that an MTC president had molested a sister missionary, and Church members who called for changes in doctrine about marriage or for leaders to be more definitive in statements about transgender individuals—these and many more issues made their way to the First Presidency for deliberation, decisions, and, sometimes, response.

President Nelson was not oblivious to criticism and had had his share of experience with it. As just one example, after the change to the *Handbook 1* in November 2015, indicating that same-sex couples who entered into marriage were engaging in apostasy and that the children of gay parents might not be eligible for baptism at the age of eight, President Nelson referred to these changes in his worldwide YSA devotional message in January 2016.

"Filled with compassion for all, and especially for the children, we wrestled at length to understand the Lord's will in this matter," he said. "Ever mindful of God's plan of salvation and of His hope for eternal life for each of His children, we considered countless permutations and combinations of possible scenarios that could arise. We

President Nelson uses his hands to bless, to pray, and to serve.

met repeatedly in the temple in fasting and prayer and sought further direction and inspiration. And then, when the Lord inspired His prophet, President Thomas S. Monson, to declare the mind of the Lord and the will of the Lord, each of us during that sacred moment felt a spiritual confirmation" (Nelson, "Becoming True Millennials").

Social media heated up immediately with reactions. Some commenters were supportive of President Nelson's remarks; many others couldn't believe his claim that the handbook change had been inspired. And yet others asked to plead their cases in person.

"It is in the nature of mortality that there must be opposition in all things," said President Dallin H. Oaks. "Given that fact, I think we have to be sensitive to the positions of people who don't agree with us, and we need to have a setting in which different points of view can be worked out."

Opposition comes from some members, from journalists, from

antagonists of the Church. "President Nelson agrees with the need to handle opposition with respect," President Oaks continued. "Out of it comes improved understanding and more appropriate policies and a better understanding of doctrine. Some people confuse doctrine and policy. Policy can be changed; doctrine can't" (*Church News*/KSL Interview, January 10, 2018).

"President Nelson is very wise, very bright, and very thoughtful," said President M. Russell Ballard. "He wants to know the facts, and he's very decisive."

He added how important it is to understand the foundation upon which President Nelson stands: "President Nelson is a total disciple of Jesus Christ, and he will defend the plan of happiness in a world today that is unraveling. He will stand for what God has revealed. He understands there are some rules, some commandments, some doctrine we have to accept and abide by. Life isn't just what everybody wants it to be. President Nelson will teach that and hold to it. His desire is to do what the Lord Jesus Christ would expect His Apostles to do" (*Church News*/KSL Interview, January 9, 2018).

"We never hesitate to bring up a particular subject. . . . We're never afraid to talk to him about any particular matter."

—President Dallin H. Oaks

President Nelson's leadership style has been developed through a myriad of life experiences, informed by the leadership strengths and weaknesses of others, and honed over decades of practice.

His Brethren and other leaders at Church headquarters who dealt with him frequently found him to be as he had been as President of the Twelve: open to new ideas, willing to discuss problems and opportunities openly and without recrimination, and eager to hear from everyone in the room—including senior employees throughout the Church's departments, divisions, and companies.

"We never hesitate to bring up a particular subject or feel that doing so is a bother to him," wrote President Dallin H. Oaks in a tribute to the new President of the Church. "We're never afraid to talk to him about any particular matter. President Nelson is very open, very approachable, and very easy to talk to."

Further, wrote President Oaks: "He is good at thinking through the probable effect of a decision or policy or application of doctrine on various groups of members. I have seen that quality in other leaders, but President Nelson's vision on this subject is exceptional. Perhaps it stems from his experience as a doctor who cannot prescribe medicine for one part of the body without considering its effect on other parts" (Oaks, "President Russell M. Nelson").

President Oaks added that President Nelson's leadership style is congenial yet disciplined. "He is easy to approach. And that is not

President Dallin H. Oaks shares a thought with President Nelson.

always true of senior men in Church leadership. We've sometimes hesitated to bring something up with them or have been reluctant to bother them. But what's really behind it is that we're afraid to talk to them about that subject. President Nelson is very easy to talk to" (*Church News*/KSL Interview, January 10, 2018).

President Henry B. Eyring said that President Nelson has "a remarkable gift for receiving revelation and allowing others to participate in the process. He wants all involved to have the chance to receive the revelation as well" (interview with author, August 10, 2018).

President M. Russell Ballard, acting President of the Quorum of the Twelve, added, "He has been outstanding in drawing from the members of the Twelve their best thinking. He guides the discussion until we finally get to what the Lord wants us to do. He is masterful at that.

"It won't be difficult for him to make decisions," President Ballard continued. "Anyone who's had somebody's heart in their hands doesn't have to have countless meetings to decide what to do.

He's made life-and-death decisions his entire life. I believe Russell M. Nelson was born to lead. He's been doing that in every capacity he's found himself in. I think I speak for all of the Twelve when I say that we have great affection for him. He is open, he listens, he gives direction, and then he makes decisions and moves us forward. I don't think there's an issue you could hand to Russell Nelson that, given a little time, he wouldn't be able to dissect and come up with the right answers. He has that kind of a trained mind" (*Church News*/KSL Interview, January 9, 2018).

After spending ten days traveling with President Nelson in South America, Elder Gary E. Stevenson remarked that President Nelson employed a kind of "divine leadership. It's so inclusive. It's arm-in-arm. We are accustomed to leadership models in the world that are often lacking. But with President Nelson, he doesn't just meet our expectations for our leader. He is exceeding them" (conversation with author, October 28, 2018).

After a particularly meaningful meeting of the First Presidency and Quorum of the Twelve, Elder Holland penned a note to President Nelson expressing gratitude for his unique leadership: "While the spirit of the moment is still upon us all, I must thank you for yet another gift to the Brethren who serve with you. None of us will ever forget the spirit and impact of having our beloved prophet plead with the Lord at the altar of the holy temple. If we love you so much, how must our Father in Heaven love such humility and such devotion? There are many blessings that come with our callings, but such a rare one as this morning's will linger in our hearts forever" (Jeffrey R. Holland to Russell M. Nelson, March 15, 2018).

As he had demonstrated as President of the Twelve, President Nelson treasured each of his Brethren and relished serving with them. His leadership approach was simple but effective: "Get good people and give them a track to run on."

"For the first time in anyone's memory,
the carts came back empty."

—Alan Parker, Church Security

The campus of Church headquarters spans several blocks in downtown Salt Lake City that include Temple Square, the Conference
Center, and the Church History Library as well as the block contain-
ing the Joseph Smith Memorial Building, the Lion House, the Church
Office Building, the Relief Society Building, and the Church Administration Building. These blocks are connected by an intricate series of
underground tunnels that make it possible for Church leaders to move
easily between buildings without respect for weather or crowds.

Golf carts transport Church leaders through the underground tunnels at Church
headquarters.

The distance underground from the Church Administration Building to the Salt Lake Temple isn't far—perhaps a few hundred yards. But for men in their eighties and nineties who at times deal with the physical limitations induced by age, the distance is farther than some have felt able to walk. Golf carts have been the answer, with a line of them available to whisk the Brethren over to the temple each Thursday morning for the weekly meeting of the First Presidency and Quorum of the Twelve, and then waiting to bring them back at the conclusion of the meeting followed by their lunch together. A team from Church Security always handles the transportation.

The second week President Nelson presided over the meeting of the First Presidency and Quorum of the Twelve in the temple, the security officers waiting with a line of carts afterward saw something they had never seen before. President Nelson emerged from the temple walking with both of his counselors, and every member of the Twelve walking behind them—fifteen prophets, seers, and revelators walking back from the temple to the Church Administration Building. "For the first time in anyone's memory," said Alan Parker, an officer with Church Security, "the carts came back empty." If the Church's ninety-three-year-old President could walk, everyone could walk.

President Nelson's health seemed to influence his Brethren's. At the conclusion of the meetings of the First Presidency and Twelve, held on the fourth floor of the Salt Lake Temple, "some take the elevator down to the lower floor and some walk down the stairs from the upper room in the temple," said President Dallin H. Oaks. "That is several flights of stairs on those beautiful circular stairs in the northwest corner of the Salt Lake Temple. President Nelson always goes down the stairs, and I always try to keep up with him, and I can't do it. I grab hold of the banister to balance me and skip along as well as I can, and it's always apparent that he can move faster on those stairs than I can" (*Church News*/KSL Interview, January 10, 2018).

President M. Russell Ballard concurred: "He's so healthy. When

Enjoying a moment outdoors.

President Nelson and Russ Jr. show off their catch.

A day in the garden.

Taking a walk in the mountains.

Touring Machu Picchu in Peru.

President Nelson loves outdoor activities.

you're not feeling well, you don't complain because it doesn't do any good. It's like being around President Hinckley. It never did any good to complain around him, either. You can't keep up with him when he's walking—at least I can't. Of course, both my knees have been replaced. So I hobble along trying to keep up, but it's not easy. He walks every chance he gets. He's vibrant" (*Church News*/KSL Interview, January 9, 2018).

Elder Gregory A. Schwitzer remembers walking the streets of Turkey with Elder Nelson and wondering if this man, then in his late eighties, could handle the terrain. "I was thinking, 'How is he going to take this hill?' He kept right up with me, no problem, talking to me the whole time. I thought, 'This is a unique man'" (*Church News*/KSL Interview, January 8, 2018).

Daughter Sylvia explained her father's approach to fitness: "He has taken care of himself; he always exercises. He doesn't like to lift weights or walk on a treadmill. He's got to be outdoors" (*Church News*/KSL Interview, January 10, 2018). Even into his nineties, he would shovel the snow from his and the neighbors' walks, walk up and down the neighborhood rolling garbage cans back up to garages on trash-collection day, and during the summer weed and prune and putter in his yard for hours at a time.

Until he became President of the Church, at which point Church Security put the kibosh on hitting the slopes, he skied as often in the winter as his schedule allowed. Family members knew that if their father and grandfather was in town on a winter Monday (the "day off" for General Authorities), and if it was a "bluebird ski day," they had a standing invitation to join him on the slopes. They also knew that if they went, they'd get a workout.

Oldest grandson Stephen McKellar, himself a heart surgeon, skied

Skiing has been a favorite way to enjoy time with his family.

with his grandfather whenever he could be away from his patients for a few hours: "Grandfather is a very good snow skier. He was past ninety the last time I went with him, and I could barely keep up. He has his routine down, and we take breaks when he wants to. I was ready for a break before he was" (*Church News*/KSL Interview, January 11, 2018). Russ Jr. added: "At about 1:00 p.m. we'll start thinking we want to stop for lunch and take a break, and he'll say, 'Oh, no, let's keep going while it's still good and sunny and take advantage of the good weather we have.' He'll go all day and he's good. We're beat, but he's great" (*Church News*/KSL Interview, January 2018). Typically, fifteen or sixteen runs later, when everyone else was ready to cry "uncle," they would finally stop.

"The man can ski with the best of them," Elder W. Craig Zwick admitted from personal experience. "I've had him on black diamond runs at Snowbird, scared to death for me and for him, but it was what he wanted to do" (*Church News*/KSL Interview, January 5, 2018).

His combination of good genes and wise health practices has served President Nelson well and allows him to serve with vibrancy into his nineties. Wendy Nelson put a fine point on her husband's energy when she commented on what it's like to travel with him: "We spend two or three weeks traveling somewhere internationally, and he comes home and hits the ground running. I just hit the ground."

President Nelson had spent his professional career trying to heal bodies. Nowhere did he indicate his respect for the gift of a body more than in the way he cared for his own.

"We will implement a newer, holier approach to caring for and ministering to others."

—President Russell M. Nelson

Members of the Church looked forward to the April 2018 general conference, knowing there would be a solemn assembly to sustain the new President of the Church. That alone would have distinguished this general conference as one for the record books. But as it turned out, that was just the beginning.

When President Henry B. Eyring announced early in the Saturday evening priesthood session that President Nelson would give brief remarks, those versed in Church protocol wondered what was happening. The presiding officer always speaks last. Why was the President of the Church walking to the pulpit after the first speaker?

President Nelson quickly answered that question. "Tonight we announce a significant restructuring of our Melchizedek Priesthood quorums to accomplish the work of the Lord more effectively," he began, then explained that high priests groups and elders quorums in each ward would now be combined into one elders quorum. The reason? "This adjustment will greatly enhance the capacity and the ability of men who bear the priesthood to serve others" (Nelson, "Introductory Remarks").

He testified that these adjustments were inspired of the Lord and then indicated that Elders D. Todd Christofferson and Ronald A. Rasband would elaborate on the change (see Christofferson, "The Elders Quorum"; Rasband, "Behold! A Royal Army"). All three made it clear that these changes were to take place throughout the Church as soon as possible. Stake presidents the world over no doubt left that meeting with their heads spinning about what the realignment of Melchizedek Priesthood quorums would mean for the priesthood bearers in their stakes. General conference had come with a bang.

The next day, in the concluding session of general conference, it became clear that the change regarding the restructure of priesthood quorums, as monumental as it was, was actually part of a much bigger picture. Early in the session, President Dallin H. Oaks announced that President Nelson would again offer brief remarks, and the prophet then made a second stunning announcement: "We have made the decision to retire home teaching and visiting teaching as we have known them. Instead, we will implement a newer, holier approach to caring for and ministering to others. We will refer to these efforts simply as 'ministering.'" Elder Holland and Sister Jean Bingham, Relief Society General President, then explained further what this meant for the Church (see Holland, "'Be With and Strengthen Them'"; Bingham, "Ministering as the Savior Does").

In President Nelson's concluding remarks, he summarized not only the emphasis of the conference but something he had focused on throughout his life: healing hearts and homes. "This general conference marks the beginning of a new era of ministering. The Lord has made important adjustments in the way we care for each other. Sisters and brothers—old and young—will serve one another in a new, holier way. Elders quorums will be strengthened to bless the lives of men, women, and children throughout the world. Relief Society sisters will continue to minister in their unique and loving way, extending opportunities to younger sisters to join them as appropriately assigned" (Nelson, "Let Us All Press On").

In short, this dramatic shift was designed to help followers of Christ better care for each other. "The hallmark of the Lord's Church is that there is an organized method for caring for every individual," President Nelson later elaborated. "No other church can make that statement. The Lord wants it done His way, and we felt that home teaching and visiting teaching were only steps in that direction. We thought we could do better. Ministering means following your feelings to help someone else feel the love of the Savior in his or her life."

In some parts of the world, visiting in the home is not possible or, in some cases, culturally acceptable. Further, the very nature of home and visiting teaching suggested an almost checklist-like approach to caring for one another as opposed to a "continuous assignment. There is no more counting. No more checklist," President Nelson added. "The question we each should ask ourselves is, 'What would Jesus do?' The answer? He would make sure that people were okay."

The amalgamation of Melchizedek Priesthood quorums made ministering possible. "Many of us in the First Presidency and the Twelve had lived in various parts of the world," President Nelson explained, "and we had been in smaller wards or branches where all Melchizedek Priesthood holders met together. We knew it worked well and helped improve service the men could offer. Further, we saw

"Ministering means
FOLLOWING YOUR FEELINGS
to help someone else feel
the **LOVE OF THE SAVIOR**
in his or her life."

—RUSSELL M. NELSON

Ministering takes many forms as people work to meet others' needs.

the pattern the sisters had in Relief Society and thought that was a pattern the men could emulate. We were not only instructed by the model of women but could see that that was the ideal. It was how the sisters visit taught that inspired our upward shift to ministering. And of course we studied the scriptures at length, and there is nothing about high priests groups in wards."

Both major changes were put in place because, as President Nelson summarized, "we could see that it was time to take a step higher."

"President Nelson, I don't know how many more 'rushes' we can handle this weekend. Some of us have weak hearts. But as I think about it, you can take care of that too. What a prophet!"

—Elder Jeffrey R. Holland

Reactions from Church members to President Nelson's initial announcement meeting were largely enthusiastic and positive; however, some reactions from the press were less so and varied widely. Apparently unaware of President Nelson's pioneering past, one Associated Press reporter, quoted widely, predicted that "Nelson's record during his three decades in church leadership suggests he will make few changes" (see, for example, McCombs, "Mormon church appoints"). Such journalists, along with many others who assumed that President Nelson's advanced age equaled stodginess and status quo, were in for a surprise—or surprises.

During the first six months of the new administration, Melchizedek Priesthood quorums were reorganized; visiting teaching and home teaching were "retired" in favor of a new effort called ministering; the Church announced the end of its century-old relationship with the Boy Scouts of America; President Nelson called the first men of Asian and Brazilian descent to the Quorum of the Twelve Apostles; he announced alongside Derrick Johnson, president of the National NAACP, a joint education initiative (see Walch, "Inside the collaboration"); right after the April 2018 general conference, he undertook an around-the-world trip, visiting members in eight countries in twelve days; in September and October 2018, he delivered what are believed to be the first addresses by a President of the Church in a language other than his own—in Spanish in the Dominican Republic and Puerto Rico and then in five countries in South America; and also in September, with a bill proposing that medical marijuana use be legalized in Utah, the Church announced its opposition to that particular piece of legislation but its support of medical marijuana to relieve suffering. "It's really remarkable the Lord's chosen prophet at this time has great empathy and understanding," said Elder Jack H. Gerard of the Seventy, speaking on behalf of the Church. President Nelson understands human pain and suffering, he added, "not only as a loving, compassionate leader of the Church, but he also understands it more from the medical perspective. That's why it really is quite significant that [the Church has] come out to support a broader coalition to work for appropriate medicinal marijuana use with appropriate safeguards" (Walch, "Church leaders want").

At the April general conference, where visiting and home teaching were retired and priesthood quorums were reorganized, Elder Jeffrey R. Holland began his remarks by paraphrasing Ralph Waldo Emerson as having said that the most memorable moments in life were those in which we could feel the rush of revelation. "President Nelson, I don't know how many more 'rushes' we can handle this weekend. Some of us have weak hearts. But as I think about it, you can take care of that too. What a prophet!" (Holland, "Be With and Strengthen Them").

In a touch of delightful irony, there was still another "rush" to come in that session, the conference's last. A relative few minutes after Elder Holland declared that Church members had about as much change as they could handle for one weekend, President Nelson again walked to the pulpit for brief concluding remarks. In less than five minutes, he announced that the Church would build six new temples, including one in Bengaluru, India, and another in a city yet to be

determined in Russia—both of which brought audible gasps throughout the capacity audience in the Conference Center.

Though these changes came in what felt like rapid-fire succession, senior Brethren had weighed them carefully for some time—in
some cases, for years. In an earlier general conference, Elder Nelson
had addressed the unique aspects of Church government that affected
such major changes: "The calling of 15 men to the holy apostleship
provides great protection for us as members of the Church," he taught.
"Why? Because decisions of these leaders must be unanimous. Can
you imagine how the Spirit needs to move upon 15 men to bring about
unanimity? These 15 men have varied educational and professional
backgrounds, with differing opinions about many things. Trust me!
These 15 men—prophets, seers, and revelators—know what the will

Elders Gerrit W. Gong and Ulisses Soares take their places on the stand with the
Quorum of the Twelve.

of the Lord is when unanimity is reached!" (Nelson, "Sustaining the Prophets").

After President Nelson's first six months in office, Patrick Mason, a Latter-day Saint historian at Claremont Graduate University in southern California, observed that "virtually every change that has been made under President Nelson's tenure has clearly been with the global church front and center. . . . Nelson clearly has an authentically global outlook" (Stack, "Mormonism was born").

Speaking to a group of young married British members of the Church inside the Church of England's Pembroke College Chapel at Oxford in November 2018, Elder Jeffrey R. Holland spoke of President Nelson's administration: "We travel with him by relay. We pass the baton to keep up with him." He then added that he wished Church members could be with him in the weekly temple meetings of the Council of the First Presidency and Quorum of the Twelve Apostles. "The windows of revelation seem free and open and abundant," he said. "Since the moment he became President of the Church, Russell Nelson has been particularly open, particularly receptive, and particularly entitled to revelation that is more public, is more shareable" (see Walch, "Q&A: Elder Holland opens up").

The new First Presidency and the Quorum of the Twelve Apostles were moving the work forward.

Just a couple of weeks after President Nelson's ordination as President of the Church, he attended the funeral of Elder Von G. Keetch of the Seventy, who died suddenly from unanticipated complications associated with a long bout with cancer. The service was inspiring, with tender remembrances from his children, a powerful yet poignant message from Elder Lance B. Wickman—Elder Keetch's longtime friend, legal compatriot, and fellow General Authority—and concluding remarks from President Nelson.

For some, however—and perhaps many—the most moving moment came after the closing prayer. As the congregation stood for the family to file out behind the casket, President Nelson walked off the rostrum and greeted Elder Keetch's wife, Bernice, her children, and then members of the extended family—at least those he could reach in the first few rows. Then, and contrary to long-held tradition that all remain standing as the President of the Church leaves any gathering first, he remained standing in front of the chapel until the large family filed out. Said one senior employee of the Church well versed in Church protocol: "I've never seen anything like it. That show of respect from the President of the Church moved me deeply. As wonderful as the funeral was, those minutes with President Nelson standing at attention in honor of the Keetch family spoke volumes to me about the greatness and gentleness of President Nelson's heart."

For President Nelson, it felt like the most natural thing to do.

Those associating with President Nelson quickly saw that such displays of generosity were typical. General Authorities, General Officers, and other leaders from various Church divisions and organizations soon found that when they entered the north boardroom in the Church Administration Building to meet with the First Presidency, President Nelson and his counselors stood to welcome them. "I've met with the First Presidency hundreds of times over the years," said one leader in a Church-owned company, "and I don't ever remember the First Presidency standing when I entered the room. It took my breath away."

Four days prior to the beginning of the April 2018 general conference, for the first time in anyone's memory, the President invited every General Authority and his wife to greet him and Sister Nelson in a receiving line in his office and a reception in nearby rooms in the Church Administration Building. Chris Wonnacott helped orchestrate the event and was present to hear the comments from the parade of General Authorities as they filed in and out of his office. "They were amazed, honored, humbled, and thrilled and openly expressed their feelings of love for the prophet," she said. "I felt the same way when he and Sister Nelson insisted that I also greet them in his office" (email to author, October 15, 2018).

In Bengaluru, India, in April 2018, President Nelson instructed the Area President conducting the meeting to invite a woman out of the audience to bear her testimony. As she approached the large stand filled with twenty or more individuals, most of them men, it was President Nelson who stood from his chair, walked over to the stairs leading up onto the rostrum, and offered his hand as she climbed the stairs.

In May, when the First Presidency met with the leaders of the National Association for the Advancement of Colored People, President Nelson met, among others, the Reverend Amos Brown, pastor of the Third Baptist Church of San Francisco. "I was blessed

President Nelson with the Reverend Amos Brown.

with a great feeling of love for that good man," President Nelson said later. During the subsequent press conference, he stood next to him and slipped his arm through Reverend Brown's. Some commented afterward that the instinctive gesture of camaraderie was more powerful than anything stated in the press release.

In late June 2018, at the conclusion of the first session of the annual new mission presidents' seminar—again for the first time in anyone's memory—President and Sister Nelson, along with President and Sister Oaks and President Eyring—greeted every mission president and his wife to express gratitude for their service and consecration.

When Elder Dale G. Renlund and his wife, Ruth, traveled with

Thanking a young Helping Hands volunteer.

Greeting a religious leader in Russia.

Sharing a moment with Elder Dale G. Renlund.

Making a new friend in Kenya.

President Nelson to the Caribbean over Labor Day in 2018, they experienced his native kindness firsthand. "Sensing that my wife might have been a little chilled on the flight from San Juan, Puerto Rico, to Salt Lake City, President Nelson procured a blanket from the flight engineer and gave it to my wife," Elder Renlund said. "I asked myself afterwards, 'Why am I not that thoughtful towards my wife?' He summarized, "Being with him made us want to become better people" (Taylor, "Experiences from pulpit's 'other side'").

The event coordinator handling a luncheon for General Authorities during the General Authority training held just prior to the October 2018 general conference was stunned when President Nelson called her over to his table, expressed gratitude for all she had done to arrange the luncheon, and introduced her to the other General Authorities at his table. "I've been trying to process this experience all afternoon," she later told Sister Nelson. "His kindness and graciousness to me during a special social gathering with his Brethren amazed me. He is a remarkable treasure" (Chris Wonnacott email to Wendy Nelson, October 3, 2018).

Elder Jeffrey R. Holland put these and other acts of generosity into perspective: "President Nelson is a gentle man. He is the consummate gentleman. In fact, he may be the man for whom the word *gentleman* was created. He is very, very kind" (*Church News*/KSL Interview, January 9, 2018).

Elder Holland had one of his first experiences with Russell Nelson's giving nature in 1981. Then serving as the president of Brigham Young University, Elder Holland was in the midst of negotiating for the university to build a center in Jerusalem. He decided to take his wife, Pat, and their three children with him on one of the many trips he made there, at his own expense. Russell Nelson was part of the entourage.

The Hollands' youngest son, David, had just turned eight, and while in Israel the boy's father baptized him in the River Jordan.

An avid photographer, Russell Nelson took these pictures in 1981 of Jeffrey R. Holland baptizing his son David in the Jordan River while on a trip to the Holy Land.

"I still didn't know Russell Nelson very well at that point," Elder Holland remembered, "but he made that experience more than memorable for our family. He became the chief photographer of David's baptism. All of the photos we have of that event were taken by Russell Nelson. He mailed us copies afterwards and then sent copies to my mother. Now, who would think of that? There was Alice Holland, a widow who missed this opportunity with her family. Who would stop to think that she needed pictures of that event? Russell Nelson thought of it, and sent her a whole packet of photos. Well, it's easy to understand who Alice Holland adopted as her favorite General Authority. I am only her second favorite Apostle" (*Church News*/KSL Interview, January 9, 2018).

President Henry B. Eyring articulated the essence of President Nelson: "He has a combination of confidence and humility that is rare. And he is so generous."

That generosity of spirit was nothing more than President Nelson's attempt to live the first two great commandments—to love the Lord and to treat others as he himself would wish to be treated.

There are six Presidents of the Church whom President Russell M. Nelson never met in this life: Joseph Smith, Brigham Young, John Taylor, Wilford Woodruff, Lorenzo Snow, and Joseph F. Smith. The other ten are a different story, however. In one way or another, he interacted with, was acquainted with, or was mentored by each of the other ten who preceded him.

"Beginning with Heber J. Grant and continuing through Thomas S. Monson, President Nelson has had remarkable exposure to the Presidents of the Church," said President Dallin H. Oaks (*Church News*/KSL Interview, January 10, 2018). Though it's likely no one realized what was happening at the time, such mentoring by this succession of Church leaders helped Russell Nelson's view of that office expand and mature through the years.

President Grant lived on the Avenues in Salt Lake City, and some of his grandsons were friends with the young Russell Nelson. From time to time, Russell found himself in President Grant's home. "He treated me like a real human being. He was so friendly, and it was always an honor to be in his home," President Nelson remembered.

The situation was similar with President George Albert Smith, who lived on the corner of 13th East and Yale Avenue in Salt Lake City, just a block from Russell Nelson's childhood home. His family knew President Smith not only as a Church leader but as a kind and generous neighbor.

His primary interaction with President David O. McKay occurred when, as president of the Bonneville Stake, President Nelson consulted with the prophet on whether or not he should accept a tempting offer from the University of Chicago Medical School. President McKay literally changed the course of Dr. Nelson's life when he counseled him to resist the lure of fame and money and remain in Salt Lake City.

President Joseph Fielding Smith was also a neighbor, dear friend, and President of the Church when Russell Nelson was called to serve as the General President of the Sunday School.

As President Smith's first counselor, President Harold B. Lee was the person to whom Russell Nelson went when he questioned whether his title as General Superintendent of the Deseret Sunday School Union should be changed. President Lee also insisted that Spencer W. Kimball do everything possible to stay alive when heart disease threatened his life. This threw Dr. Nelson into a quandary about how to handle the complicated operation President Kimball needed but ultimately facilitated Dr. Nelson's relationship with the Church President, which went far beyond medicine.

President Spencer W. Kimball's influence on Russell M. Nelson was profound. He saw President Kimball in the worst of times, particularly severe ill health, but he also witnessed him rise up as a prophet of God. Because of their unique doctor-patient relationship, Dr. Nelson was in a position, time and again, to talk as they walked after surgery, to sit at his bedside, and to literally hold the prophet's life—as well as his heart—in his hands.

President Kimball called Russell Nelson as a stake president when everyone else said he was too busy. And he emerged from months of frail health and foggy memory to receive the revelation that Russell M. Nelson was to be called as an Apostle and member of

Some of the prophets President Nelson knew personally: Heber J. Grant, George Albert Smith, David O. McKay, Joseph Fielding Smith, Harold B. Lee, and Spencer W. Kimball.

President Ezra Taft Benson greets Elder Nelson.

the Quorum of the Twelve Apostles. Their relationship was tender and personal.

Ezra Taft Benson also mentored Russell Nelson when they met in Washington, DC, in the early 1950s. Elder Benson was living in the nation's capital as Secretary of Agriculture in the cabinet of U. S. President Dwight D. Eisenhower when Lieutenant Nelson's army orders took him to the area for a stint at the Walter Reed Army Medical Center. For a short time, Lieutenant Nelson served as second counselor in the bishopric of the Washington Ward, and the cabinet secretary took a liking to him.

When the Nelsons moved to Boston for Dr. Nelson's work at Massachusetts General Hospital, Elder Benson asked Russell to help activate a family friend, Robert Walker. He did so, and Bob Walker subsequently married one of the Benson daughters and went on to give extensive leadership in the Church.

Russell Nelson's impact on the Benson family went even further, however. One night he and Dantzel were at a concert at the Huntsman Center on the University of Utah campus. President Benson and his wife, Flora, were sitting directly in front of them. Suddenly, Flora went into cardiac arrest, and Dr. Nelson sprang into action, positioning himself to reach around her from behind and do CPR. "She was gone. She died there," President Nelson said. "As I did chest compression to get her heart pumping again, the sweetest words she ever uttered were, 'I wish you would stop doing that.' Gratefully, we were able to get her back."

President Benson sold Russell and Dantzel four acres in Midway, Utah, for a country getaway for their large family, and he was the one who gave Elder Russell Nelson the assignment to open up eastern Europe for the Church—which assignment provided its own unique tutoring for the newly called Apostle.

In President Howard W. Hunter, President Nelson saw gentleness combined with strength of testimony and conviction. And though President Hunter's time as President of the Church was short in length, Elder Nelson found it powerful in terms of influence—particularly because of President

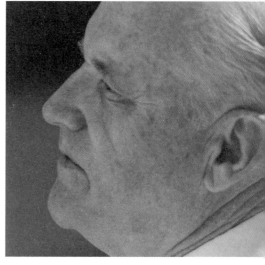

Elder Nelson took this picture of President Howard W. Hunter in a contemplative mood.

Hunter's emphasis on the temple and his encouragement for every member to have a current temple recommend.

Then, he marveled at the vision, energy, and sheer prophetic genius of President Gordon B. Hinckley. "President Hinckley doesn't expect to be bowed to and prefers to be treated as though he is an ordinary worker," Elder Nelson said at the time. "But he isn't ordinary in any respect. . . . Whether it is medicine or law, education or plumbing, it doesn't seem to matter. He grasps things quickly, has an amazing breadth of knowledge, and can apply what he knows" (Dew, *Go Forward with Faith*, 449). He added, giving a glimpse into meetings with the First Presidency and the Twelve: "We sit with him each Thursday. We throw curve balls and hard balls to him, difficult problems. And he fields them all and makes wise decisions. He is brilliant at decision-making" (Madsen, *Presidents of the Church*, 425).

It was President Hinckley who extended the call, at President Kimball's instruction, to Russell Nelson to serve in the Quorum of the Twelve, and it was he who ordained him an Apostle. Through the

On tour with President Gordon B. Hinckley and his wife, Marjorie.

years the Nelsons traveled a number of times with the Hinckleys, including a trip to Central America that nearly proved disastrous.

One evening while in Managua, Nicaragua, the Hinckleys and Nelsons had just finished speaking to more than two thousand Saints there and were en route to the airport when a truck nearly hit the car carrying the Hinckleys. Though the truck managed to stop in time to avoid a collision, its load of long metal channel irons flew off and hit the right rear of the car.

"Those channel irons were twelve to twenty feet long," Elder Nelson recorded. "Like javelins, they struck the rear window, the wing window, and the window of the right rear door, completely shattering all three windows. The rear window of the Hinckleys' car was totally gone! President Hinckley foresaw the event and ducked his head forward. Sister Hinckley had done the same. Both escaped without injury. Sister Hinckley had several slivers of glass on her face, but they were easily removed. When we looked at the car, . . . we realized that the good Lord had protected His prophet and Sister Hinckley in a miraculous way" (Russell M. Nelson personal record, January 21, 1997).

Seven years later to the month, in January 2004, the Nelsons were returning from the dedication of the Accra Ghana Temple with the Hinckleys when Sister Hinckley had a medical event on the plane. Elder Nelson did all he could to comfort and help her, though at 30,000 feet he was limited in what he could do. Sister Hinckley never fully recovered from that incident and passed away three months later, on April 6, 2004. Ten months later, when Dantzel passed away, President Hinckley was one of the early visitors to check on Elder Nelson.

President Nelson's association with President Monson went back decades, to the season when Elder Monson was on the University of Utah alumni board and Dr. Nelson was president of the University of Utah medical alumni association. "Just call me Tom," Elder Monson greeted Dr. Nelson as they met, beginning a long and enduring friendship.

Elder Nelson had been with President Monson on October 28, 1988, when they met with Erich Honecker, chairman of the State Council of the German Democratic Republic, to ask for permission to send full-time missionaries to his country. The chairman responded with a thirty-minute lecture about the progress of the GDR under his leadership. But then Honecker opened a door that had been years in the making. "I watched the miracle happen when Erich Honecker said, 'President Monson, we trust you,'" Elder Nelson recorded. "All those years they had been keeping track of him. The Communists keep really good records of people who come in and out. They had monitored his sermons, and Erich Honecker said, 'We trust you. Therefore your requests are granted.'" The Church's request for missionaries was approved. Honecker also agreed that ten young men from the GDR could be called to serve outside their country (see Swinton, *To the Rescue*, 331–35).

Just over a year later, the Berlin Wall came down, and eleven months after that, Elder Nelson had the privilege of joining with President Monson to realign stake boundaries throughout Berlin, uniting the Saints in East and West Berlin for the first time in decades. It was a red-letter day filled with gratitude and emotion for Saints who had long been separated by the wall.

On June 1, 2008, Elder and Sister Nelson had the privilege of accompanying President Monson to the dedication of the temple in Curitiba, Brazil. There they again witnessed the greatness of President Monson's heart as well as his ability to receive revelation.

Prior to the dedication, Elder Nelson received a request from leaders in Brazil, asking if he could visit a boy stricken with a high-grade malignancy and currently undergoing chemotherapy while he was there. Because he was President Monson's "junior companion" on this trip and subject to his schedule, Elder Nelson did not immediately make an appointment to see the boy but hoped to find a time while he was in the area.

President Thomas S. Monson with Lincoln Vieira Cordeiro at the cornerstone laying of the Curitiba Brazil Temple.

Then the Lord intervened. At the cornerstone laying ceremony, as part of the first dedicatory session, President Monson applied the ceremonial mortar sealing the cornerstone in place. Then he scanned the audience and spotted a particular young boy. "He looks cold. Let's have him come up," he said. As he did, a photographer suggested the little boy take off his hat, which he did, revealing his bald head. Elder Nelson knew immediately, instinctively that the boy was the same child he'd been told about. Lincoln Vieira Cordeiro was his name, and President Monson helped him apply mortar to the cornerstone.

At that point, Elder Nelson, who was trying to keep the President on schedule, suggested they go back inside the temple to resume the first dedicatory session. But President Monson lingered, saying he wanted to invite another person to come forward. Again he scanned the crowd and ultimately noticed a woman far in the back and motioned her to come forward and put some mud in the crack. It wasn't until the next day that Elder Nelson learned the woman, Odilene Cordeiro, was Lincoln's mother. Rather than a visit with one Apostle, she and her son had met the prophet.

That was President Monson, according to Elder Nelson. "He [knew] how to draw revelation from God Almighty to bless the life of one person" (Swinton, *To the Rescue*, 520–21).

It was such experiences with President Monson that showed President Nelson that "there are things more important than the clock. I've tried to be more like him when I am meeting with people. Even with my family. Don't be so overridingly concerned with what time it is; just make sure that you are blessing the people while you are there, that they go away from that interchange better than they would have been" (Swinton, *To the Rescue*, 434).

In retrospect, President Nelson said of his relationship with President Monson: "He trusted me. He trusted me to help him when Frances was in ICU for long periods of time. He trusted me to follow in his footsteps in Eastern Europe and help there. He just trusted me."

President Nelson's various experiences with Presidents of the Church only reconfirmed and accentuated what he believed: that they led the Lord's Church under His direction; that they communicated with God in behalf of His people; and that heeding their counsel was spiritually wise. He had personally witnessed too many evidences of their prophetic gifts to ever conclude otherwise.

"Our sustaining of prophets is a personal commitment that we will do our utmost to uphold their prophetic priorities," President Nelson taught. "Our sustaining is an oath-like indication that we recognize their calling as prophet to be legitimate and binding upon us" (Nelson, "Sustaining the Prophets").

> "From his birth he's been intrigued
> with how things tick."
>
> —Elder Jeffrey R. Holland

Throughout his life, Russell Nelson demonstrated an inquisitive nature. His pioneering efforts in open-heart surgery are prima facie evidence, but there are other indicators as well. He is a classic "early adopter"—one of the first General Authorities to get a computer, one of the first to adopt new technologies, to get the latest iPhone, iPad, or other invention. Katie Irion Owens says her grandfather is the one who taught her how to AirDrop photos.

He tried to encourage his Brethren and other leaders to stay abreast of ever-changing technology. Ardeth G. Kapp remembers a day during her term as General President of the Young Women, from 1984 until 1992, when Elder Nelson proudly showed her the new computer he had in his office—one of the first in a General Authority's office. She suggested that the women serving as General Officers might be advantaged by a computer, and in less than a week she had one in her office.

He once tried to demystify the computer for Elder Neal A. Maxwell, a literal genius with

President Nelson's enthusiasm for technology is reflected in this 2016 picture of him in his office with two monitors for his computer and a tablet.

President Nelson played the organ in Quorum of
the Twelve meetings for nearly thirty-four years.

words, but "it made him feel like he was in the cockpit of a B-29"
(Hafen, *Disciple's Life*, 165).

When President Nelson became President of the Church, it was
the first time the President's office had Wi-Fi installed, the first time
there was a computer—with two monitors, no less—in the room.

President Nelson has always been an insatiable student. "I've
been in a car driving through the streets of Moscow, Russia, with
him," said Elder Gregory A. Schwitzer, "and he's always reading the
billboards and asking, 'What does that say? Tell me how you say that
word.' He wanted to learn languages, visit in members' homes, and
stop at historic sites in various countries, all to better understand the
people" (*Church News*/KSL Interview, January 8, 2018).

"I have this theory about President Nelson," said Elder Jeffrey R.
Holland, "that from his birth he's been intrigued with how things tick.
First of all he wanted to know how a heart ticked, so he learned how to
make them tick better. But after a phenomenal professional academic
career, he's brought that same approach to the Church. He wants to
know what makes people tick. He wanted to know what made the

Quorum of the Twelve tick. He's a Renaissance man, and he has the unusual ability to tell the world and tell the Church how the gospel ticks, how the Lord works, and what the Restoration of the gospel means for everyone" (*Church News*/KSL Interview, January 9, 2018).

President M. Russell Ballard summarized President Nelson's propensity for learning: "I think Russell Nelson got in every line in the premortal world. He plays the organ for us in our temple meetings. He knows the scriptures forwards and backwards. He knows languages. He goes some place and he's not there very long and is speaking to them in their language. When I go down to South America and try to say a little Spanish, they have to translate my Spanish into Spanish. That's the difference between the 'Russells.' But he is a born leader, and we will sustain and support him with all of our hearts" (*Church News*/KSL Interview, January 9, 2018).

President Dallin H. Oaks concurred, adding that he "is also the best writer in the Quorum of the Twelve. That may come as a surprise to some. I have spent my professional life working with words. I am very careful with words. But I have found as I give my talks in draft form to various members of the Quorum of the Twelve, there is no one who has a greater capacity to improve my talks than Russell M. Nelson. That came as a surprise to me, because doctors are not renowned for legible handwriting or clarity of expression. He is contrary to the expectation in both of those qualities. And over the years he has blessed my life greatly in the messages I've given in general conference" (*Church News*/KSL Interview, January 10, 2018).

From his earliest years when he skipped a grade in school, graduated early from medical school first in his class, became chief resident at the University of Minnesota Medical School, and helped pioneer open-heart surgery, Russell Nelson had been known for his intellect and curiosity. And regardless of his assignments or areas of responsibility, he wanted to understand not only how things ticked, but how to make them tick better.

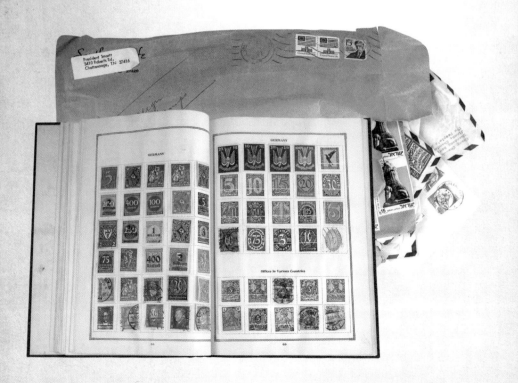

A few of President Nelson's hobbies are represented here: stamp and coin collecting, finding unusual figurines of doctors in other countries, and putting together jigsaw puzzles.

"Whenever I'm comfortably situated in our home, I'm in the wrong place. I need to be where the people are."

—President Russell M. Nelson

With his ordination as President of the Church just three months old and his first general conference as President of the Church in the books, President and Sister Nelson, along with Elder Jeffrey R. and Sister Patricia Holland, headed out on a twelve-day, whirlwind trip around the world. It was President Nelson's first international trip as President of the Church, and he built his itinerary with two clear messages in mind. First, by going directly to Jerusalem (after an overnight stop in London), he signaled his—and the Church's—highest priority: that members of The Church of Jesus Christ of Latter-day Saints are followers of Jesus Christ, and that the Church is the Lord's Church. It belongs to Him and is led by Him. And it is infused with all of His power to help build, strengthen, heal, perfect, and exalt His followers.

President Nelson, with Old Jerusalem in the background.

Second, the President was eager to show how deeply he cares about members everywhere in the growing, international Church he now led. In less than two weeks, the Nelsons and Hollands flew just shy of 30,000 miles to meet with the Saints in London, Jerusalem, Nairobi, Harare,

Bengalaru, Bangkok, Hong Kong, and Laie, Hawaii. "We met multitudes," said Elder Holland, "as many as could get into the venues" (see "Global Ministry Tour").

In Africa, some of the Saints traveled upwards of twenty hours to get to Nairobi or Harare, walking, taking long bus rides, doing whatever it took to be in the presence of a prophet. At least five of the gatherings—in Thailand, India, Hong Kong, Zimbabwe, and Kenya—were historic: in each case believed to be the largest gathering of Saints ever in those cities and countries.

In India, President Nelson told the members what a thrill it had been for him when he received clear revelation just prior to general

President Nelson speaks during the Jerusalem District Conference at the BYU Jerusalem Center.

The Nelsons and the Hollands in Bangkok, Thailand.

Receiving traditional leis with Sister Jean B. Bingham in Laie, Hawaii.

Greeting Saints in Bengaluru, India.

Sharing a moment with a child in Bangkok.

conference that it was time to build a temple there. In Kenya, he assured the Saints that they were pioneers in their own right. In Bangkok, Elder Holland was visibly moved when he saw the large convention center ballroom filled with 3,200 members. "I wish every missionary who has ever served in Thailand, and especially every early "pioneering" missionary, could see what I am looking at this evening," Elder Holland said with emotion at the outset of his address (transcript of Bangkok address, recorded by the author, April 20, 2018).

President Nelson spoke about the temple soon to be constructed in Bangkok and promised they would build it as soon as they could. "But it is up to you to build yourselves to the point where you can go to the temple," he urged the large congregation. "Prepare yourselves to be compliant with the commandments of God. Stop doing things you shouldn't do and start doing things you should do. . . . As you prepare yourselves to go to the temple, you will prepare you and your families for all the blessings God has in store for His faithful children" (Bangkok Devotional, transcript of message, April 20, 2018).

Throughout the trip, Elder Holland had a unique vantage point

Examining possible temple sites in Bengaluru, India.

Saints in Kenya line up to hear the prophet speak.

from which to observe the prophet: "When President Nelson was at the pulpit, almost easier than looking at him was to look out at the audience and watch them looking at him," he said. "I could get my impressions of him and my feelings about what he was saying by watching their faces to see what it did to them.

"I'm a member of the Church like everybody else out there," he continued, "and Russell M. Nelson is my prophet as well as theirs. I'm as adoring as they are because this is my prophet, this is my President. The members in each of those locations had it one time; Pat and I got to have it more than a half dozen times in sequence. In that sense, we were very much like members—it's just that we had more of a ringside seat and loved every minute of it" (Taylor, "Experiences from pulpit's 'other side,'" 3–4).

The Nelsons and Hollands kept a punishing pace, but as Wendy Nelson explained, "We don't have time for jet lag." They spoke, met with thousands of members—including in some members' homes— hugged hundreds of children, shook countless hands, and were photo-graphed constantly—all to communicate a central message, which

President Nelson and Sister Nelson meet with media representatives at the Hyde Park chapel in London, England.

President Nelson made clear: "Our message to the world is simple and sincere. We invite all of God's children, on both sides of the veil, to come unto their Savior, receive the blessings of the holy temple, have enduring joy, and qualify for eternal life" (see Nelson, "Let Us All Press On"; also transcripts of messages on Global Ministry Tour).

The travel was wearing for everyone, let alone a man in his nineties. But it was also rejuvenating to be with the members. "Broadening" is how President Nelson described it. "We enjoy meeting the people—they energize us. We learn their names, their culture, their language."

Dubbed the "Global Ministry Tour," this voyage actually was that. The gathering of Israel—the gathering of those who would hear the Lord's voice and follow Him—was in process all over the world. After introducing "ministering" in the April 2018 general conference, President Nelson set out around the world to show how it is done.

"Would you like to be a big part of the greatest challenge, the greatest cause, and the greatest work on earth today?"

—President Russell M. Nelson and Sister Wendy W. Nelson

President Russell M. Nelson has for decades studied and spoken frequently about the gathering of Israel on both sides of the veil. His October 2006 general conference address, "The Gathering of Scattered Israel," was a reflection of an untold number of messages he'd given through the years in less public settings on the same topic. The subject compelled him, and he returned to it again and again.

While serving as a mission president in Dallas, Texas, Elder Brian K. Taylor of the Seventy attended a mission presidents' seminar in the Midwest with Elder Nelson as the presiding authority. "He said he had been skiing with President Uchtdorf that morning, caught a flight, and then arrived at the seminar in time to teach us for two hours straight about the gathering of Israel. He opened my eyes to the gathering in a new way" (conversation with author, June 5, 2018).

Repeatedly, President Nelson emphasized how vital the doctrine of gathering is to the Lord's Church. Why? "Because the gathering of Israel is necessary to prepare the world for the Second Coming," he told incoming mission presidents on June 26, 2013. "The coming forth of the Book of Mormon is a tangible sign to the world that the Lord has commenced gathering Israel and fulfilling covenants He made to Abraham, Isaac, and Jacob. We not only teach this concept, but we also get to participate in it! We do so as we help to gather the elect of the Lord on both sides of the veil" (Nelson, "The Book of Mormon, the Gathering of Israel, and the Second Coming").

So it was not a surprise to anyone who'd paid attention to President Nelson's teachings through the years when he and Sister Nelson turned to this topic in a worldwide devotional for the youth of the Church on June 3, 2018. Speaking in tag-team fashion, with President Nelson beginning, followed by Sister Nelson, and then sandwiched again by the President to conclude, they invited every youth in the Church between the ages of twelve and eighteen to "enlist in the youth battalion of the Lord," focused on gathering Israel.

Sister Nelson asked the youth if they'd ever wondered why they hadn't been born in the 1880s, or, for that matter, thirty years from now. "Why are you here on earth *right now*?" she asked, and then she shared an experience she'd had in Moscow, Russia, on June 15, 2013, that opened her eyes and literally changed her view of living in the latter days.

As she began to address a group of about a hundred Russian sisters, she found herself saying something she had not anticipated saying. "I'd like to get acquainted with you by lineage," she began. Then, as the names of the Twelve Tribes of Israel were mentioned, she invited the sisters to stand when the tribe identified in their patriarchal blessings was named. Benjamin. Dan. Reuben. Naphtali. Zebulun. And so on. She, and everyone else, watched in amazement as women from every tribe but one—Levi—stood. Members from eleven of the twelve tribes of Israel were represented in that one small audience in Russia's capital city that day.

That afternoon, she and President Nelson flew to Yerevan, Armenia, and there she met a young elder (from Gilbert, Arizona, of all places) who was from the tribe of Levi. So in a twenty-four-hour period, she met someone from each of the twelve tribes.

"When I was a little girl attending Primary in Raymond, Alberta, Canada, I learned that in the last days—before the Second Coming of the Savior—the twelve tribes of Israel would be gathered," she told the youth. "So imagine what it was like for me to be with members of all twelve tribes of Israel within one twenty-four-hour period of time!"

At the worldwide devotional, she then turned the pulpit back to her husband with the charge to the youth: "Premortally, you and I committed to do a great work while we are here on earth. And with the Lord's help, we will do it!"

President Nelson built on his wife's experience, declaring that these *are* the latter days, that the Lord *is* hastening His work to gather Israel, and that "if you choose to, if you want to, you can be a big part of it. You can be a big part of something big, something grand, something majestic!"

He taught the youth that gathering Israel essentially means giving every one of Heavenly Father's children, on both sides of the veil, the chance to hear the message of the restored gospel of Jesus Christ and decide for themselves if they believe it. He then posed the question: "Would you like to be a big part of *the greatest* challenge, *the greatest* cause, and *the greatest* work on earth today?" If they would accept five challenges, he said, they would be better prepared to help gather Israel:

- Hold a seven-day fast from social media.
- For three weeks, make a weekly sacrifice of time to the Lord.
- Keep on the covenant path. If you have wandered off, immediately get back on the road of repentance.
- Pray daily for all to receive the blessings of the gospel.
- Stand out. Be a light. Set the standard. Give away one copy of *For the Strength of Youth*.

President Nelson concluded with the invitation to join the Lord's youth battalion. "You are among the best the Lord has *ever* sent to this world," he assured them. "You have the capacity to be smarter and wiser and have more impact on the world than any previous generation!" (Nelson and Nelson, "Hope of Israel").

Reactions were swift, powerful, and enduring. Many youth

The audience in the Conference Center for the worldwide youth devotional.

Inset: President and Sister Nelson at the worldwide devotional for youth.

deleted their social media apps before arriving home from the meeting. Others spoke about it publicly or went online to the Church's youth website or other locations to post their feelings. One young man leaving on his mission to the Philippines said he had given up treasured time with family at a nearby lake, a family favorite, during the last two weeks before his mission and instead had chosen to go the temple every day—and that he felt much more ready to enter the mission field. Another young man, a priest, spoke powerfully in sacrament meeting about the invitation to join the Lord's youth battalion and then declared, "President Nelson, my answer is yes. I want to be part of the Lord's youth battalion." Many later went to the Youth section of lds.org to record their reactions and experiences:

- "I really enjoyed President Nelson's counsel to take a break from social media. I found that as I took his counsel into account, I found that I felt different and wanted to extend my social media fast to one month and see how it went."

- "Thank you, President Nelson, for being so clear and distinct about what the youth need to do and why we are needed. So many confusing messages are online that distort why we came to earth and what we were sent here to do. These messages cleared my confusion and made sharing the gospel a thrilling mission to complete, rather than a burden."

- "I have been in an odd spiritual slump for a while now. I became so obsessed with my grades and work that I have been losing focus and precious time. . . . I almost didn't go to see this devotional . . . but I'm so glad that I went! . . . I began to tear up in the first song. . . . I am back in my groove with the Spirit and I can feel the daily sunshine in my soul. It's been months and I am so eternally grateful! Thank you President Nelson and Sister Nelson for answering questions and prayers of us all! We love and sustain you!"

- "I have been putting off watching this devotional for about a week now. Because I knew as soon as I watched it I would be accountable for my actions in either living what you have so diligently taught or putting aside the only thing that really should matter in my life. I don't want to go into detail, I just want to thank you for sharing this message. It's just what I need to get my life in line."

- "I have never felt so inspired in the course of my entire life. While this is a worldwide movement, I feel that it's also a personal call."

The social media fast, in particular, elicited hundreds, if not thousands, of pieces of feedback over time:

- It was amazing!!! I went to my phone, disabled my account, and deleted the app from my phone! I was excited to see how fast I would realize the difference that following President Nelson's invitation would manifest itself to me! It was almost immediately! It was amazing to me how much happier I was and how well things were going at home! The contention between my mother and I and my brothers and I diminished! I was so surprised I decided to add ANOTHER week to my fast!

- IT WAS ABSOLUTELY CHALLENGING YET FULFILLING! I ended mine yesterday and surprisingly, I did not feel the need to reinstall all of my social media apps anymore. The first few days of my fast felt like pure torture but as the days passed by, I came to realize how much time I spend on scrolling and reading stuff that did not help me at all.

- I hear all of the people saying how amazing it was, and I'm just laughing to myself bc for the first half of the week I literally hated it SO MUCH. Like I thought about quitting, the only reason I didn't quit was bc I told God I was gonna do it and I didn't want to disappoint Him like that. but yeah the first 3–4 days were probably the worst I've had in a long time, but I noticed that I was getting so much done. I went to the lake twice, temple twice, read 25-ish chapters in the BOM, got my oil changed, took some awesome naps, hung out with three different friends, I literally did so much. Doing this social media fast was the first time I've ever noticed myself listening to and following the counsel of the prophets and it seriously helped me gain a testimony that applying their words to my own life will be such a blessing in my life. It has proven to me that President Nelson is truly God's prophet on the earth and that he really does speak with Heavenly Father and receive revelation for our Church.

The first step in mobilizing the youth of the Church to help gather Israel was to invite them to experience what it felt like to disengage from the pull and tug of the world's voices. And for some, it was both revealing and life altering.

As Elder Brian K. Taylor of the Seventy remarked, "Imagine, President Nelson took one of the most difficult doctrines to teach, the gathering of Israel, and made it relevant to teenagers!" (conversation with author, June 5, 2018).

"I think my husband was hoping for a more concrete answer from my grandfather, but then when he stepped back, he thought that what he told him was exactly what he needed to do."

—Granddaughter Katie Irion Owens

As intent as he was on doing what the Lord needed and wanted him to do, nowhere was President Russell M. Nelson more invested, more connected than with his own family. With the increased demands as President of the Church, his schedule and visibility forced some things to change. But important family traditions remained intact. Children, grandchildren, and even great-grandchildren knew that if they texted their grandfather, he would respond, regardless of where he was in the world. Church leaders hosting him in various countries frequently saw him pull out his phone, dial a family member, and with Wendy sing "Happy Birthday" to a member of his huge clan. Family members scheduled blessings, baptisms, ordinations, sealings, and endowments so that

President Nelson congratulates a great-granddaughter at her baptism.

he and Wendy could be there. To them, he was still "Daddy" and "Grandfather."

"My grandfather is just so encouraging," said Katie Irion Owens. "He's always known just what to say. When he's traveling, he'll run into someone who knows a family member and then we'll get an email or a text telling us about it. He'll say something like, 'As a grandparent, that just makes my buttons burst.' As a granddaughter, to hear that is just so endearing. He is always in our corner and makes us feel like we can face anything" (*Church News*/KSL Interview, January 10, 2018).

During the solemn assembly at the April 2018 general conference, when the young women were invited to stand, Ashlyn Owens caught her great-grandfather's eye. "He smiled at me and gave a little wave, and I started to cry. I loved sustaining my great-grandfather" (remarks at President Nelson's ninety-fourth birthday devotional, recorded by author, September 9, 2018).

Stephen McKellar, now a cardiac surgeon at the University of Utah specializing in heart and lung transplants as well as artificial hearts, often comes to family events with the telltale messy hair of someone who's worn a surgical cap all day. "Tell me what you did today," his grandfather will quiz him with keen interest.

"Being a surgeon in the fifties and sixties and seventies is very different from today," Dr. McKellar said, "and he's always interested in what I'm doing and how I'm doing it. I've always felt he was one of my biggest cheerleaders. He convinced me over the years there was nothing I couldn't do. Next to my spouse and my parents, he has been the most influential person in my life. When I finished my training, he pulled me aside and gave me a briefcase and said, 'You'll need this as you start your career.' It was an emotional moment for the two of us that I'll never forget" (*Church News*/KSL Interview, January 11, 2018).

Family members were not immune, though, to their father's increased visibility as well as the heavy load he carried. "I shed tears of love for him and concern about the added burdens he would now be called upon to bear," said Gloria Irion from her home across the street from the Nauvoo Temple, where her husband was presiding as president and she was serving as temple matron when her father became President of the Church. "But his family has seen firsthand how he has been preserved and prepared," she admitted (conversation with author, May 8, 2018). Many family members had the same experience, vacillating between the joy of seeing Church members better know and appreciate their father and grandfather and concern about the additional burden he carried. But there were also privileges and insights into the growing gospel kingdom.

For decades, family members had benefited from their family patriarch's assignments around the world. Virtually anywhere any of them traveled, he had been there and left his mark. "I grew up

Then-Elder Nelson accompanies daughter Rosalie Ringwood at a mission presidents' seminar in Korea in November 2005.

hearing stories about establishing the Church in eastern bloc countries," said Stephen McKellar, "and when I went to a professional meeting in Prague, he said, 'My footprints are all over that town.' I distinctly remember having a conversation with him when I was a kid and he said, 'Stephen, these are some of the most pure people in the whole world.' It gave me a broader view of the work of God" (*Church News*/KSL Interview, January 11, 2018).

Russ Jr. was a teenager when he accompanied his father on a trip to Eastern Europe. "I got to pass the sacrament in Prague, Czechoslovakia, in the late eighties," he said. "The Church was brand-new there and I was one of two that passed the sacrament to maybe twenty people. That left a very deep impression on me and underscored that the Church is more than a place we go to or something we do. It is part of us" (*Church News*/KSL Interview, January 2018).

Near the end of Russ Jr.'s subsequent mission to Russia, he was helping prepare the members and others for the arrival of his father in the city where he was serving. "I was doing an interview on a local radio station," he said, "explaining the importance of having a member of the Quorum of the Twelve come to our city, when it dawned on me that this was my dad I was talking about. That was one of the first times the magnitude of my father's calling came together for me" (*Church News*/KSL Interview, January 2018).

As President Nelson's posterity grew, and grandchildren as well as great-grandchildren began to reach adulthood, his family faced the kinds of challenges most families encounter. And with the sheer number of individuals involved (at the time of this writing, more than 220), there were bound to be disappointments, trials, and setbacks. While several granddaughters chose to serve missions, not every missionary-age grandson chose to serve, and not every missionary grandson who began a mission finished it. While the majority of grandchildren were married in the temple and subsequently, with the birth of their children, were examples of righteous, intentional

With a great-granddaughter.

parenting, a couple of grandchildren left Church activity and a few others wrestled with questions and wondered if they had testimonies.

Two daughters dealt with divorce, which in both cases turned to their good. Serious health challenges were an ongoing part of the lives of several in each generation, and, reflective of the times in which we live, gender identity issues were present in the grand-children's generation. However, the strength of the extended Nelson family provided a buffer and place of security for those who chose to seek it, which most did.

In addition, President Nelson tended to take a long view when confronted with family members' challenges. "My husband has tre-mendous confidence in his children, as the parents and grandparents

Many members of President Nelson's family gathered to witness the announcement when he became President of the Church.

and great-grandparents of his posterity," Wendy Nelson explained.
"He trusts them to nurture and
strengthen and guide their children.
Naturally, he does whatever he can
to help as well. But he has faith that,
in time, the Lord will help with even
the most serious challenges in his
family."

And through all of the joys and
challenges, family members continued to learn from their patriarch's vast experience, some of it
immensely practical. Katie Irion
Owens's husband, Casey, a doctor
specializing in gastroenterology,
pulled his wife's grandfather aside
at a family gathering and asked him
how he had juggled it all as a young

Enjoying time with great-grandchildren at
his ninety-fourth birthday celebration.

doctor, father, and member of the Church asked to serve in many
ways. President Nelson's grandfatherly advice was straightforward:
"When you put the Lord first, you gain a great perspective and everything just falls in its rightful place." Katie said afterwards, "I think
my husband was hoping for a more concrete answer from my grandfather, but then when he stepped back, he thought that what he told
him was exactly what he needed to do" (*Church News*/KSL Interview,
January 10, 2018).

Putting the Lord first had always included, for President Nelson,
his family. At a family devotional the evening of his ninety-fourth
birthday, he and Wendy arrived at 5:00 p.m. for an event that wasn't
to begin until 6:30 to make sure he could greet every member of
his large family as they arrived. For an hour and half, he stood to

welcome and hug and, in his own unique way, encourage every child, grandchild, and great-grandchild, every son-in-law, daughter-in-law, and person who had married into the Nelson family. His nature to minister to every one of them was not diminished in the least by the fact that he now had the entire Church to worry about.

President and Sister Nelson at his ninety-fourth birthday celebration, September 9, 2018.

> "We are living in the most crucial era in the history of the world."
>
> —President Russell M. Nelson

L ines began to form around Safeco Field, the iconic home of the Seattle Mariners, early on Saturday, September 15, 2018. As the stadium filled to near capacity with what would be the largest non-sporting event ever held there, one almost expected Kevin Costner to emerge from the dugout. "If you build it, [they] will come," Costner's character heard a voice telling him in the classic 1989 film *Field of Dreams*, about an Iowa farmer who mowed down a cornfield to build a baseball diamond.

Instead it was a ninety-four-year-old prophet and his wife who emerged from the tunnel opposite first base and walked past 2,200 Laurels and priests seated on the infield to the large rostrum constructed at second base. Never mind that Seattle is one of the least religious cities in one of the least religious states in the U.S. (according to a 2017 Gallup poll, 47 percent of the adults in the state say "religion is not important to them, and they seldom or never attend services"). When Church leaders in the Seattle area learned President and Sister Nelson, along with President Henry B. Eyring,

President and Sister Nelson enter the stadium.

President Nelson addresses the crowd at Safeco Field.

would visit their city, they looked for the largest facility they could find, confident that members would fill it to the rafters. And on a chilly, rainy Saturday evening, 49,089 people did in fact come, filling the large baseball stadium.

Prior to the devotional, President and Sister Nelson and President Eyring spoke briefly to and greeted more than two hundred guests at a reception of local community and religious leaders. President Nelson thanked them for their contributions to the greater Seattle community and pronounced a blessing on Seattle's decision makers.

Meanwhile, as the large crowd filling the park waited eagerly for the Church President to appear, they shared their experience via social media. At various points during the evening, the hashtag #followtheprophet trended in Twitter's top ten in the country.

During the devotional, President Eyring bore his witness that

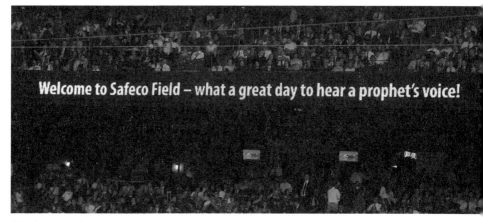

Celebrating a landmark event.

the Lord "directs His prophet even in the details of His kingdom" and that members can "take joy in new messages coming from God through the prophet." The gospel will not change, he assured the large audience, "but we will need personal revelation to feel the hand of the Lord when practical ways of doing things are changed by the Lord through His prophet. It will also take personal revelation to be able to see that a new way of doing things is better than the ways we have enjoyed." His summary was clear: The privilege of hearing "the word of God from a living prophet," he said, "is one of the great joys of being a member of The Church of Jesus Christ of Latter-day Saints."

Sister Nelson bore her unique testimony about the witness the Lord had blessed her with of her husband's prophetic call—but not without commenting on the unusual venue: "For some reason

President Henry B. Eyring at the Safeco Field event.

the song 'Take Me Out to the Ball Game' keeps coming to mind," she quipped. "And I have a craving for a hot dog."

Just the previous Sunday, President Nelson had celebrated his ninety-fourth birthday. Being still in the time of reflection birthdays tend to bring, he offered the large stadium audience lessons he had learned during his nine-plus decades of living. He began by recounting the time on the Colorado River when he'd been thrown from a raft and nearly drowned, then likened our journey through life to a river trip marked by both beautiful vistas and perilous rapids.

"If I've learned anything in my life," he taught, "it is that our ultimate security and our only enduring happiness lie in holding on to the iron rod of the restored gospel of Jesus Christ, complete with its covenants and ordinances. When we do so, we can safely navigate through rough waters because we have access to God's power."

President Nelson continued, proclaiming that "we are living in the most crucial era in the history of the world. Since the beginning of time, prophets have foreseen our day and prophesied about what would take place during this winding-up period before the Savior comes again." As a Church, he said, "we need to be doing what the Savior wishes us to do. And as a people we need to be looking and acting like true followers of Jesus Christ."

He pleaded with the large audience not to let the temptations of the world "distract you from the real reason you are here on planet earth." The real reason, he declared, was to determine if "you will use your agency to choose Jesus Christ and His gospel."

Members young and old were moved by the experience. "We were part of history," said one woman, who with her husband had brought six of their seven children to the stadium to hear the prophet. "Our kids will remember that forever." And another attendee echoed the feelings of many when he said that when President Nelson entered Safeco Field, the stadium became "holy ground" (see Weaver, "Seattle crowd").

> "One question we've wrestled with is how to take the gospel in its simple purity and the ordinances with their eternal efficacy to all of God's children without having basketball hoops get in the way."
>
> —President Russell M. Nelson

As President of the Quorum of the Twelve, President Nelson encouraged frequent conversations with his Brethren about the "imbalance between what we are doing as a Church and what we must do," as he described it.

Those who drive by or enter Latter-day Saint chapels see beautiful landscaping, nice parking lots, and handsome buildings with basketball courts inside. And yet most of the people of the earth live in China, India, and the Middle East—areas where billions live stacked on top of each other, wall-to-wall.

"One question we've wrestled with," President Nelson said, "is how to take the gospel in its simple purity and the ordinances with their eternal efficacy to all of God's children without having basketball hoops get in the way. We are accustomed to a church that is supported at home but accomplished in the chapels. We need a complete turnaround, where we have a home-centered church supported by what takes place inside our buildings. The only buildings that are absolutely essential are temples. Stake centers and chapels are a luxury. This imbalance is on our worry list—*high* on the list. One Muslim man said it this way, 'When your Christianity is simple enough that I can take it with me on the back of a camel, I will be interested.' Faith, repentance, baptism, the endowment, and the sealing ordinance are

A home-centered church is supported in the meetinghouse, not focused on it.

essential. Everything you'll see happening in the Church from this point forward will be in that direction."

In a letter dated June 29, 2018, the First Presidency announced a series of resources to help Church members and their families study the scriptures at home: *Come, Follow Me—For Individuals and Families*, essentially, the "Come, Follow Me" approach for individual and home learning. "Living by and reading the word of God," the First Presidency wrote, "will build faith in Heavenly Father and His plan of salvation and in the Savior Jesus Christ and His Atonement."

For years leaders had been emphasizing that home was, ideally, where primary gospel learning should take place. Leaders hoped members would use the new resources to strengthen their faith, deepen conversion, and increase their knowledge of the gospel (see "LDS Church to Release 'Come, Follow Me' Curriculum").

Or at least, that was what it looked like in July, when the resources were announced. But the full impact and purpose of *Come, Follow Me—For Individuals and Families* became clear when, in the Saturday morning session of the October 2018 general conference, President Russell M. Nelson stepped to the Conference Center pulpit and announced another historic decision: "As Latter-day Saints we have become accustomed to thinking of 'church' as something that happens in our meetinghouses," he explained. "We need an adjustment to this pattern. It is time for a home-centered church, supported by what takes place inside our branch, ward, and stake buildings"

(Nelson, "Opening Remarks"). He then said that Elder Quentin L. Cook would explain in detail what this meant.

In a change that had been rumored, in one fashion or another, for years, Elder Cook explained that the three-hour meeting block on Sunday would, as of January 2019, be shortened to allow more time at home that day for family gatherings and gospel study. The first hour would be devoted to sacrament meeting and the second to Relief Society, Young Women, and priesthood quorum meetings every other Sunday, with alternate Sundays using that hour for Sunday School. Primary would be held the second hour every week.

The new "Come, Follow Me" curriculum.

"Our purpose is to balance the Church and the home experiences in a way that will greatly increase faith and spirituality and deepen conversion to Heavenly Father and the Lord Jesus Christ," Elder Cook declared. He also underscored the ongoing revelation that had led to this significant modification: "As leaders have sought revelation, the guidance received over the past few years is to strengthen the sacrament meeting, honor the Sabbath day, and encourage and assist parents and individuals to make their homes a source of spiritual strength and increased faith—a place of joy and happiness."

Elder Cook concluded with his testimony of all that had transpired leading to this announcement: "I testify to you that in the deliberations of the Council of the First Presidency and the Quorum of the Twelve Apostles in the temple, and after our beloved prophet petitioned the Lord for revelation to move forward with these adjustments, a powerful confirmation was received by all. Russell M. Nelson is our living President and prophet. The announcements made today will result in profound blessings for those who enthusiastically embrace the adjustments and seek the guidance of the Holy Ghost" (Cook, "Deep and Lasting Conversion").

During the same session, Elder David A. Bednar added his witness about the restructured Sabbath day schedule combined with emphasis on gospel learning in the home: "We live in a remarkable and revelatory season of the restored Church of Jesus Christ. The historic adjustments announced today have only one overarching purpose: to strengthen faith in Heavenly Father and His plan and in His Son, Jesus Christ, and His Atonement. The Sunday meeting schedule was not simply shortened. Rather, we now have increased opportunities and responsibilities as individuals and families to use our time for enhancing the Sabbath as a delight at home and at church" (Bednar, "Gather Together").

It was a landmark change, one discussed in various iterations over many years and now designed, the Brethren believed, to help members make home their primary place of religious instruction. "The new home-centered, Church-supported integrated curriculum has the potential to unleash the power of families, as each family follows through conscientiously and carefully to transform their home into a sanctuary of faith," President Nelson promised in his concluding remarks at the conference. "I promise that as you diligently work to remodel your home into a center of gospel learning, over time *your* Sabbath days will truly be a delight. *Your* children will be excited to learn and to live the Savior's teachings, and the influence of the adversary in *your* life and in *your* home will decrease. Changes in your family will be dramatic and sustaining" (Nelson, "Becoming Exemplary Latter-day Saints").

Response to the announcement ran the gamut. While there seemed to be an almost universal appreciation for a shorter block of time at Church on Sunday, some parents felt overwhelmed and worried about whether they could make the extra time teaching their

"I promise that as you diligently work to REMODEL your HOME into a **center of gospel learning,** over time your SABBATH DAYS will truly be a delight."

—RUSSELL M. NELSON

children at home meaningful. Many mothers, in particular, felt the weight of providing experiences for their children that would make a difference. Some parents with adult children wondered how to encourage family members living away from home to increase and improve their gospel study. Some single parents or unmarried members wrestled with what it meant for them. Others welcomed the change and relished additional time on the Sabbath to serve, study, and ponder as well as spend time with family members. One sister summarized the feelings of many when she said, "I think the prophet has given us all a hastening. This changed only one hour each Sunday at church, but it feels like a much bigger shift for all of us."

For members wherever they lived and whatever their circumstances, this change signaled the Lord's confidence, communicated through His servants, in the members of His Church to take a major step forward in their own personal worship.

"It is *not* a name change.
It is *not* rebranding. It is *not* cosmetic.
It is *not* a whim. And it is *not* inconsequential.
Instead, it *is* a correction."

—President Russell M. Nelson

Under President Nelson's leadership, there continued to be new areas of emphasis. On Thursday, August 16, 2018, the Church issued a press release directed largely to news media that caught the attention of not only journalists but members and even the general public alike. The opening lines left no doubt about where the statement originated, and why: "President Russell M. Nelson of The Church of Jesus Christ of Latter-day Saints has made the following statement regarding the name of the Church: 'The Lord has impressed upon my mind the importance of the name He has revealed for His Church, even The Church of Jesus Christ of Latter-day Saints. We have work before us to bring ourselves in harmony with His will. In recent weeks, various Church leaders and departments have initiated the necessary steps to do so'" ("Name of the Church").

The statement included a style guide explaining that the Prophet Joseph Smith received the full name of the Church by revelation in 1838, and that when referencing the Church, writers and others should use its full name whenever possible, though it could also be referred to as the "Church of Jesus Christ" or the "restored Church of Jesus Christ." "Please avoid using the abbreviation 'LDS' or the nickname 'Mormon' as substitutes for the name of the Church, as in 'Mormon Church,' 'LDS Church,' or 'Church of the Latter-day Saints.'"

When referencing members of the Church, *Latter-day Saints* was preferred. "We ask that the term *Mormons* not be used, though the word *Mormon* could be properly used in the Book of Mormon and in other historical expressions such as the 'Mormon Trail.'"

The announcement and style guide raised questions about the future of the names of many well-known, and even famous, Church institutions. The institutional Church itself was, in many respects, the worst offender, with the last decade or so bringing the advent of the Mormon Channel, the *Meet the Mormons* movie, the "I'm a Mormon" campaign, Mormon.org, Mormon Messages, Mormon Helping Hands, Mormonandgay.org, and the Church's main website (lds.org) as well as the address for all official Church emails (@ldschurch.org). Ironically, the announcement came via one of the Church's official websites, mormonnewsroom.org.

Reaction was swift and varied. Some thought it was much ado about nothing. Others were struck by President Nelson's clear declaration that the Lord had spoken to Him about this issue. Skeptics doubted it was possible. The Church had tried before, they said, to encourage the use of the full name of the Church, and it had never lasted.

President Marion G. Romney of the First Presidency had said in a 1979 general conference address that the term *Mormon Church* was inaccurate. In 1990, Elder Russell M. Nelson reemphasized the importance of the correct name of the Church, also in general conference (see Nelson, "Thus Shall My Church Be Called"). Prior to the 2002 Winter Olympics held in Salt Lake City, the First Presidency issued an official letter posted in meetinghouses encouraging the use of the full, official name of the Church—or shortened versions that included the name of Jesus Christ. Most recently, in 2011, Elder M. Russell Ballard said the nickname "Mormon" was acceptable but encouraged use of the full, official name of the Church and discouraged using "Mormon Church."

Despite skeptics who claimed that this had been tried before, and that the word *Mormon* was too ingrained in the Church's and world's lexicon to ever be successfully eliminated, many members responded quickly and positively. Some Latter-day Saints quickly changed the names of their Twitter accounts and Facebook pages. Operators of Latter-day Saint websites began to look for solutions and alternatives. Many responded in ways that suggested they sensed something was different this time. As one woman summarized her reaction, "It sounds as though President Nelson is saying, 'Enough. We have offended the Lord long enough by endorsing the use of nicknames that omit His name."

Indeed, something was different this time. In a series of many meetings during the preceding months, the First Presidency and Quorum of the Twelve Apostles had discussed this issue at length, including how difficult it would be to effect a sustained change among Church members, and they were united about its importance. They consulted with experts and sought the direction of heaven. Ultimately, President Nelson tasked the quorum to lead the effort to honor the Lord's instructions about what His Church should be called.

At the seminar for new mission presidents in June 2018, President Nelson referred to the "hope of his heart," that we would begin to call the Church by its correct name. Other meetings for General Authorities and General Officers emphasized the importance of this undertaking.

In a meeting just days before the press release announcing the course correction, President M. Russell Ballard convened a meeting of Church department heads and leaders from other Church organizations to discuss the coming announcement. In that meeting, Elder Jeffrey R. Holland declared that "names matter," adding that "if we don't take the name of Christ, by definition we take some other name." Elder Dieter F. Uchtdorf emphasized that the senior Brethren

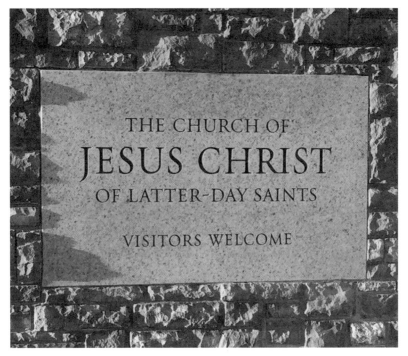

More than twenty years ago, in 1996, the Church changed its logo to "reempha-size . . . the official name of the Church and the central position of the Savior in its theology" ("New Church Logo Announced").

were united in understanding that there was no need to take the monumental effort to make this course correction unless they were prepared to see it through to the end. And President Ballard emphasized that point in his concluding remarks: "This is a revealed concern to the prophet today, and he has laid at the feet of the Quorum of the Twelve the responsibility to make this happen," he said. "We *are* The Church of Jesus Christ of Latter-day Saints. We realize this will not happen overnight, but this time, this effort to use the correct name of the Church will not dwindle in unbelief" (meeting with Church department and organizational heads, August 13, 2018, author's personal notes).

Two days after the press release, President Nelson told a large group of Saints at a devotional in Montreal, Canada, that the name of the Church was not negotiable because the Lord has told us what His Church should be called. "We're not changing names," he confirmed. "We are correcting the name—that's important to note."

In a post-devotional media interview, he acknowledged it was going to be a challenge to undo traditions of more than a hundred years, and that we don't have all the answers, but that "we are correcting an error that has crept in over the ages." He also reaffirmed that he wanted to be careful to protect the name of Mormon, a prophet and record keeper whom we honor. "All we know," he said, "is the Lord has said, 'Thus shall my church be called. . . . The Church of Jesus Christ of Latter-day Saints.' That's enough for me" (Taylor, "'We're correcting a name'").

If there were any question about how serious the senior leaders of the Church were about making this correction, those wonderings were put to rest the day before the October 2018 general conference when leaders of the venerable Mormon Tabernacle Choir announced that the choir's name had been changed to the Tabernacle Choir at Temple Square.

Then, at conference, President Nelson addressed the issue head-on. Acknowledging that reactions to the earlier press statement about the name of the Church had been mixed, he began by stating what this effort was *not*: "It is *not* a name change. It is *not* rebranding. It is *not* cosmetic. It is *not* a whim. And it is *not* inconsequential," he declared. "Instead, it *is* a correction. It is the command of the Lord. . . . It was the Savior Himself who said, 'For thus shall my church be called in the last days, even The Church of Jesus Christ of Latter-day Saints.'" (Nelson, "Correct Name of the Church").

President Nelson made the crux of the issue crystal clear: "What's in a name or, in this case, a nickname? When it comes to nicknames of the Church, such as the 'LDS Church,' the 'Mormon Church,' or the 'Church of the Latter-day Saints,' the most important thing *in* those names is the *absence* of the Savior's name. To remove the Lord's name from the Lord's Church is a major victory for Satan. When we *discard* the Savior's name, we are subtly *disregarding* all that Jesus Christ did for us—even His Atonement." (Nelson, "Correct Name of the Church").

This was not a change; it was a course correction—and one that, admittedly, called for heavy lifting. But there were also promised blessings for respecting the Lord Jesus Christ anytime His Church was mentioned. "I promise you that if we will do our best to restore the correct name of the Lord's Church," President Nelson concluded, "He whose Church this is will pour down His power and blessings upon the heads of the Latter-day Saints, the likes of which we have never seen" (Nelson, "Correct Name of the Church").

The Lord had spoken to His prophet, and President Nelson had now conveyed the message and set in process the course correction. "In a coming day," he said, "I will report my stewardship to the Prophet Joseph Smith and Brigham Young and Spencer W. Kimball and others, and I want to be able to tell them I've done what the Lord wanted me to do."

"Con su permiso, quisiera hablar en español."

—President Russell M. Nelson

___

On Saturday evening, October 20, 2018, President Nelson stepped to the pulpit in a large sports arena in Lima, Peru. Nearly 6,000 Latter-day Saints of every age had packed the Coliseum, and another 35,000 were viewing from various stake centers throughout Peru. Elder Enrique R. Falabella, president of the South America North Area, and his wife, Ruth; Elder Gary E. Stevenson of the Quorum of the Twelve and his wife, Lesa; and Wendy Nelson had already addressed the large audience. Then something unexpected, something almost magical, happened.

President Nelson began by saying, "My heart is filled with feelings of love and gratitude for you." He told the Peruvian Saints about meeting with their president, the president of Peru, that morning at the Presidential Palace in Lima. President Martín Vizcarra had thanked President Nelson for the Saints there being such good citizens as well as for humanitarian aid in the form of wheelchairs and other significant contributions the Church had made to his country. "We thank you for being such good examples," President Nelson said to the

Meeting with President Martín Vizcarra of Peru. Left to right: Elder Gary E. Stevenson, President Nelson, President Vizcarra, and Elder Enrique R. Falabella.

President Nelson delivers his address to Peruvian Saints in Spanish.

Saints. He then thanked his translator, told him he wouldn't need him any further, and said: *"Con su permiso, quisiera hablar en español."* ("With your permission, I would like to speak in Spanish.")

From his ideal vantage point on the large rostrum, Elder Stevenson saw the reaction throughout the hall: "We watched from the stage as complete surprise registered on the faces of so many and then as tears began to flow," he described. "Then, unable to contain their excitement, the audience began to spontaneously applaud. It was a moment to remember" (conversation with author, October 28, 2018).

There were tears and smiles all around. Husbands hugged their wives and mothers leaned over and whispered to their children as, for more than twenty minutes, they listened to their prophet speak to them in their own tongue. President Nelson's message was straight-forward and clear: He encouraged them to keep the commandments, to teach their children the gospel, to grow together as families, and to build their faith in Jesus Christ.

Earlier that day, the Nelsons, Stevensons, and Falabellas had spoken to missionaries from the five Lima-area missions who had jammed into the largest stake center in Peru's capital city. "I went fishing last July," President Nelson told the missionaries, "and we didn't put a worm on a hook and hope to catch a fish. We were on a boat with a fish-finder. We went where the fish were. You are fishers of men, and you have been assigned to labor where the fish are, because most of those you teach in Peru are of the lineage of Joseph. As Sister Nelson explained earlier, their ancestors are pulling and pleading for you to find and baptize or activate those who will do their work for them. You are in a rich field of labor" (Lima, Peru, missionary meeting, October 20, 2018, author's notes).

From Lima, the Nelsons, Stevensons, and Falabellas flew to La Paz, Bolivia, where the Saints turned out again in record numbers. More than 9,000 members filled a large sports arena, with another 15,000-plus viewing the proceedings throughout Bolivia. The mile-long row of buses painted in every color of the rainbow lined up outside the sports arena reflected the effort of thousands who came on foot, by bus, and via every conceivable mode of transportation to hear the prophet of God.

President Nelson had been to South America many times over the years, beginning with professional invitations to teach open-heart surgery and then continuing during his ministry as an Apostle. But visiting as President of the Church was new, and he seized the opportunity to minister to the Saints in the way only the President of the Church can. He shook hands with hundreds of missionaries, met with small groups of young adults, teenagers, and families before each devotional, and was drawn to members young and old.

"What I have felt as much as anything on this trip is the almost universal connection President Nelson has to the members," said

Surrounded by children in Asunción, Paraguay.

Elder Gary E. Stevenson. "You think that he's connected to the children. And yes, he is. But he's also connected to the youth. And to young adults and young marrieds. And then you see how sweet he is with seniors. The connection he has to every age group is profound, and they seem to all feel that they own him, because he reaches out to them. I feel that I've been mentored in ministering" (conversation with author, October 28, 2018).

President Nelson connected by sharing his love openly, which often included sharing his heart as well.

In Lima, a small group of teenagers had the chance to meet with the Nelsons, Stevensons, and Falabellas prior to the devotional. One teenage girl asked how to stay actively involved in the Church when other family members are not. President Nelson readily shared his own background—that he hadn't been raised in a home where the gospel was taught but that it is very possible to have a testimony even when one's personal circumstances aren't perfect. Several youth wiped away tears as President Nelson left their small gathering to join the large congregation waiting for him.

As President and Sister Nelson prepared to depart various venues in Lima, La Paz, Asunción, Montevideo, and Concepción, they waved, and thousands of hands waved back. But the children near him weren't always as circumspect, sometimes rushing up to greet him, even surprising security officers standing nearby. In Asunción, when President and Sister Nelson exited the stage and walked down to the first row of the congregation to greet government and religious dignitaries who had honored him with their presence, a group of children saw an opportunity and together rushed forward for hugs. Before anyone knew it, President Nelson was on his knees surrounded by a dozen adoring children.

"I was totally caught off guard by what I experienced on this trip," Sister Lesa Stevenson admitted. "For example, when we walked into that large sports coliseum in La Paz, Bolivia, the love and joy the people had for him, and he for them, was palpable. In that moment I realized that I hadn't known what to expect when we were invited to accompany the President of the Church and his wife to South America. I thought I knew, but I didn't. Being with the prophet out ministering to the people is an experience that changes you" (conversation with author, October 28, 2018).

President Nelson's ten days in South America provided other unique opportunities. While in Montevideo, he was interviewed by Sergio Rubin, the official biographer of Pope Francis, who traveled from Buenos Aires to meet him. One of the most respected journalists in the southern cone of South America, Rubin posed questions about everything from the relevance of religion in an increasingly secular society to President Nelson's views on gun control, immigration, abortion, polygamy, same-sex marriage, gender rights, and the role of women in the Church.

After Rubin asked about extremists whose violence is motivated by religion, President Nelson repeated something he said several times while in South America: "The teachings of the Lord are clear. There is to be no contention, no disputation." President Nelson quickly added that Muslims unfairly suffer discrimination for the acts of radicalized Muslims. "They are our brothers and sisters," he said, "and we don't like adversarial proceedings between them and us."

On the volatile topic of immigration, President Nelson said, simply, "We teach that we should build bridges of cooperation instead of fences of opposition," adding, "I don't like fences."

Rubin, with a dual Argentine and Italian citizenship, asked about the temple soon to be dedicated in Rome, and President Nelson spoke of his appreciation for "the kindness of the Pope and the Vatican. They have been most gracious and welcoming to us." Rubin characterized the temple in Rome as an "exercise in interfaith coexistence."

When Rubin asked if the U.S. Supreme Court would reverse abortion laws, President Nelson responded that current law appeared to be "settled law. I don't see that as a very likely possibility, but nonetheless we teach our people to have respect for human life from conception to the grave. It is a sacred matter, and people offend the Creator when they interfere with His plans, so we strongly support the sacredness of the body." At Rubin's second question on the topic, President Nelson added, "Each body is a temple of God. As a doctor, I know that little fetus has life. About two weeks after conception, a little heart starts to beat. For us, that is a very sacred thought."

President Nelson responded with optimism to Rubin's assertion that religion is under retreat in many areas of the world: "Generally speaking, the family is under attack and religion is under attack," President Nelson agreed, "but we are confident the family will prevail and religion will prevail" (Russell M. Nelson interview with Sergio Rubin, October 26, 2018, author's notes).

After the interview, Rubin agreed to be interviewed by the

President Nelson gives a copy of his biography to Sergio Rubin, Argentine journalist and biographer of Pope Francis, after an interview in Montevideo, Uruguay, on October 26, 2018. Carlos Aguero, center, interprets.

journalists who were following President Nelson on the trip, and he reflected about meeting President Nelson: "He is very warm. He is a man of faith, he's a man of the spiritual world, and this means that he conveys at a very special frequency—very human and way beyond the human way. Like every church, The Church of Jesus Christ has its peculiarities and differences, but the truth is, at the core, all religions have the same teachings. Religions teach peace, brotherhood. It's good that The Church of Jesus Christ wants to spread spirituality to the world. The Church shows characteristics of solidarity" (Sergio Ruben interview with journalists, October 26, 2018, audiofile in author's possession; see also Walch, "President Nelson condemns religious violence").

President Nelson concluded his visit to five South American countries with what he called a "heavenly crescendo"—the dedication of the Church's 160th operating temple, the Concepción Chile

Temple, on Sunday, October 28, 2018. Elder Stevenson built on that theme, adding: "Today just felt absolutely heavenly. It was punctuated by the spirit and the people and their preparation spiritually" (Walch, "President Nelson calls Chile temple dedication 'heavenly crescendo'").

President Thomas S. Monson had announced the Concepción Chile Temple in October 2009, but just four months later a massive 8.8-magnitude earthquake struck Chile, delaying construction but significantly influencing the unique engineering of the new edifice. The temple was essentially constructed on two foundations—one that holds up the temple and the other that holds up twenty-four ball bearings on top of pedestals that allow the temple to move or roll up to two feet in any direction in the event of earthquake, with large shock absorbers in all four corners designed to slow the acceleration of any movement. As a result, a 10-magnitude earthquake would feel more like a 2-magnitude inside the temple.

Referring to the dedication of this unique structure, Sister Wendy Nelson, who spoke at every meeting with members and missionaries as well as in one temple dedicatory session, added that her husband had "seen the faith of the people. He has seen the love of the people for the Lord. Now he has seen the love of the people for the temple. That means everything to my husband to see that."

After the VIP luncheon the day prior to the dedication, Chilean Senator Jacqueline van Rysselberghe shared her reaction to the construction of a temple in Concepción: "When we have had emergencies—and in this city we have had many emergencies," she said, "many members of the Church volunteer to help, to serve, and to assist on behalf of other people. Therefore, what we see here today, the beauty of this building, reflects the beauty of the souls of the members of the Church" ("President Nelson Dedicates Concepción Chile Temple").

Such comments from respectful dignitaries who attended

At the cornerstone-laying ceremony for the
Concepción Chile Temple dedication.

President Nelson greets a missionary grandson in Uruguay.

Bolivian Saints gather to hear the prophet's words.

In front of the Concepción Chile Temple.

various events with President Nelson, as well as the large numbers the Nelsons and Stevensons met throughout Peru, Bolivia, Paraguay, Uruguay, and Chile, represented what felt like a miracle to President Nelson. On December 25, 1925, Elder Melvin J. Ballard had dedicated the land of South America for the preaching of the gospel in a park in Buenos Aires, Argentina. At the time, there were no known members of the Church there. And though the Prophet Joseph Smith had prophesied that the gospel would fill both North and South America, Elder Ballard and his colleagues completed their assignments in South America in 1925 feeling they had failed to inaugurate the conversion process to any degree.

Russell Nelson was just fifteen months old when Elder Melvin J. Ballard delivered that dedicatory prayer. So, in the span of President Nelson's lifetime, South America had been transformed from a land where the gospel was absent into a center of gospel strength with more than four million members. It had grown from "an acorn to a mighty oak," as Elder Melvin J. Ballard had also prophesied. South America was exhibit A for the gathering that President Nelson repeatedly spoke of with energy and urgency.

With more than two hundred countries in the world, the number of places President Nelson visited in his first ten months as President of the Church seemed like "a small drop in the bucket," he admitted. But he was not finished. "We will get around, but we will still miss more than we will touch. But we will try. We won't give up just because it is a big job" (Walch, "President Nelson calls Chile temple dedication 'heavenly crescendo'").

When asked after interviewing President Nelson how leaders can help people embrace religion, Sergio Rubin answered that "closeness, humanity, reaching out is very important. Leaders have to get close to the people to see that religion is an everyday matter. It is a normal thing. That God is right next to the person. So others can see them as normal people. In the future, closeness will define this religious question" (Sergio Rubin interview with journalists, October 26, 2018, audiofile in author's possession; see also "Popes and Prophets").

It was the desire to get close to the people that took President and Sister Nelson to South America, where during ten days there they spoke to an estimated 224,000 Saints. And there was more to come. "We're witnesses to a process of restoration," the prophet said before departing Concepción at the conclusion of his trip to South America. "If you think the Church has been fully restored, you're just seeing the beginning. There is much more to come. . . . Wait till next year. And then the next year. Eat your vitamin pills. Get your rest. It's going to be exciting" ("Latter-day Saint Prophet").

President Nelson with Elders Gary E. Stevenson and Enrique R. Falabella after meeting with the president of Peru.

Bidding a fond farewell to the Saints in South America.

EPILOGUE

While working on this book, I had the privilege of joining President and Sister Nelson along with others in a sealing session in the Bountiful Utah Temple. That day we acted as proxies for fifty deceased couples who were to be sealed. This meant, of course, that we listened to that stunning ordinance fifty times in a row. The repetition that day did something for me. I "heard" things I had never heard before and found myself pondering the implications of several words—and promises—in the ordinance in a new way.

As we concluded, before we left the sealing room, I asked President Nelson one of the questions I'd been pondering. He answered quickly and without apology: "I don't know the answer to that, Sheri. What I do know is that what the Lord has in store for those who make and keep these covenants with Him goes far beyond what we can comprehend right now. All of the promises in the sealing covenant are possible because of Him." As he spoke, I heard echoes of, "Ye are little children and ye cannot bear all things now; ye must grow in grace and in the knowledge of the truth" (Doctrine and Covenants 50:40).

In that brief interchange, President Russell M. Nelson did what prophets always do. He testified of Jesus Christ and, in the process, offered a glimpse into the majesty of eternity. This depth of knowledge—and the promise of even more to come in the future—provides a kind of security and confirmation that can't be found anywhere else.

Not long ago I heard a mission president ask a group of his elders and sisters what they thought the most difficult commandment to live would be after they were released as full-time missionaries and then throughout their lives. Their answers were varied, with many revolving around the challenge to live the law of chastity. The mission president listened intently, and after the missionaries had each shared his or her response, he said: "You will each have challenges, and, for some of you, temptations with morality will be among them. But I invite you to consider something: Throughout the rest of your life, your most difficult challenge will probably be to follow the prophet. There is going to be an increasing gap between his counsel and what the world insists is acceptable and reasonable. There will likely be moments when you don't agree with something he says. But I hope you'll remember what I'm telling you today, that your greatest safety will be in following the prophet. The prophet will always see things you can't see and help you avoid pitfalls you otherwise might not recognize in time."

There are not many guarantees in this life. There isn't a car made with a warranty that covers everything. No bank can guarantee your money will be safe under every circumstance. Plenty of leaders let us down. Politicians often don't do what they promised. On occasion, even Amazon Prime fails to deliver on time.

But the Lord has given His followers, members of His Church, an ironclad guarantee, a supernal spiritual safety net—that *He* will choose His prophet, and that He will never let that man lead us astray. In a world of noisy, competing, conflicting voices constantly jockeying for customers or followers or adherents to their points of view—voices for whom self-interest too often rules the day—this is a stunning guarantee.

One of the surest ways to *get on,* or *get back on,* or *stay on* the covenant path is to follow the prophet.

———

A good while before President Nelson became President Nelson—meaning, before he became President of the Quorum of the Twelve, let alone President of the Church—I had an unexpected and, for me, unique experience. In the middle of one night I awoke suddenly, sat straight up in bed, and had one of the clearer impressions of my life: "Russell M. Nelson is going to be the President of the Church." In that moment, it seemed so curious. I've rarely had impressions about callings before they occur. And besides, President Monson was doing well, and President Boyd K. Packer and Elder L. Tom Perry were senior to then-Elder Nelson. I wasn't sure what to make of that experience. All I knew to do was to tuck it away and, like Mary, keep "all these things, and [ponder] them in [my] heart" (Luke 2:19).

I still don't understand why the Lord shared that information with me when He did. But because of that nighttime message, I had a witness long before President Monson died not only that President Russell M. Nelson was a prophet, seer, and revelator but that he would become the senior Apostle and thus President of the Church.

Even with that, over the past months as I've labored on this project, the Spirit has repeatedly borne witness again that President Nelson is a prophet of God. As I have examined so many details from his life, it has become even more clear that the Lord has had him in His tutelage from day one. He, meaning the Lord, has taught and mentored and tried and tested and refined and guided him again and again and again.

I bear witness of the prophetic call of Russell M. Nelson. He, like the sixteen men who have preceded him in this office—beginning with the Prophet Joseph Smith—and like those the Lord is preparing even now to succeed him, has been prepared and seasoned by heaven for the specific hour and season his leadership is needed. I am certain of that. This is not something I believe. It is something I know.

I am also certain that one of the greatest gifts our Father and His Son have given us, and one of our greatest mortal safety nets, is the gift of a living prophet. I testify that all who sincerely want to know if this is true can know it for themselves. And I testify also that the safest course in life is to listen to and follow the prophet.

SOURCES CITED

Andersen, Neil L. Facebook post. @lds.neil.l.andersen, August 15, 2018.

———. "A Holier Approach to Ministering." BYU Devotional, April 10, 2018.

———. "The Prophet of God." *Ensign*, May 2018.

———. "The Voice of the Lord." *Ensign*, November 2017.

Bednar, David A. "Gather Together in One All Things in Christ." *Ensign*, November 2018.

Bingham, Jean B. "Ministering as the Savior Does." *Ensign*, May 2018.

Christofferson, D. Todd. "The Elders Quorum." *Ensign*, May 2018.

Church News/KSL Interviews. January 5, 8–11, 2018.

Condie, Spencer J. *Russell M. Nelson: Father, Surgeon, Apostle.* 2003.

Cook, Quentin L. "Deep and Lasting Conversion to Heavenly Father and the Lord Jesus Christ." *Ensign*, November 2018.

Cowdery, Oliver. "Dear Brother." *Messenger and Advocate*, vol. 1, no. 1 (October 1834): 14–16.

Dew, Sheri L. *Ezra Taft Benson: A Biography.* 1987.

———. *Go Forward with Faith: The Biography of Gordon B. Hinckley.* 1996.

"Discovering a Surgical First: Russell M. Nelson and Tricuspid Valve Annuloplasty." *BYU Studies* 17, no. 3 (1977): 319–37.

Eaton, Robert I., and Henry J. Eyring. *I Will Lead You Along: The Life of Henry B. Eyring.* 2013.

"Elder Russell M. Nelson of the Quorum of the Twelve Apostles." *Ensign*, May 1984.

"Elders Maxwell, Nelson welcomed in China." *Church News,* April 29, 1995.

"Funeral Services for Elder Richard L. Evans," *Ensign,* December 1971.

Gardner, Barbara Morgan. Interview with Russell M. Nelson. Salt Lake City, Utah, August 30, 2013.

Gardner, Marvin K. "Elder Russell M. Nelson: Applying Divine Laws." *Ensign,* June 1984.

"Global Ministry Tour." Video released by *Church News*, 2018.

Greenberg, Heidi. Interview with Russell M. Nelson. University of Utah School of Medicine, November 13, 2015.

SOURCES CITED

Hafen, Bruce C. *A Disciple's Life: The Biography of Neal A. Maxwell.* 2002.

Hinckley, Gordon B. "Small Acts Lead to Great Consequences." *Ensign,* May 1984.

———. "Stand Strong against the Wiles of the World." *Ensign,* November 1995.

Holland, Jeffrey R. "Be With and Strengthen Them." *Ensign,* May 2018.

Johnson, Lane. "Russell M. Nelson: A Study in Obedience." *Ensign,* August 1982.

Kimball, Spencer W. *Teachings of Presidents of the Church: Spencer W. Kimball.* 2006.

———. "The Uttermost Parts of the Earth." Regional Representatives' Seminar, September 29, 1978.

———. "When the World Will Be Converted." *Ensign,* October 1974.

"Latter-day Saint Prophet, Wife and Apostle Share Insights of Global Ministry." Video, October 30, 2018. www.mormonnewsroom.org/article /latter-day-saint-prophet-wife-apostle-share-insights-global-ministry.

"LDS Church announces historic changes to missionary age requirements," ksl.com, October 6, 2012.

"LDS Church to Release 'Come, Follow Me' Curriculum in 2019 for Home, Primary and Adults," ldschurchnews.com, July 6, 2018.

Madsen, Truman G. *The Presidents of the Church: Insights into Their Lives and Teachings.* 2004.

McCombs, Brady. "Mormon church appoints 93-year-old ex-surgeon as president." *Chicago Tribune*, January 16, 2018.

"Missionaries perform humanitarian service." *Church News,* December 7, 1991.

Monson, Thomas S. "The Power of the Book of Mormon." *Ensign,* May 2017.

———. "See Others as They May Become." *Ensign*, November 2012.

———. "Welcome to Conference." *Ensign*, November 2012.

"The Name of the Church." Newsroom statement, August 16, 2018.

Nelson, Russell M. "Becoming Exemplary Latter-day Saints." *Ensign*, November 2018.

———. "Becoming True Millennials." Worldwide Devotional for Young Adults, January 10, 2016.

———. "Begin with the End in Mind." BYU Fireside, September 30, 1984.

———. Benemérito de las Américas address. January 29, 2013; transcription in author's possession.

———. "The Book of Mormon, the Gathering of Israel, and the Second Coming," *Ensign*, July 2014.

———. "The Book of Mormon: What Would Your Life Be Like without It?" *Ensign*, November 2017.

———. "Call to the Holy Apostleship." *Ensign*, May 1984.

———. "Children of the Covenant." *Ensign*, May 1995.

434

———. "The Correct Name of the Church." *Ensign,* November 2018.

———. "Drama on the European Stage." *Ensign*, December 1991.

———. "Drawing the Power of Jesus Christ into Our Lives." *Ensign,* May 2017.

———. "Faith and Families." BYU Devotional, February 6, 2005.

———. *From Heart to Heart: An Autobiography.* 1979.

———. "Historic Site of Translation, Revelation, and Restoration," September 19, 2015. https://www.mormonnewsroom.org/article priesthood-restoration-site-dedication-transcript.

———. "Identity, Priority, and Blessings." BYU Devotional, September 10, 2000.

———. "Introductory Remarks." *Ensign*, May 2018.

———. "Lessons Life Has Taught Me." Seattle Area Devotional, September 15, 2018.

———. "Let Us All Press On." *Ensign*, May 2018.

———. "The Lord Uses the Unlikely to Accomplish the Impossible." BYU– Idaho Devotional, January 27, 2015.

———. "Opening Remarks." *Ensign*, November 2018.

———. "A Plea to My Sisters." *Ensign*, November 2015.

———. "The Price of Priesthood Power." *Ensign*, May 2016.

———. "Revelation for the Church, Revelation for Our Lives." *Ensign,* May 2018.

———. "The Sabbath Is a Delight." *Ensign,* May 2015.

———. "Spencer W. Kimball: Man of Faith." *Ensign*, December 1985.

———. "Sustaining the Prophets." *Ensign*, November 2014.

———. "Sweet Power of Prayer." *Ensign,* May 2003.

———. "Thus Shall My Church Be Called." *Ensign,* May 1990.

Nelson, Russell M., and Wendy W. Nelson. "Hope of Israel." Worldwide Youth Devotional, June 3, 2018.

———. RootsTech Family Discovery Day—Opening Session 2017. https://www .lds.org/topics/family-history/familydiscoveryday/nelson.

Nelson, Russell M., Jr. Remarks at President Nelson's ninety-fourth birthday devotional (author's notes), September 9, 2018.

"New Church Logo Announced." *Ensign*, October 1996.

Oaks, Dallin H. "The Plan and the Proclamation." *Ensign,* November 2017.

———. "President Russell M. Nelson: Guided, Prepared, Committed." *Ensign*, May 2018.

Pinegar, Ed J. *What Every Future Missionary and Their Parents Need to Know.* 2016.

"Popes and Prophets." *Church News* video, October 27, 2018. https://www.you tube.com/watch?v=fFQV7rOQRn0.

"President Hinckley Says Lord, Not Men, Called Pair." *Deseret News,* April 9, 1984.

"President Nelson Dedicates Concepción Chile Temple." www.mormon

newsroom.org/article/president-nelson-dedicates-concepcion-chile -temple, October 28, 2018.

Rasband, Ronald A. "Behold! A Royal Army." *Ensign*, May 2018.

Smith, Joseph. *Teachings of Presidents of the Church: Joseph Smith.* 2007.

Stack, Peggy Fletcher. "Mormonism was born in the USA but, under Nelson, is quickly embracing its growing multiculturalism as it aims to become a truly global religion." *Salt Lake Tribune,* July 24, 2018.

Stevenson, Gary E. "The Heart of a Prophet." *Ensign*, May 2018.

Swinton, Heidi S. *To the Rescue: The Biography of Thomas S. Monson.* 2010.

Taylor, Scott. "Experiences from pulpit's 'other side.'" *Church News*, September 15, 2018.

———. "'We're correcting a name,' President Russell M. Nelson tells Latter-day Saints in Canada." *Deseret News,* August 18, 2018.

Walch, Tad. "Church leaders want Utah Legislature to legalize medical marijuana by year's end." deseretnews.com, September 16, 2018.

———. "Inside the collaboration between the LDS Church and NAACP." *Deseret News,* July 22, 2018.

———. "President Nelson calls Chile temple dedication 'heavenly crescendo' for 5-nation tour." deseretnews.com, October 28, 2018.

———. "President Nelson condemns religious violence in wide-ranging interview." deseretnews.com, October 26, 2018.

———. "Q&A: Elder Holland opens up about personal life struggles, speaks with young married Latter-day Saints in Anglican Oxford chapel," the churchnews.com, November 24, 2018.

Weaver, Sarah Jane. "Dantzel Nelson Succumbs at Age 78." *Church News,* February 17, 2008.

———. "Get to Know President Russell M. Nelson, a Renaissance Man." *Church News,* January 16, 2018.

———. "Seattle crowd of nearly 50,000 hear President Nelson call today 'the most crucial era in the history of the world.'" *Church News*, September 15, 2018.

INDEX

Numbers in *italics* indicate photographs.

Abortion, 137–38, 421

Acupuncture, 134

Adultery, 212

African tribal king, 310–11

Age change for missionary eligibility, 264–72; reactions to, *267*

Agency, 325

Aguero, Carlos, *422*

Airplane: prayer for rerouted, 199–201; catches fire, 259–60

Alcohol, 5, 31, 185

Andersen, Dwayne N., 138

Andersen, Kathy, *282*

Andersen, Neil L., 282–83, 317, 329, *277, 282*

Anderson, Joseph, 90–91

Anniversary card, *233*

Aortic valve surgery: mortality rate on, 87, 88; on Spencer W. Kimball, 103–9

Area conference(s): in Manchester, England, 100–101; in South Pacific, 117–21

Arnold, Mervyn B., 190

Artemova, Svetlana, 178–79

Artificial heart-lung machine, 31–36, 53–56

Ashton, Marvin J., *209*

Asunción, Paraguay, 420

Atonement, 154

Auditorium in medical center named for Dr. Nelson, *320*

Baby boy, Dantzel dreams of, 78–79

Bacterial toxemia, 33–34

Balance, in gospel, 405–9

Ballard, Melvin J., 426

Ballard, M. Russell, *277;* on President Nelson as student, 13–14; on President Nelson's time management, 122; on President Nelson's care for General Authorities, 316, 318; on President Nelson's personality, 335; on President Nelson's leadership style, 337–38; on President Nelson's health, 344; on President Nelson's propensity for learning, 375; on name of Church, 411, 413

Bangkok, Thailand, 382

Baptism(s): of Russell M. Nelson, 6; of Beverly and Derwin Ashcraft, 42–44; of Zhang Zhen-Xiang and Zhou Qingguo, 146–47; of Eastern European citizens, 178–80; of Joseph Smith and

Oliver Cowdery, 286; of David Holland, 360–62
Barnard, Christiaan, 30
Baronofsky, Ivan, 31
Bednar, David A., *277*, 408
Bengaluru, India, *381*
Benson, Ezra Taft, 126, 165–66, 169, 171, 174–75, 197–98, *366*, 366–67
Benson, Flora, 366
Bible, Russian, 178–79
Bingham, Jean B., *380*
Birth announcement for Russ Jr., *80–81*
Blood, donated for money, 27–28
Body, President Nelson's admiration and respect for, 148–50
Bolivia, gathering of Saints in, *425*
Bonneville Stake, 86–88
Book of Mormon, *179*, 290–91, 310–14, 385; President Nelson's personal copy of, *313*
Brigham City Temple dedication, *276*
Brinton, Gregory S., 295, *295*
Brinton, Sally, 295, *295*
Brinton, Sam, *295*, 295–96
Brown, Amos, Reverend, 356–57, *357*
Budapest Stake, 185
Bulgaria, 195–97
Burdette, Walter J., 75–76, 77
BYU Jerusalem Center, *379*

Cabin, 126–27, *128–29*
Campbell, Beverly, 183, 189
Car accident(s): Wendy Nelson survives, 259; in Nicaragua, 368–69
Card celebrating anniversary, *233*
Card, Kathy, 236
Carrel, Alexis, 32

Centro Escolar Benemérito de las Américas, 269–70
Chastity, 212
Children, 25–26, 420
China, 132, 135–36, 142–47, 167, 168–70, 205–7, 302–4
"Chore-girls" scrubbing pads, 54
Christofferson, D. Todd, *277*
Church campus in downtown Salt Lake City, 339–44
Churchill, Edward D., 45
Church meeting schedule, 407–9
Church of Jesus Christ of Latter-day Saints, The, name of, 410–15, *413. See also* Gospel
Clayton, Kathy, *276*
Clayton, L. Whitney, *276*
Coin collection, *377*
Collaboration, among surgeons, 57–58
Colorado River, rafting on, 110–11, 404
"Come, Follow Me" approach to gospel learning, 405–9; curriculum for, *407*
Comfort, 63
Commitments, keeping, 167
Communist countries. *See* Eastern Europe
Competition, among surgeons, 57–58
Computers, 373–74
Concepción Chile Temple, 422–23, *424, 425*
Condie, Spencer J., vii
Confidence, spiritual, 73–74
Cook, Quentin L., *277*, 407–8
Cordeiro, Lincoln Vieira, *370*, 371
Cordeiro, Odilene, 371
Countries: visited by Elder Nelson, *221, 262*; dedication of, 261–63
Cowdery, Oliver, 285–86

Crawley, England, 199–201
Criticism, 333–35
Curiosity, of Russell M. Nelson, 12, 373–75
Curitiba Brazil Temple, *370*, 370–71
Curtis, Jan, 157–58
Czechoslovakia, 191–94, 396

Davis, Netta, 35–36
Death: preparedness for, 73–74; dealing with, 215–17; separation after, as temporary, 231
Delegating responsibilities, 281
Dennis, Clarence, 31, 33, 36
Derrick, Allie, 321
Desk from medical school days, *27*
DeVries, William, 16
Dew, Sheri, 236–38
Discouragement, 61–63
Discrimination, faced by President Nelson, 75–76
Divine law, 48–50, 152–54, 160–62
Doctor bag, *153*
Doctors, unusual figurines of, *376*
Dogs, experimental surgery on, 32, 33–35, *34*
Doty, Don, 77, 166–67
Dream(s): of A. C. Nelson, 8–11; Dantzel's, of baby boy, 78–79
Drowning, 110–11
Dunn, Paul H., *115*, 115–16

Eastern Europe: President Nelson assigned to open, 174–75; efforts to open, 175–78, 180–81, 191, 395–96; map of, *176*; baptisms of citizens of, 178–80; Church granted recognition in Russia, 181–82; efforts to open Hungary, 183–85; efforts to open Romania, 186–89; President Nelson builds relationships with Church members in, 189–90; efforts to open Czechoslovakia, 191–94; efforts to open Poland, 194; efforts to open Bulgaria, 195–97; lessons learned from opening, 197; President Nelson visits, 294–96, 307–8
East High School, 13–14
Eddy, Frank, 33
Eder, W. Phil, 33
Effort, 197
Efimov, Galina, 309
Efimov, Viacheslav, 309
Emotions, controlling, 64–65
English as a second language volunteer teachers, 207
Europe East Area, visit to, 294–96
Exodus 31:13, 94–96
Eyring, Henry B., 317–18, 326–27, *331*, 331–32, 337, 362, 402–3, *403*

Falabella, Enrique R., 416, *416*, *427*
"Family: A Proclamation to the World, The," 208–13, *211*
Family challenges, 396–99
Family history work, 117–18
Fang Rongxiang, 168–70, *169*, 302; son and grandson of, *303*
Faust, James E., 190, 209, *209*
Finances, lean, 27–29
First Presidency, *331*: and "The Family: A Proclamation to the World," 208–10; and "The Living Christ," 224–25; reorganization of, 326–27, *327*; responsibilities of, 330–31; works in sync, 331–32; challenging decisions facing, 333–35
Fishing, *342*, *344*; missionary work compared to, 418
Fowles, Robert, 226

Gabor, Klinger, 185
Gardening, *342*

Gateway We Call Death, The (Nelson), 217, *217*
Gathering of Israel, 385–92
Gatwick Airport, 199–200
Gay marriage, 212
Genealogy work, 117–18
General Authorities: President Nelson called as Apostle, 158–64; President Nelson looks after, 309, 315–20; reception for, 356; luncheon for, 360. *See also* First Presidency; Quorum of the Twelve Apostles
General Sunday School Presidency, *97, 99*; Russell M. Nelson called to, 97–99
Generosity, of President Nelson, 131, 355–62
Gerard, Jack H., 352
German Democratic Republic, 369–70
Global Ministry Tour, 378–84
God: healing as gift from, 149–50; accepting will of, 214–18; timing of, 240–41
Golf carts, *339*, 339–40
Gong, Gerrit W., *353*
Goodman, Louis, 16
Gorbachev, Mikhail, 182
Gorbachev, Raisa, 182
Gospel: clinging to, 110–11, 404; simplicity and balance in, 405–9
Grades, transcript of, *47*
Grandchildren, 130–31, 160, 230, 252, 393, 396–400
Grant, Heber J., 363, *365*
Gromyko, Andrei, 101

Hafen, Bruce C., 185
Haight, David B., *209*
Hales, Brook, 321
Hales, Mary, 317
Hales, Robert D., *277*, 315–17, *315*

Hallstrom, Donald L., 294
Hallstrom, Diane, 294
Harmony, Pennsylvania, dedication of, 285–91
Harris, Martin, 290
Harvard Medical School, 45–47
Hatfield, Gay Lynn, 61–63, 298, 299–301
Hatfield, Jimmy, 61, 298–301, *299*
Hatfield, Jimmy Jr., 61
Hatfield, Laural Ann, 61, 298, 299–301
Hatfield, Ruth, 61, 298–300, 301
Hatfield, Shawn, 300–301
Havel, Vaclav, 192
Haycock, Arthur, 118, 120, 171
Hayfoot, Strawfoot, 18, *19*
Healing, 148–50
Heart: laws governing, 48–50; diagram of, *70*
Heart-lung machine, 31–36, 53–56, *56, 76*
Heart surgery: experiments for, 31–36; first, in Utah, 56–57; discouragement and grief over failed, 61–63; revelation in, 68–72; death as possible outcome of, 73–74; mortality rate for, 87, 88; on Sabbath, 94–96; on Spencer W. Kimball, 103–9; for Paul H. Dunn, 115–16; for Fang Rongxiang, 168–70
Hecht, Hans, 56–57
Hillam, Harold G., 238
Hinckley, Gordon B., *368*; on prophets, viii, ix; and President Nelson's calling as Apostle, 158, 160, 162; counsels President Nelson, 167, 169, 234–35; and death of Spencer W. Kimball, 171; conducts President Kimball's funeral, *172*; and "The Family: A Proclamation to the World," 210;

offers condolences following
Dantzel's death, 230; President
Nelson's relationship with,
367–69

Hinckley, Marjorie, *368*, 368–69
Holland, Alice, 362
Holland, David, 360–62, *361*
Holland, Jeffrey R., *277, 380, 382*;
on President Nelson's refusal of
University of Chicago position,
93; and change in missionary
age, 265; on President Nelson
as listener, 279–80; receives
priesthood blessing from
President Nelson, 319–20;
on President Nelson's calling
as Church President, 329; on
President Nelson's leadership
style, 338; on changes under
President Nelson, 352; on
President Nelson's receptivity
to revelation, 354; on kindness
of President Nelson, 360–62;
baptizes son in Jordan River, *361*;
on President Nelson's curiosity,
374–75; and Global Ministry
Tour, 378–79, 382–83; on name
of Church, 412

Holland, Patricia T., *361, 380*
Holmstrom, Emil, 16
Home, as site for primary gospel
learning, 405–9
Home teaching, 348–49
Honecker, Erich, 369
Horn Creek rapids, 110–11
Hromadka, Josef, 193, 194
Humility, of President Nelson,
355–62
Hungary, 183–85
Hunter, Howard W., *209*, 367, *367*

Immigration, 421
India, 379–82

Inspiration. *See* Revelation
Internal Revenue Service, 202–4
International Cardiovascular
Society meeting, 100–101
International Surgical Society
meeting, 100–101
Interns, classmates of RMN, *14*
Irion, Gloria Nelson (daughter of
RMN), *28, 46, 80, 81, 124, 125,
229, 297*, 395
Iron rod, holding to, 404
Islam, 421
Israel, gathering of, 385–92

Janko, Vladimir, 191–92, 194
Jarvik, Robert, 16–17
Jensen, Amanda (grandmother of
RMN), *9, 11*
Jenson, Conrad, 77, 168–69, 170
Jerusalem, *378, 379*
Jesus Christ: apostolic testimonies
of, 223–25; Book of Mormon as
testament of, 310–11; and name
of Church, 410–15; and sealing
ordinance, 429
Jigsaw puzzle, *377*
Jinan, China, 135–36, 142–44, 302–3
John the Baptist, 285–86
Jones, Kent, 77
Journals, personal, *323*
Joyce, Lyle, 59–60
Judgment, preparedness for, 73–74

Kapp, Ardeth G., 373
Karlson, Karl E., 33
Kay, Jerome, 71
Keetch, Bernice, 355
Keetch, Von G., 355
Kemppainen, Jussi, 179
Kemppainen, Raija, 179
Kennedy, David M., 183
Kenya, Saints line up in, *383*
Kharchev, Konstantin, 176–77

Kimball, Camilla, 104, *107*, 108, 118, 171–72

Kimball, Spencer W., *365*; calls President Nelson as stake president, 86–88; undergoes heart surgery, 103–9, 151–52; with Russell M. Nelson, *105*, *107*; becomes Church President, 112–14; walking in snow, *113*; addressing the Saints, *114*; attends area conferences in South Pacific, 117–21; prayer for healing of, 120–21; on taking gospel to China, 132, 135; and vacancies in Quorum of the Twelve, 157–58; calls Nelson and Oaks as Apostles, 162–63; death of, 171–73; funeral of, *172*; on reaching beyond iron and bamboo curtains, 198; on women and church growth, 293; President Nelson's relationship with, 364–66

Kindness, of President Nelson, 189–90, 355–62

Korean War, 36–42

Kremlin, *178*

Kruger Park game reserve, *254*

Lake Baikal, *295*, 295–96

Languages, spoken by President Nelson, 219–22, 417–18. *See also* Mandarin

Lantos, Tom, 183

La Paz, Bolivia, 418, 420

Larsen, Ralph, 237

Larsen, Sharon, 237

Lava Falls, 111

Lee, Harold B., *97*, 97–98, 99, 104, 107–9, 112, 364, *365*

Lee, Vivian, 50

Library, 12

Li Lanqing, 205–6, *206*

Lima, Peru, 416–18, 419–20

Lindbergh, Charles, 32

Listening, 279–80

"Living Christ, The," 223–25

Li Xiaolin, 206

Lladro figurine, broken, 130

Love poems, *250–51*

Lowder, Marjorie Nelson (daughter of RMN), *80*, *81*, *125*, *229*, *297*

Lyman, E., 68–72

Machu Picchu, *343*

Madsen, Ann, 253

Madsen, Truman G., 253

Manchester area conference, 100–103

Mandarin, 132–35, 142, 144–45, 147, 207

Map of Eastern Europe, *176*

Marijuana, medical, 352

Marsh, Laurie Nelson (daughter of RMN), 78, *80*, *81*, 83–85, *124*, *125*, *229*, *297*

M.A.S.H. units, 38-39, *40*

Mason, Patrick, 354

Massachusetts General Hospital, 45–47

Maxfield, Wendy Nelson (daughter of RMN), *28*, *46*, *80*, *81*, *124*, *125*, *228*, *229*, *297*

Maxwell, Neal A., 163–64, *203*, 205–6, 209, *209*, 318, 373–74

McConkie, Bruce R., 325

McKay, David O., xi, 90–92, *92*, 364, *365*

McKellar, Stephen, 60, 130, 230, 293, 345–46, 394, *395–96*

Medical marijuana, 352

Meeting room in Church Administration Building, *281*

Melchizedek Priesthood quorums, restructuring of, 347–48, 349–50

Memory, President Nelson's capacity with, 283

Metcalf, Robert, 17

Midway cabin, 126–27, *128–29*

Mikhailusenko, Igor, 178

Miklos, Imre, 183–85

Miles, Brenda Nelson (daughter of RMN), *46, 80, 81, 124, 125,* 130, *229, 297*

Ministering program, 347–50, *350*

Missionary Executive Council (MEC), 265–72

Missionary Training Center(s): in São Paulo, Brazil, 219, 220; in Provo, Utah, *268*; expansion and construction of, 269–70; in Mexico City, *271*

Missionary work: in spirit world, 9, 10; tax exemption for, 202–4; lowering of required age for, 264–72; advancements in, 270–72; in German Democratic Republic, 369–70; in Lima, 418

Monson, Thomas S., *203, 370*; and opening of Eastern Europe, 197; gives President Nelson priesthood blessing, 202–3; and change in missionary age, 264, 269; encourages members to read Book of Mormon, 310; death of, 321; President Nelson's relationship with, 369–72

Moon cakes, 144

Moscow, Russia, *178*

Moses, 197

Motherhood, importance of, 292–97

Mount Gellert, *184*

Mourning, 217

Mozambique mission home, *255*

Mozambique, robbery in, 253–59

Music, 18, 124–25, *250–51*

Muslims, 421

National Association for the Advancement of Colored People, 356–57

Nelson, Andrew Clarence (A. C.) (grandfather of RMN), *8, 8–11, 11*

Nelson, Britney, *297*

Nelson, Dantzel White (wife of RMN): dating and courtship of, 18–22; early married years of, 23–26; finances of, 25–29; patience of, 46–47; helps build oxygenator, 53–56; encourages President Nelson, 62–63; dreams of baby boy, 78–79; as mother, 83–85, 122, 123, 124, 130; personal sacrifices of, 123; love of, for music, 124–25; designs Midway cabin, 126–27; as grandmother, 130; learns Mandarin, 132–34; visits China, 142, 143–44; on President Nelson's calling as Apostle, 159; treated for non-Hodgkins lymphoma, 215–17; faith of, 218; death of, 226–35; President Nelson's support for, 248

Nelson, Dantzel White, photos of: *63,* dating RMN, *20*; in wedding dress, *21*; on honeymoon, *23;* as young adult, *24;* with two children, *26*; with young family on pier, *28*; in Boston with family, *46*; with ten children and first grandchild, *80*; with children and grandchildren, *84*; with husband, *101, 161, 227–29, 232*; in South Pacific, *119*; with family in matching outfits, *124*; at Midway vacation home, *128*; with Dr. Wu Yingkai, *135*; outside China's Forbidden City, *136*; with Neil and Kathy Andersen, *282*

Nelson daughters. See Irion, Gloria
Nelson; Lowder, Marjorie
Nelson; Marsh, Laurie Nelson;
Maxfield, Wendy Nelson; Miles,
Brenda Nelson; Ringwood,
Rosalie Nelson; Webster, Sylvia
Nelson; Wittwer, Emily Nelson;
Workman, Marsha Nelson
Nelson, Floss Edna Anderson
(mother of RMN), 3, 4, *6*, 7, 22,
34–35, *80*
Nelson, Margrethe Christensen, 9
Nelson, Marion Clavar (father
of RMN), 3–4, *6*, 7, *11*, 22, 30,
34–35, *80*
Nelson News, 216
Nelson, Olivia, *297*
Nelson, Russell M.: biography of,
vii–viii; spiritual schooling of,
ix, 166–67, 431–32; parents and
ancestry of, 3; childhood of, 3–4;
learns gospel, 4–5; education of,
5–6, 12–17, 24–25, 30–36, 45–47;
baptism of, 6; early church
attendance of, 6–7; sealed to
parents, 7; spiritual heritage
of, 8–11; inquisitive nature of,
12, 373–75; musical talent of,
18; dating and courtship with
Dantzel, 18–22; early married
years of, 23–26; finances
of, 25–29; serves in Korean
War, 36–42; performs open-
heart surgery for first time,
56–57; as teacher, 57–60, 65–67;
discouragement and persistence
of, 61–63; faces religious
discrimination at University
of Utah, 75–76; as father and
grandfather, 79–83, 122–23, 126,
130–31, 252, 393–400; called as
stake president, 86–88; called
to Sunday School Presidency,

97–99; time management skills
of, 122–23; deals with daughters'
suitors, 127; generosity of, 131,
355–62; languages spoken by,
132–35, 142, 144–45, 147, 207,
219–22, 417–18; called as Apostle,
158–64; preparation of, for
Apostleship, 166–67; humility
and kindness of, 189–90,
355–62; remarriage's impact
on, 245–46, 247; as husband,
247–48, 252; survives robbery
in Mozambique, 253–59;
survives airplane fire, 259–60;
dedicates six countries in four
days, 261–63; as President
of Quorum of the Twelve
Apostles, 275–83; memory of,
283; given title "Old Friend of
China," 302–3; testimony of
Book of Mormon, 311; called
as Church President, 321–25;
ordained Church President,
326–29; responsibilities of,
as Church President, 330–32;
leadership style of, 336–38;
health and energy of, 339–46;
policy changes under, 347–54;
interactions with previous
Church Presidents, 363–72;
intelligence and talents of, 375;
worldwide tour undertaken by,
378–84; challenges in family of,
396–99; ninety-fourth birthday
celebration of, 399–400
Nelson, Russell M., photos of:
portrait, *vi*; as child, *3, 4, 5*;
in graduation robes, *15*; as
young adult, *17, 20, 24*; wedding
portrait, *21*; on honeymoon, *23*;
with young family on pier, *28*;
with rifle, *38*; in Korea, *40, 44*; in
army uniform, *41*; with family in

Boston, *46*; in doctoral robes, *47*; in surgical garb, *55*; performing surgery, *56, 152*; with model of human heart, *59*; in operating room, *62*; in newspaper articles, *76, 95*; holding baby Russ Jr., *82*; with children and grandchildren, *84*; holding great-grandson, *85*; as Bonneville Stake president, *87*; with new General Sunday School Presidency, *97, 99*; in new office, *98*; with Dantzel, *101, 161, 227–29*; with Spencer W. Kimball, *105, 107*; in South Pacific, *119*; with family in matching outfits, *124*; on horseback with granddaughter, *127*; at Midway vacation home, *129*; with Santa, *130*; outside China's Forbidden City, *136*; at Shandong Medical College, *143*; at Great Wall of China, *145*; at time of call to Twelve, *162*; with Bernard P. Brockbank, *163*; at general conference, *166*; with Fang Rongxiang, *169*; with Russian vice president Alexander Rutskoy, *181*; with Olga and Jirí Snederfler, *193*; shaking hands with President Monson, *203*; with Li Lanqing, vice premier of China, *206*; with Wendy on wedding day, *243*; with large posterity, *244, 398*; with Wendy, *245, 246, 325*; in a leisure moment, *249*; at game reserve, *254*; at press conference after missionary age change, *266*; at Brigham City Temple dedication, *276*; with Quorum of Twelve in 2015, *277*; at pulpit, *279*; with Neil and Kathy Andersen, *282*; at Priesthood Restoration Site, *287, 288–89*; at Lake Baikal in Russia, *295*; with family members on Mother's Day, *297*; with Hatfield family at Payson Utah Temple, *299*; with son and grandson of Fang Rongxiang, *303*; greeting Robert D. Hales, *315*; with President Boyd K. Packer, *316*; assisting Joseph B. Wirthlin, *319*; speaking at President Monson's funeral, *322*; with Brethren to announce reorganization of First Presidency, *327*; with counselors in First Presidency, *331*; with Dallin H. Oaks, *337*; on swing, *341*; enjoying various outdoor activities, *342–43*; fishing, *344*; skiing, *345*; with the Reverend Amos Brown, *357*; with Helping Hands volunteer, *358*; with Russian religious leader, *358*; with Dale G. Renlund, *359*; with child in Kenya, *359*; with camera, *361*; with Ezra Taft Benson, *366*; in office, *373*; playing organ, *374*; working on jigsaw puzzle, *377*; outside Jerusalem, *378, 379*; greeting Saints around the world, *380–81*; in Bengaluru, India, *382*; in London, England, *384*; at worldwide youth devotional, *389*; with great-grandchildren, *393, 397, 399*; accompanying daughter on piano, *395*; at Safeco Field, *401, 402*; with president of Peru, *416*; addressing Peruvian Saints, *417*; with children in Paraguay, *419*; with Sergio Rubin in Uruguay, *422*; at Concepción Chile Temple, *424, 425*; greeting missionary grandson in

Uruguay, *424*; waving good-bye to South American Saints, *428*; smiling, *432*

Nelson, Russell Marion Jr., 78–83, *80–82, 110, 125, 129,* 234, 249, 252, *297, 342, 346,* 396

Nelson, Wendy Watson: author's relationship with, x; on Romanian orphan program, 188; events leading to President Nelson's marriage to, 236–41; marriage's impact on, 242–49; President Nelson's love for, 252; survives robbery in Mozambique, 256, 257; survives car accident, 259; on dedication of Balkan countries, 261; on Priesthood Restoration Site, 287; on President Nelson's esteem for womanhood and motherhood, 294; speaks at member devotional, 294; on Chinese Church members, 303–4; on President Nelson as Church President, 321, 322–25, 330–32; on energy of President Nelson, 346; on gathering of Israel, 386–87; on President Nelson as father and grandfather, 398–99; speaks at Safeco Field, 403–4; and dedication of Concepción Chile Temple, 423

Nelson, Wendy Watson, photos of: on wedding day, *243*; with Elder Nelson's large posterity, *244, 398*; with husband, *245, 246, 325, 400*; in a leisure moment, *249*; at game reserve, *254*; at Brigham City Temple dedication, *276*; at Priesthood Restoration Site, *287, 288–89*; at Lake Baikal in Russia, *295*; with family members on Mother's Day, *297*; enjoying outdoor activities, *343*; in Kenya, *359*; in Bangkok, Thailand, *380, 381*; in Laie, Hawaii, *380*; in London, England, *384*; at worldwide youth devotional, *389*; at Safeco Field, *401*; at Concepción Chile Temple, *424, 425*; waving good-bye to South American Saints, *428*

New Zealand, 118–21

Nicaragua, car accident in, 368–69

Nielsen, Mads Peter, 8–11

Note to Elder Nelson from Sheri Dew and Wendy Watson, *239*

Notebooks: with medical notes, *49*; from regional representatives' seminar, *133*; small, personal journals kept in, *323*

Oaks, Dallin H., *162, 203, 277, 331, 337*; hosts Nelsons in Chicago, 89–90; called as Apostle, 159–60, 162; on "The Family: A Proclamation to the World," 208–9, 212; on President Nelson as President of Twelve, 281; on President Nelson's medical care, 317; as President Nelson's counselor, 326–27, 331–32; on President Nelson's leadership style, 326–27; on opposition, 334, 335; on President Nelson's health, 344; on President Nelson's interactions with Church Presidents, 363; on President Nelson's writing talent, 375

Oaks, June, 90

Obedience, blessings of, 48–50, 152–54

"Old Friend of China," 302–3

Olmstead, Heather, 139–41, *140, 141*

Olmstead, Nicole, 139–41, *140, 141*

Olmstead, Rick, 137–38, 140–41

Olmstead, Trudy, 137–41, *140*

Open-heart surgery. *See* Heart surgery

Operating room: controlling emotions in, 64–65; RMN's teaching style in, 66–67; revelation in, 68–72

Opposition, 333–35

Organ, RMN playing, *374*

Orphans, Romanian, 187–88

Oswald, Mickey, 73–74

Owens, Ashlyn, 394

Owens, Casey, 399

Owens, Katie Irion, 218, 231–34, 249, 373, 394, 399

Oxygenator, 53–56

Pacemaker, for Spencer W. Kimball, 151–52

Packard, Blair J., 253–54, *258*, 259

Packard, Cindy, 254–55, 256, 257–58, *258*

Packer, Allan F., *276*

Packer, Boyd K., *209*, *276*, 276–77

Packer, Donna, *276*

Packer, Terri, *276*

Paraguay, *419*, 420

Parker, Alan, 344

Pearce, Maunsel B., 69, 71

Perry, Barbara, 236–37, *237*, *276*

Perry, L. Tom, *209*, *237*, 275, 275–76, *276*

Peru: president of, *416*; addressing Saints in, *417*

Petersen, Mark E., 157, 160, 164

Pillow, *263*

Pinegar, Ed. J., 200–201

"A Plea to My Sisters," 292–93

Playbill, *19*

Plummer, Gail, 18

Pneumonectomy, 139–41

Pocatello Highland Stake, 282–83

Poems, love, *250–51*

Poland, 194

Pop, Teofil, 188–89

Porter, Bruce D., 295, 305–9, *306*

Porter, David, 307

Porter, Susan, 294, *295*, 305–9, *306*

Portuguese, 219, 220

Prayer: to heal Spencer W. Kimball, 120–21; for Spirit to be poured over Hungary, 184–85; for rerouted plane, 199–201

Prescription pad, *77*

Presiding Bishopric, 330–31

Price, Alvin, 188

Price, Barbara, 188

Price, Philip B., 16, 53, 75

Priesthood blessing: for ill doctor, 149–50; for Spencer W. Kimball, 151; as predicated on obedience to law, 152; for Jeffrey R. Holland, 319–20

Priesthood, restoration of, 285–86

Priesthood Restoration Site, 285–91, *287*, *288–89*, *290*

Proclamation on the family, 208–13

Prophet(s): learning from, vii, 102; Gordon B. Hinckley on, viii, ix; work of, viii–ix; schooling of, ix; author's testimony of, x–xii; following, xii, 430–31, 432; President Nelson's faith in, 90–93; Spencer W. Kimball as, 172–73; President Nelson called as, 321–25; President Nelson's interactions with, 363–72; sustaining of, 372

Provo Utah Temple, *7*

Puzzle, working on, *377*

Qi Huaiyuan, 206

Quorum of the Twelve Apostles: vacancies in, 157–58; President Nelson called to, 158–64;

President Nelson's early experiences in, 165–66; President Nelson's preparation for, 166–67; President Nelson as President of, 275–83; meeting room of, *281*; differences between First Presidency and, 330–31

Radicalized Muslims, 421
Rafting trip, 110–11, 404
Rasband, Ronald A., *277, 279*
Reemtsma, Keith, 77
Religious discrimination, against President Nelson, 75–76
Remarriage: President Nelson considers, 234–35; events leading to, with Wendy Watson, 236–41; challenges of, 242–47; and President Nelson as husband, 247–48, 252; Wendy's reception in Nelson family, 248–49
Renlund, Dale G., 17, *277, 279,* 357, *359,* 360
Renlund, Ruth, 357–60
Responsibility, taking, 64–65
Resurrection, 10
Revelation: in open-heart surgery, 68–72; regarding Spencer W. Kimball as prophet, 107–8; regarding health of Paul H. Dunn, 115–16; given to President Nelson, 315–17, 324; given to Wendy Nelson, 322; President Nelson's receptivity to, 354; concerning President Nelson's calling as Church President, 431
Rich, J. Charles Jr., 17
Richards, LeGrand, 86–88, 157, 160
Ringger, Hans B., 176–77, 186, *187,* 189, 195–96
Ringwood, Rosalie Nelson

(daughter of RMN), *80, 81,* 123, *124, 125,* 229, *297, 395*
Robbery, in Mozambique, 253–59
Rock Solid Relationships, 240, *240*
Romania, 186–89
Rome Temple, 421
Romney, Marion G., 411
Rubin, Sergio, 420–22, *422,* 426–27
Russia: efforts to open, 175–78, 180–81; Church granted recognition in, 181–82; President Nelson visits, 307–8; lineage of Saints in, 386
Rutskoy, Alexander, 180–81, *181*

Sabbath, keeping, 94–96
Safeco Field, 401–4, *402, 403*
Saksena, Devendra, 59
Salt Lake City, Church campus in, 339–44
Salt Lake Clinic, 77
Salt Lake Public Library, *12*
Same-sex couples, 333–34
Samoa, 117–18
Samuels, Leo T., 16
Schwitzer, Gregory A.: on President Nelson as medical student, 14; on President Nelson as inspiring, 60, 67; on President Nelson as medical teacher, 66; on President Nelson's pioneering efforts in Eastern Europe, 182, 189–90; on President Nelson's leadership style, 272; on President Nelson's interaction with Hatfields, 301; on President Nelson's health, 344; on President Nelson's curiosity, 374
Scott, Richard G., 278
Sealing: of Nelson family, 7, 9, 11; of Hatfield family, 298–301; promises of ordinance, 429
Seattle, Washington, 401–4

Second Coming, 385

Seers, 213

Self-mastery, 64–65

Shandong Medical College, 135, 142–43, *143*

Shandong University School of Medicine, 302

Signatures of prophets and apostles, *224*

Sill, Sterling W., 6–7

Simeone, Fiorindo A., 38, 39

Simplicity, in gospel, 405–9

Skiing, *345*, 345–46

Smith, Emma, 285, 290–91

Smith, George Albert, 363–64, *365*

Smith, Joseph, 223, 285–86, 287–90

Smith, Joseph Fielding, *102*, 102, 108, 260, 364, *365*

Smith, Lucy, 290

Smith, Sidney A., 146

Smolianova, Olga, 178

Snederfler, Jirí, 192–93, *193*, 194

Snederfler, Olga, 192, *193*, 194

Snow, Erastus, 9

Snow, Phyllis, 286

Snow, Steven E., 286

Soares, Ulisses, *353*

Social media fast, 390, 391–92

Sofia, Bulgaria, *195*

Solemn assembly, *328*, 329, 394

South Africa, 253

South America, ten-day tour to, 416–27

South Pacific, *119*, *121*; area conferences in, 117–21

Soviet Union. *See* Eastern Europe

Spanish, President Nelson speaks in, 417–18

Special Olympic Games, 188

Spiritual confidence, 73–74

Spirit world, 8–10

Stake president: President Nelson called as, 86–88; calling of new, 282–83

Stamp collection, *376*

Stevenson, Gary E., *277*, *416*, *427*; on President Nelson as teacher, 65–66; called as Apostle, 279; and dedication of Priesthood Restoration Site, 286; on ordination of President Nelson, 326; on President Nelson's leadership style, 338; visits South America with President Nelson, 416; on Saints' reaction to President Nelson's speaking Spanish, 417; on President Nelson's connection with members, 418–19; on dedication of Concepción Chile Temple, 423

Stevenson, Lesa, 286, 416, 420

Sunday meeting schedule, 407–9

Sunday School General Presidency, *97*, 99; Russell M. Nelson called to, 97–99

Susquehanna River, *284*, 285, *288*

Tabernacle Choir in Russia, 180–81, *181*

Tanner, N. Eldon, *97*, 97–98, *100*, 100, 101, 118, 120

Tax exemptions, for missionary work, 202–4

Taylor, Brian K., 385, 392

Technology, 373–74

Temple(s): in Samoa, 117–18; Curitiba Brazil Temple, 370–71; in India, 352, 379, 382; in Russia, 352–53, in Bangkok, 382; Concepción Chile Temple, 422–26

Teraskin, Sasha, 179–80

Terebenin, Anna, 178

Terebenin, Liudmila, 178

Terebenin, Yuri, 178, 180

Terrorists, 421

Testimony, growing, 198

Thoracic surgical training program, 77

Time management, 122

Tithing, 27–28, 29

Transcript of grades from PhD program, *47*

Transgender issues, 212

Tricuspid valve annuloplasty, 68–72, *71*

Tsvetkov, Tsviatko, 196

Tumor, surgery to remove, in Trudy Olmstead, 137–41

Two-hour meeting block, 407–9

Uchtdorf, Dieter F., 412–13

University of Chicago, *89*, 89–93

University of Utah, *13*, 13–17, 75–76, 77

Uruguay, *422*

Vacation home, 126–27, *128–29*

van Rysselberghe, Jacqueline, 423

Varco, Richard L., 35

Vieira Cordeiro, Lincoln, *370*, 371

Vision, of A. C. Nelson, 8–11

Visiting teaching, 348–49

Visscher, Maurice, 30

Vizcarra, Martin, 416, *416*

Walker, Robert, 366

Walker, William R., *276*

Wangensteen, Owen H., 16, 30–31

Warner, Richard L., *97, 99*, 99

Watson, Wendy. *See* Nelson, Wendy Watson

Webster, David, 127, 130, 234, 293

Webster, Sylvia Nelson (daughter of RMN), *80, 81*, 122, 123, *124, 125*, 126, 131, *229*, 234, 249, *297*, 345

Whipple, Walter, 194

White, Dantzel. *See* Nelson, Dantzel White

White, LeRoy Davis, 20

White, Maude Clark, 20, 28

Wilkinson, Ernest, 103–4, 151

Wintrobe, Max, 16, 75

Wirthlin, Joseph B., *97*, 98–99, *99*, 318–19

Wittwer, Bradley E., 214, *215*

Wittwer, Emily Nelson (daughter of RMN), 78, *80, 81*, 160, *124, 125*, 214–18, *215, 216*, 229

Wittwer, Jordan, 215

Women, importance of, 292–97

Wonnacott, Chris, 356

Word of Wisdom, 5, 31, 185

Workman, Marsha Nelson (daughter of RMN), 25–26, *26, 28, 46, 80, 81, 124*, 228, 229

Worldwide devotional for youth, 386–87, *388–89*

Worldwide tour, 378–84

Worthen, Vernell, 57

Writing, 375

Wu Yingkai, 134–36, *135*, 142

Yin Dakui, 206

Youth: and gathering of Israel, 386–92; President Nelson's connection to, 419–20

Zhang Xiaowen, 206

Zhang Zhen-Xiang, 142–47, *147*, 168–69, 302

Zhou Qingguo, 146–47

Zwick, W. Craig, 185, 219, 271, 281–82, 312–14, 346

IMAGE CREDITS

All photographs provided courtesy of the Nelson family unless otherwise noted.

Nelson family artifact photographs, by Kelly Sansom: pages 27, 47, 49, 133, 153, 216, 232–33, 239, 250–51, 262–63, 376–77.

The photographs on the following pages are used by permission of the *Deseret News/Church News*.

Pages ii, 267, photos by Laura Seitz.

Pages 47, 334, 373, 379, 380–81, 382, 416, 417, 418, 424–25, 427, 428, photos by Jeffrey D. Allred.

Pages 266, 331, photo by Scott G Winterton.

Pages 268, 271, photos by Jason Swensen.

Pages 322, 325, 353, photos by Spenser Heaps.

Pages 279, 328, 357, photos by Ravell Call.

Page 358, photos by R. Scott Lloyd.

Page 370, photo by Gerry Avant.

Pages 388–89, photos by James Wooldridge.

Pages 401–3, photos by Kristin Murphy.

The photographs on the following pages are used by permission and/or courtesy.

Page 7, photo by Randy Judkins/Shutterstock.com.

Pages 12, 13, 281, 332, 339, photos by Richard Erickson.

Page 54, photo by Ugorenkov Aleksandr/Shutterstock.com.

Page 70, photo by SumHint/Shutterstock.com.

Page 71, illustration based on a technical drawing.

Page 89, photo by janniswerner/iStock Editorial/Getty Images Plus.

Page 140, photo courtesy of Trudy Olmstead.

Page 141, photo courtesy of Nicole Olmstead. Photo by Jonathan Canlas.

Page 149, photo by Arunee H/Shutterstock.com.

Page 178, photo by svic/Shutterstock.com.

Page 184, photo by Brian Kinney/Shutterstock.com.